**Also by Leandro Herrero**

The Leader with Seven Faces
Viral Change
New Leaders Wanted: Now Hiring!
Disruptive Ideas

# HOMO IMITANS

# HOMO IMITANS

The art of social infection:
Viral Change™ in action

## Leandro Herrero

Published by:
**meetingminds**
PO Box 1192, HP9 1YQ, United Kingdom
**www.meetingminds.com**


ISBN Paperback edition:
10–Digit: 1-905776-07-1
13–Digit:  978-1-905776-07-8


A CIP catalogue record for this title is available from the British Library

# Contents

Never doubt that a small group of thoughtful, committed citizens can change the world. Indeed, it is the only thing that ever has.

**Margaret Mead**
Anthropologist

No social advance rolls in on the wheels of inevitability. It comes through the tireless efforts and persistent work of dedicated individuals.

**Martin Luther King, Jr.**

The greater danger for most of us lies not in setting our aim too high and falling short; but in setting our aim too low, and achieving our mark.

**Michelangelo**

If you ask a little child in Gaza today what he wants to be, he doesn't say a doctor or engineer or businessman. He says he wants to be a martyr.

**Caroline Hawley**
Special Correspondent, BBC

**To Tom and Aisling**

# 1

# Copy ergo sum (cogito is a bonus)

I am on two missions. One: I want to create epidemics of goodness and counter-epidemics to evil by applying the powers of social influence and social contagion. Two: I want to enlist you in my first mission. Grandiose language, I know. OK, I'll come down to earth. Let me translate. I want to create real change in organizations by applying the principles that create change in the macro-social world and vice versa. And I want to recruit you as a follower of these ideas:

(1) The only change is behavioural change. Pick any organization, health programme or societal change project. No matter how much you reorganize processes in the company, or how many

health awareness campaigns are in place, or how many appeals to community cohesion your government funds; nothing changes until and unless behaviours change. If you are leading change in organizations or society, behaviours must be the focus of your attention. So we'd better know how to do this and, believe me, above all, how not to do it.

(2) Behaviours don't like classrooms, PowerPoint presentations, posters or billboards. Behaviours travel through imitation and copying. So this is the second clue. We'd better know how this works and 'what' or 'who' has the power to spread behaviours. We must get this right or we will be wasting our time, money and hope.

(3) Organizational change and macro-social change are large-scale changes. How large will vary case by case, but we are not talking about changes that occur at the atomic level of management teams or in the intimacy of the one-to-one executive coaching sessions. These are important and may in some cases indeed be crucial to the organization, but the social infections I am talking about go beyond the scope of these situations.

This book is about bundling and un-bundling all the ingredients of social infection with behaviours at the core. I use the term of social infection to refer to social changes both inside the organization (i.e. the world of public and private business, as well as non-profit) and in the macro-social world. I will share with you the logic behind this and I will use the premise that there is a continuum between both worlds. We need to unbundle the components to understand and master them. Then we need to re-bundle them, put it all together again to orchestrate that change.

As you can already see, I have a passion for infections. I think there's nothing better than a good epidemic. Blame it on my previous career as a practicing physician.

2

If you are a manager or a leader in either of these worlds, you are also in the infection business. You may not know it yet, but this book is going to help you realize that this is the only hope you have of managing and leading successfully.

I want you to start thinking either like a good 'patient zero' (the term used in epidemiology to describe the first patient infecting others) or a social master of other 'patients zero'. Yes, I do love epidemics. In fact, I want to create epidemics of success inside and outside organizations. OK, so we will need to define success, I agree. And I, like you, have my own ethical filters for picking my epidemics. 'Epidemic' usually has a negative connotation, I know, but it doesn't necessarily have to. More on that later.

> If you are a manager or leader in the micro- or macro-social world, you are in the social infection business.

I hope you are ready for a long chat, because that is what this book is about! Look around. We are bound to each other by the things we do, the clothes we wear, the music we listen to, the mobile phones we use and a million other things that are a copy of what others do. You thought you made completely independent, deliberate and rational choices, but in reality you were infected by the social norms around you. And when these norms are not manifested physically around you, they are still in your head. Call it whatever you like. Social scientists use terms such as social contagion, social copying or social infections. Sometimes also more prosaic ones such as 'herd behaviour'. I know what you are thinking: "*Not me! I'm not part of a herd!*" Yep, we don't like it. Because accepting this reality feels like saying that we have surrendered our will, that one aspect of our being that makes us human. Herds are for cattle, we have free will. Yes, I know.

3

## The beauty of two brains

Don't despair. Yes, we are Homo Sapiens. Very Sapiens indeed. Our brain has evolved and has a brand new neocortex, which is responsible for all those noble things like judgement, morals and apparently free will. Descartes told us: "*cogito ergo sum*" (I think therefore I am). Sure. The problem is that when we developed the neocortex, we did not get rid of the old layers of brain (paleocortex) which control pretty much everything else, such as emotions and any other primal animal behaviours. We really have two brains. That's not bad! What makes us human is the coexistence of both and the subtle dynamics between them.

Homo Sapiens shows off in the eloquence of your speech, the complexity of your thoughts, the elegance of the scientific rationale, the richness of introspection, the beauty of poetic writing and even in the elaborate, perhaps contradictory, mysterious and baffling intricacy of your religious thoughts. Homo Sapiens takes his children to school, reads the newspapers, goes to work, fills in spreadsheets, uses machines, plays tennis, gives lectures, texts home, creates art and has drinks with friends. But inside this Homo Sapiens there is also a more primal Homo Imitans.

The threads of the rich tapestry of behaviours of Homo Sapiens are made of imitation and influence. We copy others or are influenced by others, or they copy us or are influenced by us. And this happens much more than we care to admit. Most of this copying (some good, some bad) is unconscious, but it's there. We are intellectually complex, rationally stylish, highly enlightened, unsophisticated copying machines.

Most people who buy newspapers buy the ones which have 'close-to-home' views of their world. Perhaps, simply put, you can't stomach that left/right wing, so you buy X which you will continue to buy forever. By doing so, you join the club of people who think like you and make similar choices. You are now de facto linked to a social network of individuals who read the same newspaper and see the same adverts. The belonging to the invisible club is self-reinforcing. Exposing yourself to more of the same (view of the world) will make you continue buying that newspaper. It has an influence on you. You think you make a daily rational choice (after all, you don't have to do this), but the habit and social self-reinforcement are in the driver's seat. This is a caricature example, but we are composed of hundreds of these daily caricatures.

> **We are intellectually complex, highly enlightened, unsophisticated copying machines.**

In my adopted home country, England, you send your children either to public school or private school. Those who can afford private education will shop around. Parents usually visit nearby schools, look at the facilities, talk to headmasters, listen to their 'spiel' of *"children are very happy here, this is what makes us different"*, check the fees and make a decision. All those bits of information get to your brain together with *"Mary takes her children here. You know Mary? The lawyer you met at that party?"* And the combination of all this, allows you to decide 'freely' where to send your children. So, Mary and you meet in the car park for years to come.

When somebody has just been hired and goes to the office on his first day, he is given a tour of the place and perhaps an induction plan. There are Standard Operating Procedures (SOP) to follow, training courses to join and detailed instructions on how to fill in an expense sheet. In other words, lots of formal 'onboarding' stuff.

But the SOP does not contain all the rules or the hundreds of things that occupy 90% of your time in daily life. They are not written down. Is it better to bump into each other in the corridor as a way to meet people or to request formal meetings through

Outlook instead? Is it better to desert the floor en masse at lunchtime or to unpack plastic containers and free your cucumber sandwiches in solitude instead? Is it better to wear a tie or to avoid embarrassment for being the only one who does? Is it better to chat across the dividing screens or to enjoy monastic silence behind closed office doors? Is it better to have meetings in the cafeteria or in meeting rooms? Is it better to put everything into PowerPoints or to have a dialog without visuals? By day three the new recruit has unconsciously adopted hundreds of unwritten rules which truly define 'the culture'.

We are influenced by others in an incredible way. This statement is silly. It is obvious. However, many people spend a lot of time fighting against the fact that this is actually the case. We all want to be unique, different and not part of the crowd. But we are definitely influenced by others. What's more, friends and friends of friends seem to have a particularly strong power over us. It is not entirely clear why, but many studies, some of them quoted in this book, show that this is the case. In a very important American study where more than 12,000 people were followed over three decades, it was shown that people were at a greater risk of becoming obese when a close friend became obese. We'll talk more about this later. Obesity! Friends! Interestingly, in this large study, friends were statistically well above the influence from spouse or siblings.

Yes, cogito ergo sum, but also imitator ergo sum, copy ergo sum. Ortega y Gasset, the Spanish philosopher said, "I am I and my circumstance." Today, Ortega would have explained 'circumstance' including Facebook and LinkedIn. We are what we are plus our copied routines, our conformity to social norms, our primal need to imitate. The examples of the power of social imitation, social copying or social infection (as a practitioner, I tend to use these terms as synonyms) are vast and well-documented.

I have grouped most of them under one roof in the Annex of this book so that they can be read independently. I have subtitled the Annex *A guide for the perplexed*, thinking of me more than you. You'll see how the way we vote in elections has a lot to do with how people close to us vote; how happiness spreads like a virus or how pregnancies or suicide can also be copied. These are just three examples where 'imitation' may not immediately come to our minds when thinking about 'why' these things happen.

In the last few years, a convergence of information coming from different and sometimes distant disciplines has allowed us to start making sense of Homo Imitans. To list some of them: social and behavioural sciences, network theory and epidemiology. We are moving fast from curiosity ('Oh, that's interesting') to baffling ('Is that really me? Is this how we do things?'), to defence ('That's not me, that is for the masses'), to taking charge ('If this is so, let's make use of it to do some good'). Over the years, I have travelled all over between these stations, backwards and forwards, commuting from curiosity to charge and back.

> Management has created children called 'Best Practices' and sent them to be educated at the Benchmarking High School.

My day job is organizational consulting. My team and I call ourselves organizational architects ('we don't do buildings'). The bias of our praxis is behaviours. My chronic frustration continues to be how the business world in particular has thick walls, impermeable to the reality of the outside world in terms of understanding the dynamics of human social behaviour. It sometimes seems as if the old nine-to-five world and the current 24/7 Blackberry-world are governed by laws written (mostly) by Anglo-Saxon management consultants, business schools, academics and corporate saints and heroes who have developed an impermeable system called 'management'.

This Management has created children called 'Best Practices' and sent them to be educated at the Benchmarking High School where they can obtain grades without having touched a bit of behavioural or social sciences. And even when they do touch on this, it feels like a superficial pick and mix. Even professionals of social and behavioural sciences starting jobs in Human Resources or Organizational Development seem to abandon whatever they have learnt as soon as they hit the organization chart! They swap it for 'standard management best practices' and routines, some of which are based on evidence without much consistency.

Homo Imitans (including this book) is saying, "*Hello! Anybody home over there at corporate headquarters? Could we please make a hole in those walls and open a few windows? Look outside. This is how people behave, how social interaction takes place, how 'social movements' appear, how ideas spread, how behaviours are copied, how they create some sort of 'critical mass' that is copied by another critical mass until, suddenly, new norms appear. Do you think that your corporate/organizational world is different? Would you not like to know? And for those of you in the business of 'change' ('management of change', 'change management programmes', etc.) do you really think that macro-social change (that involves people's behaviours, their social networks and some sort of influence) is going to be different from your internal micro-social change?*"

## Some initial principles

So let me make some initial statements:

1. Let me repeat this: Macro-social change (as observed in social movements, the spread of fashions, fads and new ideas, the sometimes apparently unpredictable and irrational massive consumer change in preference, political and social activism such as the Obama campaign, negative social changes such as spread of violent behaviour, health and well-being trends, etc.) has mechanisms that are equally applicable to micro-social change,

8

the kind practiced in day-to-day management of organizations, corporate transformations or the shaping of a new company culture.

2. When applying the microscope to both worlds, you will find the same components: behaviours, social networks, influence, social copying and social reinforcement of some sort.

3. We are beginning to understand the laws that link all those components and make use of them. To do so, we need to reinvent disciplines and break down some walls and silos. The traditional split between Psychology (social or not), Sociology and Anthropology, for example, may remain in schools and colleges, but is no longer useful when trying to understand the world today. Network theory, which extracts meaning and laws from digital networks to social networks, with its maths in the background, is now so close to sociology that any barrier no longer makes sense. A new Social Science is appearing. The world of management needs to embrace it fast or it will be relegated to the mechanics of closing the monthly budget.

4. Because of that growing knowledge, we have passed the stations of curiosity, bafflement and defence and all our trains should now stop at taking charge. We have the possibility of creating positive, large-scale change. We can also create the opposite. The laws are the same. Large-scale change, from very large social change to the less large internal organizational change, is about creating social infections, epidemics. Epidemiology is in. MBA management is out. If you are a leader in an organization, you can't ignore this anymore.

5. Here is another repeat. There is no change unless there is behavioural change. You can change processes and systems, reshuffle reporting lines, restructure the house or all of the above. You may call that change, but it is not change until and unless people do things in a different way and those 'new ways' become new norms. Behavioural change is not an option. It is

9

* * *

> To create a culture of accountability is to create an internal epidemic of behaviours that we can observe and can call 'accountability'.

* * *

not 'another type of change'. Whether in itself ('we need to create a culture of') or in the context of structural and process change, you must hit behaviours or you will be left with superficial refurbishments, musical chairs and a degree of 'hope' that all that will be conducive to a 'new culture'.

6. Behaviours plus influence plus networks create social infections. Let me refine this a bit. Behaviours: we don't need a million of them. A small set usually has the power to create high impact. Influence: not hierarchical influence, because its power doesn't get near that of peer-to-peer influence, the power of 'people like us' on us. Networks: not the structured (straitjacket) teams and committees, but internal social networks of fluid and semi-invisible conversations. Put it all together and orchestrate it and you have the basis for Viral Change™. It is a way of creating real change in real life with real people and now. Viral Change™ is not yet another form of change management or another formal corporate programme on top of the other 25 already running in Cluttered Inc. It is not just a methodology, but a concept of organization and a way of life.

For the last ten years in my work as a consultant, I have helped clients develop collective leadership, reorganize, innovate and in general use the best of behavioural sciences to create lasting change in their organizations. Wanting to articulate my practice, I wrote *Viral Change™: the alternative to slow, painful and unsuccessful management of change in organizations*. The book followed the practice, not the other way around.

In the last five years, I have been leading Viral Change™ programmes with my international team based upon those premises above. We treat change as a social infection, not as an indoctrination through cascaded-down workshops. For us, creating a culture of accountability is to create an internal epidemic of behaviours which can be observed and can then be called 'accountability'. Creating a culture of safety is to create a culture of safe acts, not necessarily a culture of training to avoid accidents. Creating a culture of customer-centrism is to create an internal epidemic of behaviours that, when observed and experienced (by customers as well), we can call the culture we want to have.

Note a couple of things in my language. I am unapologetically using the word 'internal' because the above examples have to do with the behavioural fabric inside the organization. Many behavioural values that a company wants to spread should be spread outside as well. This is the basis for Behavioural Branding. But I am giving modest examples of our organizational work.

The second thing is that I am de facto defining culture by the behaviours that can be observed. This is by design. If you want a culture, define the behaviours and only then label the culture. If you label the culture first, you are stuck with filters and clichés that will force very predictable traits into your culture and you may end up being undistinguishable from your next door competitor. If you are a Best Practice Lover, then that's OK. I wish you well for the few remaining months of your business life.

## Quick tour

In the next chapter, I'll invite you on a tour of the social copying landscape which is inhabited by Homo Imitans. I have artificially divided that land into ten areas. This is far from a suitable classification, but it mirrors the language used today to refer to these mechanisms. Since the knowledge is still scattered all over the place, each discipline or researcher uses their own language.

I invite you to read this next chapter, *The social life of Homo Imitans*, as a social voyeur. Let yourself go and enjoy the tour. Your mind will make judgements here and there, but this is bound to happen, sometimes even days or weeks after reading it.

⊙　⊙　⊙

> Communication is not change. The fact that a myriad of communication consultants call themselves change consultants just shows how foggy this world is.

⊙　⊙　⊙

In chapter 3, *A tale of two worlds*, I tackle the most infuriating mistake Mr. Management has ever made: mixing up the world of communication with the world of behaviours and completely muddling the field of 'change' in the process. These two worlds are entirely different: they have different channels and obtain different results. The currency of the world of communication is information, flowing in many directions (usually down from the top) from a point of departure to a point of destination. Communication is not change. In some doses, it helps change, but it is not change per se. The fact that a myriad of communication consultants call themselves 'change consultants' just shows how foggy this world is.

This communications world is the world of 'presentations', training, cascaded-down PowerPoints, education and most other management activities. Behaviours belong to another world, the world of day-to-day people doing things, copying others, exercising and receiving influence. I call these worlds world I and world II. I feel passionate about the importance of mastering the distinction between them. Mastering the distinction is the pre-requisite to establishing bridges between them and making the most of their combination. If there is a chapter on its own that you could recommend to others to read, this is the one.

In Chapter 4, *The five disciplines of Viral Change™*, I deal with all the ingredients needed. That's right, orchestrating (macro- or micro-) social infections is like cooking. There are lots of recipes around. But before you start cooking, you'd better know about the ingredients: where to source them, how to ensure their quality, getting the quantities right and the ways of mixing them. The following chapters deal with our five ingredients in the Viral Change™ way of creating change:

4.1 *It's behaviours!* Behaviours are a key ingredient. Very often behaviours are chosen poorly, with terrible consequences

4.2 *Scalable influence*, as the ingredient for social copying. And the question is: what kind of influence do we need?

4.3 *Informal networks* and why they matter and need to be nurtured

4.4 *Accelerating a new narrative*: this chapter focuses on stories as the true WMDs (Weapons of Mass Diffusion) of social change

4.5 *Leaders outside the charts*: exploring a special type of leadership you will need for this kind of cooking

In Chapter 5, *Viral Change™ in action*, I deal directly with the bundling of all ingredients into Viral Change™. Let me share upfront what Viral Change™ is, how I spend most of my professional life as a consultant and how we define it. But let me do it using an example. Take safety in organizations. Viral Change™ is a way to create a fast and sustainable culture of safety which does not rely on the rational understanding of hundreds of people attending safety training workshops. In Viral Change™, we identify a relatively small set of 'non-negotiable behaviours' which, when spread across the organization, have the power to create a behavioural fabric, a DNA of safety.

We also identify a relatively small number of individuals who have a high level of influence with peers, who are well connected and whose behaviours are likely to have an impact on others in a multiplying mode. These people may or may not be in specific layers of management, but usually occupy a variety of jobs across the organization.

We then put together these two components, behaviours and influence, in a well-designed format. From there, we let the spread and social infection take off and we backstage the management of it, without a lot of 'formal leadership visibility'. We literally engineer an internal social epidemic of safety behaviours which can be observed and measured.

We do not stop the 'push' of the training and development! We don't ask the Health and Safety people to stop doing their jobs or managers to no longer have safety at the core of their management. But we do orchestrate the 'pull' of connected and influential individuals who engage with peers in (a) conversations and (b) real life 'doing safety' and who (c) engage others in a viral manner through their role-modelling behaviours.

Viral Change™ is the only way to shape a culture of safety through behaviours spread across the board. Viral Change™ becomes the true Return on Investment (ROI) of all the training and communication programmes and a sort of mirror image of the 'command-and-control' system that Health and Safety provides. Many other examples can be found in the next pages. The formula is always the same: small set of behaviours x small number of highly influential individuals x their own natural social networks = Viral Change™. And we will see why 'small' is powerful later on.

In Chapter 6, *The art of social infection*, I step up to a higher level to describe some principles that apply both to macro- and micro-social change. If you are in either business, I'd like you to see yourself as social engineer. Wherever you are and whatever your focus is, these principles may help you to either orchestrate change or to re-think the way you are managing change today.

14

In Chapter 7, *Viral Change™ cannot fail (it can also fail)*, I share with you my views on the efficiency of Viral Change™ and on how we can track the progression of the social infection.

Finally, the Annex gives you a compilation of most of the good data we have around Homo Imitans in action. This data has been published in numerous places and I have attempted to organize it into certain categories as a way to facilitate the understanding of the richness of Homo Imitans life that we have.

*Homo Imitans* is a practitioner's book, part of a family of books. The older sister is *Viral Change™: the alternative to slow, painful and unsuccessful management of change in organizations*. They love travelling together. As sisters, they have lots in common, but also lots of differences. *Disruptive ideas – 10+10+10=1000: The maths of Viral Change that transform organizations* is a good cousin. It articulates thirty initiatives that could be seen as 'small' taken at face value, but that have the potential to create high impact and large-scale changes when spread virally. There are also two second cousins in the leadership branch of the family. The oldest is *The Leader with Seven Faces: Finding your own ways to practise leadership in today's organization* and the youngest *New Leaders wanted: Now hiring! 12 kinds of people you must find, seduce, hire and create a job for*. The family will grow and if you keep in touch, I will introduce you to any newcomers. You can reach me through www.thechalfontproject.com.

## Cogito (I think)

So, having not only declared myself an engineer of social infections, but also issued an invitation to you to join me, I need to deal with the elephant in the room, or better the elephant in the chapter. The elephant has a name: cogito. Cogito ('I think') was left as a bonus in the title of the chapter, remember? How can it be a bonus? Surely I am utterly disrespectful to Homo Sapiens. I feel as if we'll need a much longer chat just for this.

In the business of large-scale change (add your own focus here) we need to be pragmatic. You'll hear me saying that behaviours create culture, not the other way around. This is the pragmatist view. Yes, we would like people to have a good cognitive understanding of the reasons for change, good emotional engagement, good rational view, and a lot of good thinking about it. There are 'methods' for these. They are called communication campaigns, political initiatives, training programmes, educational projects, social debates, or, in the internal micro-social world of the organization, the work of 'management'. All those have a place. It even sounds ridiculous to assert this, particularly as Homo Sapiens.

> * * *
> **The power of large-scale social change is in large-scale social copying. Cogito is a wonderful bonus when you are in need of a revolution.**
> * * *

However, large-scale change—true cultural or transformational change inside the organization or macro-social change—happens as Homo Imitans: behaviours are copied, a critical mass of 'new ways of doing' is created, new critical masses copy the others, a large-scale 'new ways' becomes the norm. Whilst Homo Sapiens is thinking about it, Homo Imitans is copying somebody else's behaviours and doing as he or she does.

Ideology without revolutionaries is armchair revolution. Disease prevention and health education programmes without people changing behaviours is politically correct noise. Training workshops on X for all managers over a one-year programme produces a well-trained workforce, not necessarily a new culture of X, which will only occur when some of those very well-trained people behave in ways that can be copied and emulated by other very well-trained people.

Only behaviours have the power of pulling Homo Imitans together. Find the Homo Imitans with a high power of influence and you'll have fast change (good or bad, so you'd better choose well). The power of large-scale social change is in large-scale social copying. Cogito is a wonderful bonus when you are in need of a revolution.

COPY ERGO SUM

## 2

# The social life of Homo Imitans

Homo Imitans is at the core of evolution. We *are* because we copy. But Homo Imitans did not disappear when Homo Sapiens took over. Like a dinner guest reluctant to leave, Homo Imitans stuck around. Social copying explains so much about our behaviour that sometimes it makes you wonder if Sapiens really deserves the limelight it got. When I was a child, the word 'imitation' came linked with monkeys. Indeed, at 2 or 3 weeks old, both chimps and humans start imitating others. And then the 'monkey see, monkey do' really begins.

There is a whole world of data available on imitation in animals, but my interest in social infection centres around the social life of that odd couple in evolution: Sapiens and Imitans. People have

been documenting the social whereabouts of Homo Imitans for a long time. Some of those accounts belong to the social sciences and only surface in the media occasionally. However, some phenomena start in the media and end up being analyzed or validated by academia.

In the Annex of this book you will find a library of short summaries of the most relevant cases that illustrate this social life. The classification in the Annex is artificial, but deliberate. I grouped them as they tend to appear in public life ('clusters of examples'), but there is a great deal of overlap between the mechanisms involved. I'll take you on a short tour later, but, before that, let me set the scene by sharing some comments on six general and somehow overlapping examples of our social copying life.

## 1.   The power of emotional (super) glue

Homo Imitans is like a living chewing gum. Have you ever noticed? He gets stuck to other Homo Imitans with an emotional investment. Do you have children? Or do you know somebody who has? Or perhaps you remember those days of play and pretending? Children develop and learn from the social proximity of their parents. In the process, they copy adult behaviours, like when they pretend to be their parents by wearing mum's dress or dad's glasses. This also occurs with teachers.

Children sometimes copy not only their manners, but also their handwriting or their verbal stereotypes. And it doesn't only happen in our Western culture. Researchers studied Australian preschoolers and Kalahari Bushman children and found that this copying of adults is common among both.

Furthermore, the child Homo Imitans apparently imitates even if what is to be imitated doesn't seem to have a purpose, whilst

21

other primates don't bother if it doesn't make sense to them[1]. So, who is primal here?

Sometimes the price of emotional proximity is high. Some pairs of Homo Imitans have a toxic influence on each other. You may have seen or known couples where one gets sucked into the negativity of the other, producing a sort of shared misery. When negative emotions are copied, toxicity is high. This is not just influence per se, but copying a way of living. Gloom becomes the norm, even if one of them is far from negative, personality wise. However, the same copying mechanism applies in the opposite situation. A positive attitude and positive thinking are also emotionally copied. We speak of people who are 'contagious' or that their personality is contagious, usually said as a compliment for their enthusiasm or positive attitude... We copy emotions, both on a small and a large scale, and we do so because emotions are Homo Imitans' superglue.

> Role modelling is tricky territory. Like many aspects of the behavioural and social sciences, it contains a high dose of stereotyped thinking that is not always substantiated.

## 2. Role models: a warning

Sometimes you, Homo Imitans, have an emotional and psychological attachment to a (political, religious, literary, societal, etc.) role model. Homo Imitans may copy behaviours, mannerisms, expressions or an entire way of living of particular individuals. We know that. But role modelling is tricky territory.

---

[1] Nauert, R. 2010. Copycat behaviour drives acculturation. *Psych Central.* (http://psychcentral.com/news/2010/05/04/copycat-behaviour-drives-acculturation/13460.html) [Accessed May 2010].

Like many aspects of the behavioural and social sciences, it contains a high dose of stereotyped thinking that is not always substantiated. Take public role models, for example. The question is not whether they are powerful, but what their relative power is when compared with other mechanisms of social influence...

Eating habits are a good example. We spend a lot of time criticizing thin young girls on the catwalk. With their quasi-anorexic looks, we believe they are perverse role models for the younger generation, who will then aspire to become (and stay) a size zero. But if their influence is so powerful, why do we have an epidemic of obesity and not of anorexia? As I have mentioned before, a close friend or a friend of a friend has more power to influence your body weight than thousands of pictures of skinny people in magazines. Close ties may be more powerful than pictures on a screen.

If you navigate the waters of corporate life, as I do as an organizational consultant, you will often hear that the role modelling of the senior leadership team dictates what goes on below them. Or that people in the organization cannot behave in a particular (ethical, effective, open...) way if the leaders at the top don't behave that way. Both claims assume that the leadership or management team at the top has great powers. It is so entrenched in our management thinking that just the idea of challenging this would raise a few corporate eyebrows.

It is difficult to disagree with the idea that the top leadership must surely be behaving following the standards that they wish to be used in the organization and that if these standards are poor, it is likely that the organization is on shaky ground to say the least.

But the opposite is not necessarily true. Many leadership teams and boards behave one way, adhering to the high end of the value spectrum, presiding over an organization not entirely

23

consistent with that. I know many people who don't like to hear this.

Of course, management exercises an important hierarchical influence. But compared with other sources of influence within the organization, the top can't keep pace with the power of what has been described as 'people like me' or 'people like us'[2]. Or simply 'one of us'. People tend to rely on other people with whom they share similar status (defined in a very broad sense), similar ideas, similar worries, similar 'language'... in short, a similar life. Let's call them 'peers'. Peer-to-peer influence is greater than hierarchical influence. We will revisit this later on in the book.

Within the organization, Viral Change™ orchestrates peer-to-peer relations, as we will see in chapter 5. In the macro-social arena, if we want to create an epidemic of 'a good cause', we would be better off looking for 'friends', 'peers' and 'people like us', instead of public (moral, religious, civic) role models.

As I will repeat in chapter 6, politicians and social organizers (with notable exceptions) are barking up the wrong tree and are relying too much on the power of religious figures such as priests, imams or clan leaders who hardly belong to the 'people like me' category. In a nutshell, if you want changes in youth groups, get youngsters involved. There are some trans-cultural nuances to consider, but the weight of those 'cultural differences' must not cloud the more primal and socially scalable power of the 'peer-to-peer' or 'people like me' influence.

---

[2] Edelman's annual Trust Barometer constitutes an important data source for exploring the power of 'people like me'. This category scores higher than the CEO as a source of trust inside a corporation. The scores, however, change every year and also differ between countries. The 2011 data suggest a drop in the 'people like me' category due to the growing credibility of 'accredited spokespersons'. The CEO has regained some ground, but still only half the people are prepared to state they trust their CEO. See: http://www.edelman.co.uk/trustbarometer [Accessed May 2010-Feb. 2011].

## 3. Contagion in closed environments

The pre-existence or the engineering of a common goal very often links people together in a way that accelerates social copying. In a recent television series in England, school students with no particular singing skills or interest in singing were invited by a charismatic young (external) teacher to create a choir in a school without choir tradition. At first, the teacher was frustrated as he was not able to get many students to join. Then, a tipping point moment followed where the enrolment of some induced the enrolment of others and, suddenly, a very reasonably-sized choir was formed. At some point ('threshold change'), social copying (enrolling, attending class, singing, rehearsing) took over and singing in a choir became acceptable. Eventually, this brand new choir entered a large public competition at a first-class venue[3].

Many of the components of social contagion that will be addressed in this book were present in that television series. The champions: mainly the young teacher and the head of music. The backstage leaders: the headmaster and other teachers. At first, they were baffled, but then they understood that their role was to support the choir in the background and to be seen doing so; not to come along to choir rehearsals and pontificate about 'the importance of singing'. The behaviours: joining the queue for enrolment, rehearsing, being punctual and talking about it. The attitude of the students: initially sceptical and even hostile, but then turning into positive when they saw a critical mass (a group of their own peers) on board. The threshold change: slow intake and change at the beginning, then things speeding up quite quickly. The social reinforcement: being able to sing per se and in front of people; the visit from other young choir singers from another school of similar social status ('people like us') and, probably, the presence of the cameras.

---

[3] See: http://www.bbc.co.uk/sing/choir/about.shtml [Accessed May 2010].

What a fantastic showcase of (1) behavioural change management and (2) social infection! It could have become viral change if those students would then have engaged other students in other schools to repeat the process.

The declared focus of 'the project' (to prove that young people could sing) missed the point. The real potential was not only that young people *could* sing, but that the social epidemic of singing (read: joining in, learning, singing, performing, celebrating) could be scaled up, spreading the positive social consequences which were vastly greater in magnitude than just singing.

## 4. Joining the crowd

The crowd is group contagion on a larger scale and with broader borders. Crowd behaviour has been studied from many angles and in a nutshell, two streams are apparent. People join a crowd because of a conscious or unconscious, rational or irrational affinity to something or the desire to behave in a particular way. This is called convergent theory. But the crowd itself, for whatever reason, also makes people behave in a particular way. This is called contagion theory. You can see that both are possible and likely to appear together.

Homo Imitans has some characteristics that make him find affinity with others (convergence). Once inside the crowd or large social group, he can see others 'going with the flow'. It's a visible phenomenon. And so, he will become infected by the collective behaviour (contagion), which will reinforce his belonging to the crowd. But there is a third element. The collective itself may also create its own emergent and somehow invisible rules. This trio of crowd rules also explains quite a lot of what is going on inside organizations even if strictly speaking organizations are not crowds. People may join an organization because they want to be part of it. There may be many reasons. Once inside, 'the organization joins them'.

Now, some crowds are one-off phenomena, others are transitory, some recurrent (civil rights protests) and some are established rituals (religious gatherings). In some crowds the stability is often precarious. The crowd's own rules can be broken very easily by small deviations, particularly if Homo Imitans has 'converged' from different 'positions' and uses the crowd as a vehicle of expression. In crowd mode, sometimes all it takes is a minority of rule-breakers to exacerbate hidden emotions in Homo Imitans. The anti-Iraq war demonstrations in the UK and other parts of the world saw enormous (largely self-organized) crowds composed of a variety of unlikely companions. On the surface, they all had the anti-war theme in common, but the motivations behind their anti-war stance and the 'crowd-joining' mechanisms were extremely diverse. The crowd, which can have its own personality and emotions, is the perfect social copier and amplifier. An old classification of primal emotions is useful here[4]. It is said that if the dominant emotion is fear, the crowd could convert it into panic. If it's craze, the crowd produces joy. If it's anger, the crowd breeds hostility.

Incidentally, I believe my parents may have inadvertently been very fond of the convergent theory, as they often used the Spanish expression 'Dios los cria y ellos se juntan'. This translates roughly as 'God creates them and then they get together', pretty much meaning people always seem to be able to find like-minded people and associate themselves with those. The English say 'birds of a feather flock together', but in my parents' opinion that always meant something more. It meant trouble...

## 5. Self-regulation and the closed group

In the seventies, I was a practicing psychiatrist in Spain and I frequently observed a curious phenomenon of conformity self-regulation in groups. At that time, there were numerous groups of young people living in the countryside, sharing a communal

---

[4] Smelser, N. 1962. *Theory of Collective Behaviour.* New York: Free Press.

life. As much as there may have been a noble, idealistic and counter-cultural aim, they all looked weird to everybody else. They were all carbon copies of each other in clothing and physical appearance. This is how they expressed their rejection of the rest of us in suits and ties.

Life inside these communes was pretty intense, even if their members told you otherwise. There was a tight, unwritten set of rules which held the community together. Under the appearance of a free world, there were lots of borders and 'regulations', even if the latter were not recorded in a Standard Operating Procedure manual. They were typical cases of the 'Dios los cria y ellos se juntan'.

This environment attracted lots of young people from many categories: disillusioned youngsters, counterculturalists, those rejecting their parents, people wanting to save the world or refusing to join the capitalist society, music lovers, love lovers, sex lovers, drug lovers and chronic hippies. It also attracted mentally ill people.

In psychiatry, a delusion is a firm, unshakeable belief in something that has no basis in reality. For example, my thoughts are stolen by a third person. The thought process behind this belief is solid and unbreakable. Rational counter-arguments don't work, because there is nothing rational about the logic of interaction of the deluded, mentally ill person. A psychotic person thinks and behaves in a strange manner and changing that will not happen by any rational means. That is why psychotherapy or 'talk therapies' don't work here.

As you can imagine, there was a lot of irrationality in those communities and very often it was difficult to distinguish between the counterculturalist with an intact brain (or perhaps a brain partially challenged by a recreational substance) and the psychotic who was convinced that an extra-terrestrial visited him every night and took energy from him.

28

In the context of day-to-day life in the rural commune, all behaviours were constantly mixed together and even the most astute anthropologist would probably not have grasped the differences or spotted the mentally ill. But the commune people did. The rest of the counterculturalists, hippies, strange-looking, weird, bizarre and obviously wacky people rejected the psychotic, which in some cases would simply be translated as *"you need help, man!"*

> *Tribal Homo Imitans copies clothing, hairstyle, lexicon, behaviours and rituals. In the era of the cult of diversity, our similarities are embarrassingly colossal.*

This self-regulation of belonging to the group took place all the time as a means to protect the integrity and homogeneity of the group. To you and me, that homogeneity looked pretty heterogeneously wild. But the group conformity mechanism could spot 'the real alien' better than any of us. Conformity is an incredibly powerful phenomenon which has been studied hundreds of times. Homo Imitans uses it to accommodate to the social group, to belong. Most of it happens unconsciously. This case of communal self-regulation may be extreme, but it contains many of Homo Imitans' evolutionary ingredients. Belonging has a price. It is called conformity and it works nicely in the next example.

## 6. Tribes and rituals

Forget tribes in Polynesia. Open your windows and you'll see urban tribes, corporate tribes, religious tribes, political tribes and sports tribes. The 'social proof' mechanism of influence operates nicely here, sometimes even without saying a word. This mechanism ensures that 'everybody here says, does, behaves, wears X, Y, Z, etc'. This is the generic, largely unconscious copying and imitation that has been well-studied by sociologists

29

and social psychologists for many years under the broad label of 'conformity' mechanisms, which I mentioned above.

Homo Imitans needs to belong to and feel part of something that provides meaning, context or simply a psychological (or physical) shelter (a safe(r) place or a power/control centre). This was the case in the communes in the seventies and it still happens in day-to-day society today. Tribal Homo Imitans copies clothing, look and hairstyle, lexicon, behaviours and rituals[5]. In the era of the cult of diversity, our similarities are embarrassingly colossal.

Corporate Homo Imitans is particularly interesting. One of the problems of 'modern management' is that it ignores anthropology[6]. It thinks it doesn't need it in order to calculate Return on Investment (ROI) or to deliver the five-year strategic plan. But corporate Homo Imitans is a perfect object of interest under the anthropological umbrella. It has rites of passage (talent pool goes to Harvard), rituals (annual business plan process), tribal ceremonies (offsite conferences for the entire company) and other gluing mechanisms.

Some of those corporate rituals practiced by Homo Imitans on the payroll are completely inefficient from the organizational or business perspective (in some cases even utterly useless). This is a fact well-known by many corporate leaders.

---

[5] See www.exactitudes.com for a visual treat on the similar looks of Homo imitans

[6] With almost anecdotal exceptions, corporate anthropology is not part of the mainstream management disciplines. Today, there are relatively small groups of anthropologists who have traded remote tribal observations for the boardroom or teambuilding programs. As with many other social scientists (psychologists, social psychologists, sociologists), once they get injected into the corporate life, they seem to be swallowed by the glamour of management thinking and Best Practices and they often become indistinguishable from everybody else. This is probably an unkind judgment of those professionals trained in social disciplines. I accept that. I just get frustrated when I see some very good social psychologists converted into mediocre HR managers.

So why do intelligent, professional, efficient, sensible and often mindful managers or leaders keep doing them? Rationality is not going to get us anywhere here.

Those inefficient and largely not very cost-effective processes or 'events', such as the sales convention and the company-wide off-site conference, are alive because they are more than processes or events...they are rituals. Corporate rituals are the visible expression of the invisible logic of the organization. These events serve the extra-functionality of any ritual: they create a glue, a link, a sense of belonging (even if temporary), a 'raison d'être', a point in the calendar that provides some sort of meaning, 'something to go to' or to 'get through'. Those rituals are often a platform for intense social copying and social reinforcement.

Rituals that are effective both on the business AND the organizational level are rare. Most of the time there is a disconnect between the business functionality (poor) and the ritual and tribal functionality (very high). One of the visible effects of a sudden cost-cutting exercise in the firm is the almost automatic suppression of some rituals: no more off-site meetings, no more transcontinental travel for a meeting, no more people sent to business schools...

But rituals can't be suppressed. We can't pretend that we can get rid of them, leaving a vacuum behind. The annual sales conference can be cancelled for cost-cutting reasons, but it will probably be substituted by regional/local ones, a digital one, a series of internal meetings with lots of PowerPoints, teambuilding exercises, local dinner meetings or something else. The platform for belonging and expressing mimicked behaviours must exist one way or another. And if there is a real vacuum or a shortage, a new 'corporate initiative' will be launched for the corporate tribes. Tribal behaviour helps us understand a lot of Homo Imitans' social life. Today's anthropology should move from the jungle to Wall Street.

**'Homo Imitans in action'**

## Touring the social life

Let's tour Homo Imitans' social life. This promenade has 10 stops, highlighting 10 sections. Each of them corresponds with its own section in the Annex, which provides some extra background and references for you to explore.

### 1. Homo Imitans syncs and memes

For starters, Homo Imitans syncs, on an emotional, linguistic and psychomotor level. As we have seen, Homo Imitans has the ability to copy complex behaviours from other Homo Imitans, but is also still able to copy some simple ones. We all show primitive forms of copying that remind us that evolution only upgraded us yesterday. Why on earth do I have to yawn when I am sitting next to somebody who yawns? Why do I smile when someone else smiles? Why do 400 people clap rhythmically together at a concert instead of each clapping randomly to their own beat? And why do women living together in the same house tend to align their menstrual cycles? For some reason, evolution has given us an extraordinary ability to synchronize[7]. Maybe it got overlooked in the latest upgrade.

Sync also includes verbal behaviour. Corporate Homo Imitans tends to use business jargon and some of it seems to have tremendous memetic abilities, because fellow Homo Imitans copy and spread it easily. I am not talking about the standard business jargon that has become more or less universal, but about the sub-culture jargon that seems to come out of nowhere. Suddenly everybody (in a particular company) uses it, even if its strict linguistic meaning is far from clear. I remember three distinctive business 'memes' from my days in corporate life. They originated somewhere in the Californian headquarters

---

[7] A fascinating read: Strogatz, S.H. 2003. *SYNC: The emerging science of spontaneous order*. New York: Hyperion.

33

and then infected all the brains on the payroll: 'germane' (for relevant or appropriate), 'granular' (for detail or detailed) and 'we as a team' (for we). All that was needed was one guy saying 'granular' in a meeting and the other 20 in the room would inject 'granular' in a sentence whenever possible. This automatic imitation was perhaps a sort of mental reassurance that we all belonged to the same tribe. It was as noticeable as annoying. People outside the corporate world are sometimes amazed to hear what they call 'corporate speak': usually incomprehensible, robotic and terribly boring. Most of the time corporate dialects have less to do with corporate needs than with tribal needs. If you work somewhere with a heavy corporate dialect, you either speak it already and don't notice it, or you do notice it and feel odd about it. If it's the latter, see that as an early warning sign for rethinking your tribal membership.

## 2. Panic and collective fear

Situations with high emotional levels based on fear are natural incubators for social contagion. The Tylenol scare in 1982, where seven people died as a consequence of the action of one person, triggered copycat cases involving anything from mouthwash to sweets which were thought to be contaminated. Legions of 'poisoned' people had the same symptoms. Many 'allergy epidemics' follow the same pattern: there was no real allergy, but a physical reaction imitated socially and unconsciously.

Also, fear of a common enemy not only unites populations, but transfers and copies the same emotions thousands of times. Many politicians seem to know this. Fear of the end of the world has also created widespread contagious effects within a particular population. The fear ingredient is a universal trigger for social grouping and fast social infections. Homo Imitans finds refuge in the shelter of collective fear (see the Annex for examples).

34

### 3. Fads, fashions and consumer behaviours

Social fashions (ideas, clothing, music, consumer preferences, etc.) spread via social imitation. All of them have two things in common:

1. there is no obvious command-and-control centre.
2. in all of them behavioural copying travels through social networks.

Not that long ago you could see the curious phenomenon of crowds queuing outside Apple stores. These people were waiting—some even overnight!—to buy a phone from a company that had never produced one. Madness? By the end of 2009, more than 49 million Homo Imitans owned that black and white rectangular thing. I am one of them.

> A new movement tends to arise somewhere and spreads, not on its own merit, but on the back of social proof: company X uses Y, most companies use Y. Therefore, we must also use Y.

Fads are transitory phenomena, while social and consumer trends, like fashion, are more stable[8]. Many of those fashions tend to fully characterize a particular time. You can see those effects better than anywhere in management practices. Management 'movements' tend to have their own lifecycle[9]. For example, the Total Quality Movement (TQM), reengineering and Six Sigma have dominated management thinking for many years. A new movement tends to arise somewhere and spreads, not necessarily on its own merit, but on the back of a

---

[8] Newman, R. 2005. Fad products and brands: How to identify and market them. *Scribd.* http://www.scribd.com/doc/3682590/Newman-Marketing-Fads [Accessed May 2010].

[9] Strang, D., S. A. Soule. 1998. Diffusion in organizations and social movements: From hybrid corn to poison pills. *Annual Review of Sociology.* 24:265-90.

sort of social proof mechanism: company X uses Y and most companies use Y. Therefore, it must be good...so, we must also use Y.

Broadcasting trends, use of technology and its adoption, toys ... Wherever you look, you see social infection with its highs and lows. The most visible part of the infection is the 'threshold change' that I referred to before. This is the point where something has suddenly become 'the norm', as if in the blink of an eye. And sometimes, that 'norm' only lasts for a little while. I will explore models of influence later on in the book and will draw on social fashions to extract some principles that could be more universally applied.

## 4. Political and civic activism

The most recent American presidential election is a great source of insight into Homo Imitans in action. If you want to practice armchair social anthropology, forget textbooks about the Polynesian islands! Simply read the campaign account of Barack Obama's campaign manager[10]. The campaign focused on expanding the voter base, that is: add new voters. But besides this and other strategic components of the campaign, two things are particularly relevant to our purposes and the theme of this book:

(1) The acknowledgment and realization that voting is contagious. The probability of you voting increases significantly when somebody close to you votes. 'Turnout cascades' can be produced by the simple visible trigger of people close to you 'intending to vote'. And the 'intending' per se seems to do the trick. Data suggests that one decision to vote may trigger on average three others in the close social network.

---

[10] Plouffe, D. 2009.*The audacity to win: The inside story and lessons of Obama's historic victory.* New York: Viking.

(2) The confirmation that social networks are important. Conversations *within* the network, people talking to people ('people like us'), were actually more important than Obama talking directly to the huge social networks. The website my.barackobama.com was instrumental to those conversations. The campaign managers understood the importance of social networks and provided the technology for the network to have conversations. They literally nurtured the network in the way I refer to in chapter 4.3 where I say 'the network is the asset'. Following the campaign success, the movement 'Organizing for America' took over and now continues what the campaign started. Political and civic activism was not invented by the Obama campaigners; they just elevated it to a new high in which Homo Imitans took central stage. Interestingly, when the initial honeymoon period came to a close, some people in the US administration started looking back at the fundamentals of the campaign to see if it was possible to reuse those techniques.

## 5. Collective hysteria

Epidemics of laughter, dancing or 'poison in the air' have been documented for many years. These phenomena are extraordinarily colourful (see the Annex) and therefore they hit the news. People tend to see them as a curiosity. However, they represent examples of the extraordinary plasticity of Homo Imitans: able to infect others not just with emotions, but with clusters of real psychosomatic and physical symptoms. Because of their intense and visible nature, these epidemics have always been well studied. Physical cause has never been found.

Hysteria—manifested in the form of abnormal movements, paralysis or other symptoms such as lack of sensation without physical cause—has been fading in the Western world, but only recently. Hysteria was still a key focus of psychiatry in the nineteenth century. Jean-Martin Charcot's clinic in the Parisian hospital La Salpêtrière was pioneering what we today call neurology. Charcot described many modern illnesses such as

37

multiple sclerosis, but he also focused on hysteria, which he (wrongly) believed was a hereditary neurological condition. He was very good not only at describing it, but also at inducing it in patients. Bodies would be paralyzed and sensations blocked under the command of his larger than life presence. It was the best show in town, with student audiences coming from all over Europe.

As a young psychiatrist and academic, I was invited by the French authorities to visit La Salpêtrière more than 30 years ago. I could not help but feel that some of those walls and gardens must have seen Charcot going from session to session. The pictures I had only seen in books came to life.

Hysteria had been common, but I hardly saw any similar clinical cases during my years of medical practice. Hysteria was in the textbooks for many years, certainly still in mine, but it progressively faded when Homo Imitans decided to show more sophistication and started to express himself in a more Sapiens way. Instead of paralyzed arms and legs, ulcers, headaches and hypertension became the 'preferred bodily expression' of psychological causes.

The social hysteria phenomena of collective dancing or laughter described in the Annex are reminiscent of what the students of Le Salpêtrière must have seen within those walls.

## 6. Suicide

Clusters of suicide have been described for years in different locations, sometimes under the label of 'copycat suicides'. They tend to take place in close communities and often affect young people. The clusters get attention for obvious reasons. The number of individuals attempting to commit or actually committing suicide in those clusters is always above the statistical rate for the population. The media has been blamed for possibly spreading it even further by giving these clusters extra airtime and perhaps even glorifying the behaviour[11]. In the face of these kinds of dramatic events, people crave for logic and tend to 'find' dozens of explanations such as stress and working conditions, as was the case for a recent cluster of suicides at Foxconn, the world's biggest IT factory in Taiwan[12]. The reality is that even if such conditions were present, they are no different from hundreds of similar situations where suicide clusters do not appear.

> ⚀ ⚀ ⚀
>
> The popular profile of suicide bombers has consistently unravelled over time, showing less and less correlation with almost anything. Certainly no patterns of madness or 'disenfranchised and uneducated'.
>
> ⚀ ⚀ ⚀

Suicide bombers are a different story, but not that different. Homo Imitans plays his role and so do the media managed by Homo Sapiens. In fact, there is data suggesting that Imitans may be bigger than Sapiens where suicide bombers are concerned. The popular belief that suicide bombers are directly connected with social, political and economic conditions, or religious fanaticism, makes it harder to believe that a more basic mechanism may be in place. There is no question that suicide bombers appeared as a result of those conditions, for example, in Sri Lanka or the Middle East. But once the behaviour started to spread and was socially reinforced by the media (and the community), the pattern started to show more and more copycat symptoms. The popular profile of

---

[11] Coleman, L. 2004. *The copycat effect: How the media and popular culture trigger the mayhem in tomorrow's headlines.* New York: Paraview Pocket Books. Also see: Copycats and social contagion: copycat suicides and the media. *Samaritans.* http://www.samaritans.org/media_centre/copycats.aspx [Accessed may 2010].

[12] See: Foxconn offers pay rises and suicide nets as fears grow over wave of deaths. 28 May 2010. *The Guardian. http://www.guardian.co.uk/world/2010/may/28/foxconn-plant-china-deaths-suicides [Accessed May 2010].*

suicide bombers has consistently unravelled over time, showing less and less correlation with almost anything. Certainly no madness or psychopathology (popular belief) and no pattern of 'disenfranchised and uneducated' (another popular belief). Religious fanaticism is also invoked as 'a cause', but in the list of groups employing these tactics, the secular group is the majority[13]. The fact that political leaders may 'manipulate' people to use these tactics is not in conflict with the fact that the behaviour itself may be mainly spread through social copying. Trigger and spread are two different things in behavioural terms.

> ⬤ ⬤ ⬤
>
> The probability of you becoming obese will increase when your close friend becomes obese. Siblings and spouses are less powerful than friends in spreading obesity.
>
> ⬤ ⬤ ⬤

## 7. Health and well-being habits

Knowledge about the social life of Homo Imitans increased rapidly after the Framingham Heart Study. Started in 1948, this study followed thousands of people for many years and was focused on understanding the risk factors for coronary disease, stroke, heart failure and other physical conditions. But the researchers were very good at recording an incredible amount of 'extra' background information. This allowed Fowler and Christakis to analyze data of more than 12,000 people, which included the target population being followed as well as its close social network. Both researchers extracted incredibly valuable insights into how obesity, smoke cessation, drinking, loneliness and even happiness spread across social networks. A common finding emerged: the importance of a close friend. Take obesity. As I

---

[13] See data from The Chicago Project on Security and Terrorism (CPOST) on http://cpost.uchicago.edu/. Also see: Marsden, P., S. Attia. 2005. A deadly contagion? The Psychologist. 18(3): 152-155.

mentioned before, the probability of you becoming obese will increase when your close friend becomes obese. Siblings and spouses were less powerful than friends in spreading obesity.

The data has been published in numerous places, including the prestigious New England Journal of Medicine and, more recently, in an excellent book[14]. Similar patterns apply to smoke cessation (probability of being successful) and the other situations mentioned above (for more detail, see the Annex).

Think about it! Here we have something 'physical' like obesity, with all its genetic and environmental hooks, largely depending on what friends of yours do! Homo Imitans shows not only how dependent we are on our Ortegian 'circumstance', but also how much we depend on our close connections in our social networks. The findings of these studies have significant consequences for tackling public health issues and developing 'campaigns'. The pattern emerging from many studies and observations—from large-scale well-being initiatives to mechanisms of change inside organizations—is that the social network and the position of the individual in the network are responsible for a significant part of what happens in the reality of social contagion.

## 8. Violence/ aggressive behaviour

Although the violence of suicide bombers could easily have been quoted here, this is more about the day-to-day violence in our streets. From the myriad of cases, studies, reviews and circumstances written about in social sciences and criminology, I am fascinated most by the Chicago Ceasefire project, which uses Viral Change™ techniques without labelling them as such! The project has managed to decrease street violence and shootings by more than 42% by employing counter-epidemic techniques

---

[14] Christakis, N.A., J.H. Fowler. 2009. *Connected: The surprising power of our social networks and how they shape our lives.* New York: Little Brown and Company.

(see Chapter 6). Street violence is an epidemic of violence where behaviours are copied and spread. Not Homo Imitans' finest hour, but Homo Imitans nevertheless.

## 9. Financial contagion and behavioural economy

Homo Imitans and money make an interesting pair. The markets have seen unprecedented turmoil recently and many of the behaviours noticed can be explained by a great deal of imitation and social contagion, both at the individual and collective levels. For some reason, the term 'herd behaviour' is used more in this arena than anywhere else. Domino effects were noticed in the streets of major cities when people queued to withdraw money from bank branches after some people started doing so (Northern Rock in the UK). On a collective level, 'market behaviour' was copied over and over, creating cascade epidemics. What's more, these observations don't belong to specialized press, but could be seen on your TV screens and read about in your daily newspapers.

## 10. Conformity & contagion experimental phenomena

Social sciences have a long history of experimental studies looking at how individuals conform to the norm, how they 'obey' instructions or how they copy others. The literature is vast. The Annex highlights some key sources. Some of those experiments are decades old, but have never quite made it into the public domain, let alone across the threshold of corporate headquarters. Only recently, as a result of social events, these experiments have gained some public visibility.

In one of these experiments, Zimbardo, Professor Emeritus of Psychology at Stanford University, reproduced jail conditions for students and asked them to play the role of either an inmate or a guard. The guards (in uniforms) took their role so seriously, the experiment turned nasty and had to be stopped. As it took place in 1972, it was an old experiment.

But when the conditions of the Abu Ghraib jail in Iraq were seen on TV, showing Homo Sapiens in military uniforms inflicting inhumane psychological pain on naked fellow Homo Sapiens, The New York Times and other newspapers reflected, *"Here we go again! This is the Stanford prison experiment, but this time for real."*

To finish this chapter, I include two articles that I wrote a few years ago for my monthly column on management in Scrip Magazine[15]. You can skip them now and dive into the next chapter (returning to read them later on), or you can read them now to consider the social life of Homo Imitans once more.

It is my firm belief that the only way to orchestrate epidemics of goodness (please translate ad libitum) is to learn in a humble way how malleable we are, how Homo Imitans is always there (even in a grey suit bought with a Homo Sapiens credit card). Our human nature can go in any direction. It is up to us which one to choose.

Organizational change and macro-social change can be directed towards destruction of values, domestication of the individual or selfish goals benefitting a controlling elite. Or it can be aimed at value creation, enhancement of the individual and collective wealth, including profit. The ethical choice is not in the hands of the behavioural or social psychologists, but pretty much in yours and mine.

Understanding what Homo Imitans can do is the first step in the process of applying that energy and those possibilities to a positive change goal (read: change management).

---

[15] Scrip magazine was a monthly publication for the Pharmaceutical and Health Care industry, but has ceased publication.

## It's the system, not me[1]

Not many people knew what was going on in the psychology department. Nothing unusual about that. An advert in the local newspaper offered volunteers a few dollars for participating in an experiment, and many people from the city of New Haven applied.

The study was run by Stanley Milgram, a small curious assistant professor specializing in social experiments. This one examined the effects of punishment—administered here as an electric shock—on learning. The psychologist conducting the experiment read sequences of words to be repeated: house, money, flower, pretty, whether, cat. Each time a subject got them wrong, the volunteer, who was sitting on the other side of a one-way glass screen, administered a small electric shock. The potency of the shock increased progressively with each mistake – the lever moving from 25v to 30v, 40v and so on.

As the experiment continued, the subject's reaction changed from a grimace to expression of more and more discomfort. Invariably, the level became very unpleasant, even unbearable. The subject would be almost screaming. The administrator objected. *"Never mind,"* the psychologist said, *"this is a well-controlled experiment, you need to keep pushing the button."* Screams. *"I want to stop. He wants to get out."* *"No,"* said the psychologist, *"keep trying. It's the protocol, we can't break this experiment yet."* And so it continued until the pain was intolerable and the administrators were shaking. But they kept pushing the button. Well, some of them: 65 % to be precise. The other 35% gave up and refused to continue the torture.

The experiments were repeated and repeated, always the same: mistakes, shocks, up, up, up. And the citizens from New Haven kept pushing the button even though they were torturing the guy on the other side of the screen. Again and again, 65% complied with the instructions, and 35% told the psychologist to keep the money. More screams, more shocks and more knowledge about learning.

---

[1] First published in Scrip Magazine, May 2004.

And what we learned was that 65% of normal citizens from the normal town of New Haven were prepared to administer increasingly potent shocks to their increasingly terrified fellow human beings, for a few bucks, for science and for following instructions. But here's the trick. Nobody really got shocked. The subjects were actors pretending to get near convulsions each time the button was pushed.

For a long time, these experiments were known only to academics and they remain controversial to this day. They were subject to normal academic scrutiny and, although they were officially labelled obedience experiments, some psychologists argued they did not measure obedience but trust. Other discussions, then and now, centred on their true social meaning. Could we apply the laboratory findings to real life? There are tons of pages on this subject, half in favour, half against. For many, the experiments amounted to post-holocaust soul-searching as to why normal humans obey orders. Other groups of social psychologists have focused on what might distinguish the 65% from the other 35%. Is there a particular personality that correlates with one group or the other? Can we predict who will keep pushing the button? To this day, no-one has come up with a good answer to any of these questions and we are left with the hard facts: 65% of us ("*Not me,*" I hear you say) will keep obeying the instructions.

For people alien to the behavioural sciences these may be pretty unexpected, surprising and possibly disturbing results. Many years as a practising psychiatrist have made me slightly cynical about human nature and I am not half as disturbed as the average reader might be. I have been a spectator to many kinds of human misery, usually not in the public knowledge. But the Milgram experiments are distinctive. They did not deal with psychologically-disturbed or unfit people. These were normal citizens pushing the button. No matter how many academic papers refine the data, criticize the methodology, pontificate about the 'social transfer principle' (to decide whether laboratory findings can be applied in a less controlled setting) or argue as to whether the experiment examined obedience, trust, authority or hidden sadism, one cannot ignore the fact that real people inflicted what they thought was real pain on fellow human beings, simply because they were following orders.

The good news is that in management we don't have electric shocks. The bad news is that there is a worse kind of pain than that inflicted by voltage: psychological pain. The dynamics of power in our organizations are very rich. We exercise power, obey orders and follow instructions. We also challenge them, resist or decide not to comply. In the process, organizational life sometimes serves as a coverall excuse for many things that would not be accepted in normal life. How many times have we said, or heard, "It's not me, it's the system. If it were up to me, I would let you do it."

I have always been fascinated by the pervasive use of 'they' in organizations. 'They' want this. 'They' forced me to do that. What fascinates me even more is how often I have heard it used by senior people, even those at the very top. Who is 'they' in those cases? In my experience, it's a virtual, almost Olympic 'they' – the system, the best, most convenient and unaccountable management black hole.

We don't need the man in Milgram's lab to tell us, "Keep pushing, it's an experiment, for goodness sake. Do you think you can break the protocol just like that?" Our managers, supervisors, directors and vice-presidents, you and me—65% of us, if Milgram is right—will say "I am sorry, John, it's not me, it's the system. I have to inflict this pain on you. I don't want to, but I have no choice." In organizations, such behaviour comes in many forms and shapes. A 30-volt shock, for example, is forcing people to do something that is a hassle, unnecessary and serves no purpose other than to boost the ego of the person giving the instructions. A 50-volt shock might involve denying someone that little, perhaps one-off, opportunity for flexi-time that would make all the difference to the employee's family and no difference whatsoever to the business. A higher voltage could entail submitting somebody to unnecessary humiliation and considerable psychological pain by requesting an action that serves no purpose other than as a public show of power.

I have seen the latter done to someone going through a terrible family crisis. Nevertheless, she was told, "I am sorry, we have to do this, it's the system. There is nothing I can do." It was a fantastic lie; there was a lot the manager could have done.

An even higher voltage: a manager resigns to go to a competitor. Suddenly, panic explodes in the legal department and managing director's office. The resigning manager is escorted from the building with no time to explain his departure to his staff. He is treated like a terrorist-cum-industrial-spy, and humiliated personally and socially for hours. I have seen the practice so many times and it is stupid. It assumes, among other things, that it is maintaining company security by preventing the manager from ...doing what, exactly? Stealing his filing cabinet? Copying his hard drive? It insults the intelligence of the resigning manager (who has had plenty of time to copy the contents of the entire company computer had he wanted to). It serves no real business purpose and is humiliating and painful. The only conclusion that can be drawn from this is either that the legal department and managing director's office are populated by stupid people, or, more scarily, they are normal and follow stupid orders from 'the system'.

How we manage different levels of psychological voltage is personal to us. A low voltage for me might be a high voltage for you. But all of us, I bet, have experienced cases of *"It's not me, it's the system. A little shock, a big shock. I know you are going to scream, but there is little I can do."* The most worrying thing is that, with few exceptions, we are the normal citizens of New Haven, not personality disorders waiting to strike.

## Roles, power and uniforms[2]

The pictures that shocked the world will still be in many people's minds when the name Abu Ghraib is forgotten. The scenes of Iraqi prisoners and their American custodians made front pages and prime time everywhere. The sense of disgust was universal, but apart from this there was a varied spectrum of reactions. There were the politico-military questions. How on earth could this happen? Were the perpetrators just a few bad apples? How far up the chain of command did it go? There was the socio-political question: to what extent can this type of thing be justified? And there was the plain, 'normal citizen' question: how on earth can human beings do this to one another?

---

[2] First published in Scrip Magazine, July/August 2004.

Now the blame has gone in several directions, the buck has stopped somewhere, so we are told, and the whole thing will soon more or less evaporate into history. American writer Gore Vidal reacted to the events of 9/11 with a sharp, cynical and otherwise politically incorrect comment: "*It will be all over by the Christmas sales.*" It didn't quite happen like that, but he wanted to make the point of just how fragile our collective memory is. The Abu Ghraib saga, I suspect, will be contained one way or another, and soon consigned to the black book of black history. Period.

Among the thousands of articles and references relating to Abu Ghraib there was an unpretentious, not terribly prominent and matter-of-fact column published in *The New York Times*, which revealed that, at least for a tiny sector of the population, these events were no surprise whatsoever. Anybody with a degree in Social Psychology would have said: "*Aha! This is Milgram and Zimbardo revisited.*" These were the authors of some old psychological experiments that have since been repeated several times. The article mentioned the studies and sought the opinion of people who had taken part.

I referred to Stanley Milgram in a previous article ('It's the system, not me', May 2004). In a nutshell, it involved the citizens of the US town of New Haven who had volunteered to take part in an experiment on the effects of punishment on learning. They played the role of teacher, reciting words that the learners had to repeat correctly or receive an electric shock. The intensity of the shock rose with each mistake, and the learners screamed with each increase, eventually pleading with the teachers to stop. But the psychologist directing the experiment encouraged the teachers to continue regardless. Some refused and some carried on to the maximum voltage, which was labelled 'dangerous'. The proportion of people who continued administering the voltage was 65%. Interestingly, laughter was sometimes the teacher's first reaction when hearing the learner's initial discomfort. The catch, as students know and readers of this column will remember, was that the learners were actors.

In a second study, the Zimbardo experiments, a prison was recreated in the basement of Stanford University with cells, offices, corridors, lights and other paraphernalia. A group of students was invited to participate in a study of role playing.

The group was split into guards and detainees. Full use was made of the appropriate gear for the guards and the detainees and both halves took their role seriously. The guards gave more and more orders, and shouted more and more, as their behaviour reached abuse levels. The detainees were submitted to this and 'typical jail punishments', such as workouts. The atmosphere became progressively more tense, until some of the detainees protested. *"Hey, guys, come on, this is just a game, an experiment, time out!"* But the guards reacted more strongly still. More workouts, more punishment. Fiction became reality, and reality was hard. It was so hard that the experiment had to be stopped after a couple of days – one week before it was due to finish because somebody was going to be killed and others seriously wounded.

Social Psychology studies such topics – often labelled issues of obedience, conformity, authority, attribution and so on. Just for the record, we are not talking here about how these issues relate to psychopaths or deviants, but to normal people. This is the scary part. In theory, any of us could behave in the same way. Lecturers in Social Psychology would invariably ask their classes to guess the percentage of people who would 'obey'. Invariably, the class would be optimistic and predict a low proportion. The students were also asked whether they would do the same in similar circumstances and, guess what, they consistently said *"not me"*. I'm a bit ashamed of my old profession in this respect. Psychiatrists as a group usually put the figure on the low side. With regard to this, a friend of mine consoled me with the explanation that *"because you can cope with so much misery, you must be more optimistic than others"*. Maybe.

So give people roles (and titles) and uniforms (cloth or mental ones) and be ready for the unpredictable. Roles and uniforms allow us to exercise power in a legitimized way, under a given authority, be it the boss, the chain of command or the system. Like Zimbardo's students or the citizens in Milgram's experiment, we may take it very seriously. Roles and uniforms are powerful creators of new persona. Once we get them we are ready for a daily Greek tragedy and a chameleonic transformation into a caring manager, a despot, a Samaritan, a sadist, a teacher, a learner, a benign king, a foot soldier, a general, a preacher, a follower, a mentor, a smiling Buddhist monk or an arms dealer.

If the Social Sciences teach us anything, it is about our incredible plasticity, which we are always more ready to attribute to others than to ourselves. And this fantastic capacity is precisely the good/bad news to consider. Bad news à la Iraq, good news à la all the possible good that roles and uniforms could provide in daily life. And since most of our daily life is spent at work, all the above applies to management and leadership. The problem is that management science has developed thick membranes, as if it needed to protect itself from intrusions by Psychology, Sociology and the other Sciences de l'Homme. Milgram and Zimbardo are not taught in business schools, but I can't think of a better starting point to discuss leadership.

Back to the news. Another article I read was cynical about the 'new' Iraqi police. The occupying forces had finally realized there was no option but to bring back the old police force and the military that had been disbanded. The columnist joked about "*seeing the old moustaches and the old faces back*" and could not understand how we should expect new behaviour from them. Most people would sympathize with this point of view but the tiny minority that belongs to the Social Psychology tribe would have no problem accepting it. If the context changes (and, indeed, it has) this police force may surprise people with its ability to comply with the new regime. A change of uniform and context may create some good, even with the old moustaches. Similarly, providing a positive context in organizations (this is the leader's function) makes roles and uniforms constructive. The same roles—managers, directors, project leaders, heads of HR and vice-presidents—in a negative context create havoc.

The key is the existence or absence of agreement on non-negotiable behaviours, hopefully, but not necessarily, linked to a value system. These non-negotiable behaviours were probably absent in Abu Ghraib, or everything there was possible and negotiable in a contingent way – that is, depending on what needs to be achieved; for example, weakness in the detainees.

Contingent approaches in management and leadership are wonderfully convenient and deeply dangerous, not something that traditional business education is prepared to accept. My unofficial father of contingent leadership is Jack Welch, ex-CEO of General Electric.

He could go from nasty to caring (admittedly mostly the former) 'depending on what was needed', as he himself confessed more than once. My belief is that the most dangerous management statement of all is 'it depends' – but you may think that I am too radical. After all, what's wrong with adapting to situations and moderating behaviour according to the objectives? Milgram, Zimbardo, and my own clinical psychiatry work taught me a long time ago that it is precisely our plasticity that, when married to 'it depends', generates a recipe for disaster. That's why I prefer the concept of solid non-negotiable rules in management, even if I disagree with them in particular, rather than the loose, relativist, contingent, it-depends management that scares me more than Milgram's fake shock machines. The problem is not with the moustaches but with what they are allowed to do when they play guards or detainees, teachers or learners, leaders or followers.

# 3

# A tale of two worlds

We've been getting it wrong time after time. Change management programmes that fail to deliver, many inefficiencies in the management of organizations, the poor performance and big disappointments of government-orchestrated social change interventions, the failed civic or religious campaigns to develop and implement a 'social agenda', the slow, painful and often unsuccessful health education and promotion initiatives...in short, lots of failed attempts to change behaviours in a large population, either inside the firm or in the outside world.

They all have something in common. All these failures stem from the misunderstanding of the differences between two separate worlds, each with their own rules and their own tempo: the world of communication (world I) and the world of behaviours (world II).

These worlds are very different. I have summarized these differences in the graph at the end of this chapter. Yet we mix up these worlds all the time, like mixing apples and pears, pretending that they are the same. After all, they're both fruit. We cross the border between these two worlds at our convenience and we use their attributes indistinctively. And this is where the problem starts.

I deeply believe that achieving success in any of the goals described before, from internal management in the organization to an external macro-social change, depends on mastering both (a) the understanding of and respect for the differences between the two worlds and (b) the establishing of bridges between them without getting them mixed up. Management in particular has not learnt the distinction between world I and world II. It muddles them together as if they were one single territory. The consequences are a series of messy and wrong expectations either about people or 'management systems'.

Things that belong to world I are expected to deliver outcomes that belong to world II and vice versa. For example, behavioural change (world II) is expected to follow an information or communication cascade (world I). Every single day in the management of organizations this mistake is made. The mistake costs time, effort, and results, at the very least, in inefficient management and leadership. Let's look at this in detail.

## World I

In this world, the currency is information: verbal, written or electronic information that flows all around and between us. This is the world of facts, the world with pieces of data or packages of knowledge flowing from one place to another. Homo Sapiens and management love this world. The information is packaged and pre-cooked so that it is digestible, usually presented in PowerPoint dishes or contained in spreadsheet prisons (after all, we call the boxes 'cells'). Bullet points flood corporate life, encapsulating and summarizing thoughts.

In this world, company visions are presented and declarations of intention made. We 'send' guidelines, announcements, directions, pieces of news, congratulations, threats, tricks, explanations on the steps needed to go from A to B and anything else that the label 'communication' can accommodate. The 'organizational logic' is explained and distributed this way. It travels 'down' using traditional communication vehicles (from emails to posters, newsletters and magazines) or more modern media (video, audio or a combination of both).

Formal verbal interactions take place in world I. A significant amount of our time is dedicated to this world. We have 'collaboration devices' to facilitate the currency exchange: meetings, forums, workshops, town hall presentations, seminars, webcasts and podcasts. Technology has helped us to communicate in bigger and better ways. Fibre optics can now transfer 10 trillion bits of information per second[1].

Information can be used, reused, packaged and repackaged. And what's more, it's able to reach your eyes/screen/earphones on demand. E-mail is pervasive in this world. The corporate executive or the individual professional is 'always on', on demand, connected to a server 24/7. The arrival of a piece of information to your (big, small or minuscule) screen is announced by a blip that triggers a Pavlovian reaction. There is no way that information, the currency of world I, would not get to you.

---

[1] A 2008 version of a series of video presentations entitled 'Did you know?' contains astonishing information about the 'exponential times' we live in, as the authors put it. (See for example http://www.youtube.com/watch?v=cL9Wu2kWwSY)

In this world, big seems to be beautifully linear as well: the more information pushed down to the bottom, the more pipes or channels used, the more flow created...the better it seems. Indeed, this is a world of channels, vehicles and their language: flow, block, saturation, etc. The pathways are algorithmic, pardon my language. It means that usually the roads are more or less preset and laid out like on a geographical map. You can go from A to Z via different roads—either meandering along the scenic route or taking the highway—but you have to stick to the map. In large organizations, the organization chart represents the information highways (algorithms) for the 'cascade down'.

> ● ● ●
> **Success in world I is defined by the quality and quantity of the currency (information) going down the organizational pipes.**
> ● ● ●

Success in world I is defined by the quantity and quality of the currency that reaches its destination points. In a 1,000-employee organization, the aim of a communication campaign is to reach 1,000 points of arrival. Simple. The assumption is then that 1,000 people will understand the message and that, as a result, 1,000 people will be 'engaged' in a particular way (intellectually, emotionally). The latter is difficult to validate other than by invoking the corporate equivalent of the 'deus ex machina': the post hoc fallacy. In other words, we did communication campaign A, we improved B (results, performance, employee survey data), ergo, the communication campaign did it. In most cases, this is a very weak argument dominating a strong and convenient management belief.

World I is a 'stock economy' where the recipients of communication ('information stocks') are either full, half full or empty. More currency will fill up an empty recipient as needed to increase the stock. World I is also a push-world. Exercise enough 'pressure' from the north, the outputs will come south (and maybe west and east). It is a 'Big Splash' world or, as I called it in my previous book *Viral Change*™, a tsunami approach with the epicentre at the centre of power and the waves reaching all company shores. The push-world craves hierarchy because it needs to use the top-down channels (as described in the organization chart) and some sort of command system. As a navigation system it is very effective and predictable. The organization here is consciously or unconsciously seen as a complex plumbing system of interconnected top-down pipes. Management is in charge of the valves.

Because of this apparent predictability and obvious visibility of the currency 'going down', the temptation is to repeat that process to be more effective. To the linear mind, pushing again would be duplicating the message and duplicating the message is seen as a success factor. Indeed, many studies suggest that messages in the organization need to be 'heard' three to five times before the doors of the brain and the heart start to open. Not surprisingly, typical management mantras are 'you can never communicate enough' and 'communicate, communicate, communicate'[2].

---

[2] Advocates of the big splash communication process would say that this is a stereotype and that there is merit in ensuring that information/communication reaches all the employees consistently. This way, decisions, for example, are made based on what employees themselves learn or take from that information. This is behind the concept of 'information cascades', a term first described in the context of understanding how fashions are created (See: Bikhchandani, S., D. Hirshleifer, I. Welch. 1992. A theory of fads, fashion, custom, and cultural change as informational cascades. *The Journal of Political Economy*. 100(5):992-1026). Today, this has become more of a generic term for a systematic push of communication. Within the organization, the cascade attempts to ensure consistency and availability of facts. There is a well-understood potential flaw in many information cascades. It assumes that each 'echelon' will receive fresh and clean information and will act independently fresh as well. But in reality, the deeper the cascade flows, the greater the probability that people will follow previously interpreted information. It is the Chinese whispers of internal communications. There are many ways to manage that problem and professional communicators know how to deal with this. Unfortunately, in many cases it is all up to the power of the 'PowerPoint presentation' cascading down for managers to use and repeat.

However, anybody who has worked in large or medium-sized organizations knows that the effect of many repeated internal communication campaigns is saturation of the channels. Or, in everyday language: employee switch-off. *"We have heard it all before"*, *"Here we go again"*, *"Yeah, yeah, sure, whatever!"*

> Attrition is not only embedded, amazingly, we have come to accept that this is perfectly OK, a natural part of the process.

In an information-cluttered working environment where many 'initiatives' compete for airtime, repeated top-down communications become terribly inefficient. In Cluttered Corporate Inc, noise and signal get blurred. Eventually all is noise. The biggest health hazard of world I is information pollution.

In fact, the mathematics of world I are the maths of attrition: start with aiming at everybody and then cascade down. Information will reach initial destinations (stocks). Some people will pay attention. From those first 'receivers', some people will pay enough attention to understand. From those, some will consider doing something. From those, some will actually attempt to do something. When you get to the terminus, a relatively small percentage has been truly influenced by the communication(s). Attrition is not only embedded, amazingly, we have come to accept that this is perfectly OK, a natural part of the process.

To fight attrition, we usually have a not-so-secret weapon: repetition. A new, bigger and better communication campaign will take place. This time perhaps communication packages will be prepared for VPs. VPs will brief directors, directors will have workshops with managers and managers have meetings with staff. And this way, 'everybody will have gone through it' (this is the language you hear) to ensure consistency. It is a noble and expensive goal. Large budgets are allocated, but the programmes have relatively small impact.

In the macro-social arena we are confronted with a similar machine-gun approach every day. Health promotion and disease prevention campaigns aim at everybody, everywhere, with a lot of noise and money involved. Their goals: awareness and sensitization. People sometimes use the word 'motivation'. Motivating people here is bombarding them with enough rational and emotional appeal to get them on board. But they fail to deliver the desired significant change when the main focus is the communication. Some sensitization may take place and this is good. No question about that. But attrition maths are built in. Within world I, the only way to improve the results is to follow up with bigger sensitization campaigns. The impact is not zero, it is simply disproportionally low for the cost and effort.

> World I could also be described as an advocacy world. It is the world of the logical or emotional arguments, the pros and cons, the rational appeal.

World I could also be described as an advocacy world. It is the world of the logical or emotional arguments, the pros and cons, the rational appeal ('here is B as a better alternative to A; would you not do B? We must do B!'). Thousands of advocacy hours are spent debating those pros and cons, the rationality and the need, the logic and the direction. It's all brains and possibly some hearts. Ideas and information are conveyed, digested, analyzed, internalized, reframed, developed, improved, converted and passed on. Homo Sapiens loves it. Within the organization, world I managers are information traffic wardens.

There is nothing intrinsically wrong with world I. What we know as education and training lives in this world. Traditional change management programmes also belong here. A whole industry of consultants, trainers and change-managers live in world I. But 'activity' here is magnetic. With its magic of quantifiable and

59

visible parameters that can be accounted for or paid for, 'activity' soon takes over.

Very often, the vehicle (activity) takes over from the message. Business becomes busy-ness. Therefore, a 'change management programme' is often defined by its number of workshops and perhaps its number of consultants, paid by the number of hours they spend on the ground[3]. Remember, big is beautiful in world I. But the effectiveness track record here is about 40%...and that's if you're being generous.

If you spend most of your time preparing presentations for people who have to deliver a presentation or in meetings, workshops, brainstorming sessions, focus groups, user groups, classrooms or boardrooms, you are probably a citizen of world I.

## World II

Then there is world II. This is the world of behaviours. In this world, the currency is action itself. It is not a better world or a worse world, just a different world. World II is the world of 'day-to-day-doing' and visible behaviours[4]. Behaviours are reinforced or they're not. When reinforced (recognized, rewarded, given air

---

[3] Numbers are magic and provide immense comfort, reassurance and legitimization. That is why so often the measurement becomes the objective, the target, the real qualifier and the hijacker of airtime: a 100K salary, a 200K programme, a quarterly seminar, a 10-trainer/12-month deployment, a 30-day waiting list, a 2-million Customer Relationship Management programme. Value equals numbers in the quantitative world, which for obvious reasons dominates most of the business world. It would be crazy to disregard numbers, but it is even crazier to manage by numbers alone. (See my article *Prisoners of the numbers* that can be downloaded from the Ideas Lab Section of www.thechalfontproject.com)

[4] Behaviours are visible units of action which can be attributed to an agent (which is the social sciences way of saying 'you and me'). Not all that is called behaviour is a true behaviour. The label 'behaviour' must have unequivocal meaning. 'Collaboration', for example, sounds like a behaviour, but it only becomes a true behaviour when you and I have agreed on what exactly we want to see people doing or not doing. Those actions we are then happy to call collaboration. Until that point, 'collaboration' is a concept that only has the potential of being translated into behaviours. We'll see more of this in chapter 4.1.

time...), they will tend to increase in frequency. If not, they will fade. In world II, the consequences of the behaviours dictate how much of them we see. No matter what the 'origin' of the behaviours was, their life is governed by their consequences. Behaviours may become acceptable or unacceptable, rewarded or punished. They will lead you to a promotion or to a deserted island.

Behaviours are exhibited, displayed, demonstrated by individuals or groups. They cannot be sent via email. They do not appear on your blackberry. They are not packaged in PowerPoint. Actually, they do not like PowerPoint at all.

Yes, you can describe them verbally or on paper, on a screen, a flipchart, corporate brochures, a bullet point list or anywhere else...but they do not have a life there. Their reality is in the action. Even when we say that 'we teach behaviours', we don't. We explain them and ask people to imagine them, we warn about them, praise them or encourage people to have them. But this is reminiscent of Plato's cave. The PowerPoint shadows of the behaviours are not the behaviours themselves.

> Behaviours are exhibited, demonstrated. They cannot be sent via email. They do not appear on your blackberry. They are not packaged in PowerPoint. Actually, they do not like PowerPoint at all.

World II behaviours, its currency, are mostly copied by others. Conscious or unconscious imitation makes them scalable. Social imitation and social copying take care of most of their spread. Behaviours are multiplied through influence and travel through social networks (of the organization, of society) in a heuristic way, pardon my language again. That means spreading through the proximity and connectivity of the individuals in the social network. As I have already mentioned, in this world, being a friend, a friend of a friend, 'somebody like me', a peer or somebody you trust has far more power in terms of shaping your behaviour than any information package you may have received in your inbox.

It is also a non-linear world where small is beautiful and usually has a big impact. A small number of well-chosen behaviours has the power to create big impact in the organization when they are well-spread and reinforced. And that applies to big problems too. Once the social contagion of these behaviours has started, critical masses will appear ('this is how we do it now') and others will join in. "*We stopped doing X months ago. Everybody now does Y*", is often heard. And you perhaps wonder: "*Since when? How? What happened?*" Suddenly we seem to have a new way of doing things and it is not always obvious what triggered it or how it happened. Social scientists have that famous word for it, which we have already encountered in previous chapters: conformity. It is mostly irrational and unconscious: something that often terrifies Homo Sapiens.

> World II behaviours are mostly copied by others. Imitation makes them scalable. Behaviours are multiplied through influence and travel through social networks.

The vehicles in world II are the social networks, visible or invisible, silent or noisy. Actually, in this world, they are the organization or the macro-social fabric of society. Nurturing the network is nurturing the organization, as I will explain in chapter 4.3. By the same token, ignoring the social network is ignoring the organization, which is something no manager can afford to do. Diffusion of behaviours through these social networks has its laws. Every day, we learn more about them, what works and doesn't work, what makes a behaviour scale up and what doesn't.

For example, we know that some nodes in the social network (my apologies for calling you a node) have far more power than others in influencing the behaviours of many. The social network has no democratic or equalitarian properties. Some nodes are highly connected and well-positioned. They are hubs, always amplifying. If these powerful nodes exhibit a particular behaviour, good or bad, this behaviour will have a high probability of being copied and soon you'll have a new norm. In the organization, these hubs or amplifiers or highly connected-highly influential people can be found anywhere on the organization chart and across all layers of management and staff. Social network connectivity and organization chart connectivity have little to do with one another. I am using connectivity as a proxy for influence. Not all influence is connectivity, but there is no high connectivity without influence, good or bad.

But we also know that sometimes new social norms appear around us, inside or outside the firm, and they cannot simply be traced back to those particularly well-connected and influential people. We do not know why or how, but what we see is that 'the mountain is on fire'. Surely somebody started a fire somewhere. But we don't know who. Or perhaps there was more than one arsonist. Or maybe there were a few little fires which suddenly joined and created a big fire. Oh well! Who knows? We have a fire.

World II is a 'connect economy' where what matters is how behaviours travel around and create norms (read also: cultures). The connections dictate how behaviours spread, but also how fast and how powerful. Connectivity in world II makes the difference between a brief fad, a stable fashion or a social revolution.

World II is the world of social infections and social epidemics. In world II, success is defined by the magnitude and stability of a social infection. For example, is it an epidemic or just the behavioural sniffles? Is it the fad of the week or has it actually become the norm, 'the new way of doing things here'?

World II is a 'pull' world, not a push world. In this world, behaviours don't spread top-down or even bottom-up. They spread multi-centric. By the power of imitation and social copying, your behaviour is pulling other behaviours around you. You may or may not be conscious of it. Remember the example of the first day in the office and the power of unwritten rules.

The existence of those (incredibly valuable!) well-connected nodes means that they are pulling people together all the time and at a scale. If for whatever reason people copy them or mirror them, the pull power of a few must be worth dozens of workshops with partially awake delegates.

> World II is a 'pull' world. In this world, behaviours don't spread top-down or even bottom-up. They spread multi-centric. By the power of imitation and social copying, your behaviour is pulling other behaviours around you.

World II is a heterarchy[5] 'with no centre'. Here, 'butterfly effects'[6] are powerful because the creation of a small 'build-up

---

[5] The term has been used by many disciplines as the 'opposite' of hierarchy, but Warren Sturgis McCulloch is credited with the original use of the term to describe how the brain works. In case you didn't realize, there is no hierarchy in the brain and no command-or-control centre. The brain governs us, but has no governor itself.

[6] In my book, *Viral Change*, butterfly management of change ('the wings of a butterfly can trigger a hurricane') is my term for the opposite of the traditional top-down tsunami approach.

of behaviours' has the potential power to create widespread impact and a big infection.

To follow our previous example: 1,000 employees in world II can be 'pulled' (engaged, convinced, infected, changed, converted, influenced, transformed, enlisted...) by a small group of highly influential, highly connected, highly trusted people at a good pace. For this to work, people in that relatively small group need to be activists, not just advocates. This means that in their interactions with peers, they need to exhibit the desired behaviours, put joint commitments in place and act on the commitments agreed on. This will lead to an emerging and true change of behaviours.

> World II is the world of behavioural change and organizational change. Micro- and macro-social change live here. It's home to Homo Imitans and above all: it's viral.

In Viral Change™, we identify these highly influential, highly connected, highly trusted people because we need them as the engine of behavioural change. But let me be clear. If they were asked to just convey information (communicate the values and change objectives, communicate how we need to work differently, for example), they would at best be super-advocates (i.e. super information traffic wardens). They would perhaps create some sort of 'viral communication'[7], which would be the equivalent of moving from copper to fibre optics within the organization. But remember: communication is not change.

---

[7] Without claiming credit or falling prey to a post-hoc fallacy, the publication of my book *Viral Change* was followed by a series of publications on viral communication. But viral communication is not viral change. Viral communication is a legitimate way to communicate, a legitimate world I activity. Communication, viral or not, is not change.

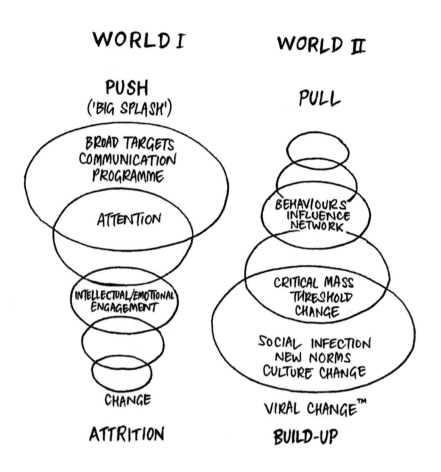

**WORLD I**

**PUSH**
('BIG SPLASH')

BROAD TARGETS
COMMUNICATION
PROGRAMME

ATTENTION

INTELLECTUAL/EMOTIONAL
ENGAGEMENT

CHANGE

**ATTRITION**

**WORLD II**

**PULL**

BEHAVIOURS
INFLUENCE
NETWORK

CRITICAL MASS
THRESHOLD
CHANGE

SOCIAL INFECTION
NEW NORMS
CULTURE CHANGE

VIRAL CHANGE™

**BUILD-UP**

However, when these influencers kick into real action, the effects are strong and noticeable. They are far more sustainable than the top-down plumbing brigades of world I could ever dream of. Their effects are faster. Later in the book I'll tackle the identification and engagement of these 'powerful people' who are sometimes hidden in the organization and perhaps have never been asked to help.

World II is the world of behavioural change, organizational change, culture building and culture change. Micro- and macro-social change and purposeful social infections live here. And it's home to Homo Imitans. The combination of a well-defined small set of behaviours, a relatively small group of highly influential, highly connected individuals and the presence of a social network forms the basis for Viral Change™. Viral change is truly world II territory.

## The two worlds side by side

Mr Sapiens and Mr Imitans live in different places, but though they should build bridges between them and then use them every day, they should also be very mindful of their different worlds. World II objectives cannot be achieved in world I territory. Social infections (world II) are not created by posters. Revolutions are not announced. Well, not usually. Social movements and cultures are not created by training. Communication (world I) is not change.

As the figure on the previous page illustrates, the maths of world II could not be more different from the maths of world I. Attrition is to world I what build/scale-up is to world II. World II effects start small, often unnoticed, with selected behaviours being practiced by a small number of individuals.

These are then copied by people in their immediate circle of influence and create 'clusters of new behaviours': true new critical masses, copied and spread by others like an infection, eventually generating 'new norms'.

Let's look at the differences between world I and world II in some real-life organizational examples. Note that there is nothing intrinsically wrong with the contents of world I, but its main problem is poor scalability and sustainability, for which it needs the help of world II as we will see later on. When you look at the highlights in each column, you may have lots of questions. Don't worry, as the rest of the book will hopefully answer all of them. For now, it's enough to simply appreciate the differences or perhaps increase your awareness of which world you spend most of your time in.

| Creating a culture of safety | |
| --- | --- |
| **World I** | **World II** |
| Health and Safety Awareness campaign (make safety understood) | Small set of non-negotiable behaviours leading to safety |
| Safety rules and manuals | 'Design' and diffusion of social infection |
| Safety communication campaign | (make safety contagious) |
| Health & Safety personnel deployment | Identification and engagement of highly |
| Obligatory training | connected and influential individuals |
| Key intervention process | ('champions'), not necessarily from |
| Safety improvement programme | management ranks |
| On-the-job training and review | Peer-to-peer conversations in the |
| Incident review and safety reports | workplace and joint commitment to |
| Repeated appeals from top management to change behaviours and avoid accidents | spread behaviours (activism) |
| | Review behaviours for sustainability |
| | Reinforcement (reward, recognition) of key non-negotiable behaviours |
| | Epidemic of safe acts |
| | Stories of success back to world I for non-viral communication |
| **Scalability:** poor. Needs continuous training and repeated campaigns for rational and emotional appeal | **Scalability:** viral. Starts small, creates critical masses or 'new norms', new 'ways of doing' |

| Continuous improvement and Lean Six Sigma (LSS) | |
|---|---|
| **World I** | **World II** |
| LSS methodology in place<br>Formal leadership training roles (Black/Green belts)<br>Training workshops for managers and lower levels<br>Process problem(s) identified<br>Methodology applied<br>Problem(s) solved<br>Lessons learned<br>Repeated appeals from management to improve processes and eliminate waste<br>Repeated training | Extract pattern of behaviours behind (systemic?) issues<br>Define non-negotiable behaviours<br>'Design' and diffusion of social infection (of behaviours to improve process, etc.)<br>Identification and engagement of champions (no formal Black/Green belts)<br>Peer-to-peer conversations and joint commitment to spread behaviours (activism)<br>Review behaviours for sustainability<br>Support small community of activists<br>Stories of success back to world I for non-viral communication |
| **Scalability:** poor. New situation, new application of same methodology. Repetition, increasing training if needed. Often unable to embed in culture | **Scalability:** viral, peer-to-peer, no formal role or authority. New critical masses of individuals create new norms and culture change |

| Creating a collaborative culture/environment | |
|---|---|
| **World I** | **World II** |
| Webcast from CEO on the importance of collaboration and teamwork<br>Define types of collaboration<br>Training in cross-discipline communication<br>Understanding people's working styles<br>Collaboration seminar<br>Training programme<br>Teamwork seminars and team building exercises<br>Use of collaborative software | Define and 'translate' collaboration into small set of non-negotiable behaviours<br>'Design' and diffusion of social infection ('make collaboration fashionable')[8]<br>Identification and engagement of champions (connected and influential, non-managers)<br>Peer-to-peer conversations and joint commitment to spread specific and well-defined collaborative behaviours<br>Measure progression of the behaviours' embedment<br>'Invisible' support to champions<br>Stories of success to world I for non-viral communication |
| **Scalability:** Poor. Retrain, team building follow-up. | **Scalability:** viral. Collaborative behaviours become the norm |

---

[8] I personally use these two sometimes interchangeable expressions: 'Let's make X fashionable' or 'let's create an internal epidemic of X'. Not only does this terminology help focus on world II, but it is also strong and memorable (and it is a real representation of what we do in Viral Change™).

69

| Deploying[9] a new corporate value system | |
|---|---|
| **World I** | **World II** |
| Communication campaign | Refined articulation of behaviours for |
| Visible presence of value system in | each value: what must be visible? |
| posters | Choice of key non-negotiable behaviours |
| Intranet presence | associated with the values |
| Town Hall meetings with senior | 'Design' and diffusion of social infection. |
| management at all sites | (make behaviours [from values] the norm) |
| Other stakeholder involvement | Identification and engagement of |
| Workshops cascaded down for | champions (non-managers, some |
| awareness , understanding and | supervisors) |
| application into specific work areas | Peer-to-peer conversations and joint |
| New values incorporated in a modified | commitment to (a) ensure understanding |
| performance management system | and (b) exhibit/practice specific non- |
| (performance appraisals) for all | negotiable behaviours connected with the |
| management levels | value system |
| | Support to champions' community |
| | Measure behaviours' progression of |
| | spread, not the understanding of values |
| | Stories of success to world I for non-viral |
| | communication |
| **Scalability:** Poor once the cascade is | **Scalability:** high, viral. Behaviours become |
| finished. Success defined by number of | the norm after new, small 'critical masses' |
| workshops and number of people | are formed everywhere |
| 'gone through' the program. Several | |
| follow-up conferences on values | |
| planned | |

World I and world II are also present in the macro-social world. Tackling an epidemic of street violence, for example, is done quite differently in both worlds as the following summary shows. These differences have tremendous implications when crafting mechanisms to tackle epidemics from a social policy perspective.

In the course of our Viral Change™ programmes, usually early on in the phase of exposing people to the techniques and the principles, there is always somebody who, for very good reasons, reacts to the world I-world II dichotomy by saying, "*This is too*

---

[9] Note the corporate language used here and commonly seen everywhere: 'deploying'. 'cascading' or 'disseminating' (on top of 'communicating' itself). It is world I, stock economy language.

| Addressing street violence, youth gangs[10] | |
| --- | --- |
| **World I** | **World II** |
| Awareness campaign: the tragedy of violence<br>'Hearts and minds campaign'<br>Schools campaign<br>Street demonstrations against violence<br>Community leaders (religious, civic) reaching out, making the case for non-violence<br>Police posters: call in confidence<br>Social workers' conference<br>Teachers' conference<br>Church services inviting to non-violence<br>Appeals to families<br>Government campaign: TV, radio | Identification and engagement of same age, same origin influential people ('champions'): no hierarchical figures of any kind<br>Recruit ex-gang members<br>'Design' and diffusion of social infection (geography, pace)<br>Very small set of key non-negotiable behaviours, including (1) real life intervention on streets and (2) confronting defeatism ('we will never get rid of this')<br>Champions' 'training'<br>Champions in action<br>Support for and cross-learning from champions<br>Counter-epidemic mode<br>Stories of success to world I for non-viral communication |
| **Scalability:** Poor. Continuous noise and presence, repeated campaigns (based upon hope of 'changing hearts and minds') | **Scalability:** viral, counter-epidemic |

*black and white!"* This is only natural. Indeed, our minds resist the categorization, as deep inside, we tend to believe that most things are grey, a mixture, a bit of this and a bit of that. That gives the mind the comfort of allowing for possibilities and often the freedom of not being forced to declare its allegiance too soon.

When people become aware of how much time they spend in the corridors of world I, they tend to panic and say, "Hey, *wait a minute. We are in world II as well. We do X and we do Y!*" However, very often, their argument is not that strong, not very convincing and even a little bit defensive.

---

[10] The Chicago 'ceasefire' project is explained in more detail in chapter 6.

The obvious source of misinterpretation is the concept of behaviours itself. Although I will address behaviours in more detail in chapter 4.1, let's clarify something here straight away. When a cascaded-down communication programme takes place, perhaps gratuitously labelled 'change programme', and workshops start popping up like mushrooms, there will be lots of discussions and interactions between people, lots of note-taking and lots of action points agreed upon.

The 'employee engagement' industry, having a ball, claims that all this is 'behaving', i.e. doing something practical and therefore surely an ingredient of world II. I can hardly disagree with the fact that verbal behaviour is a form of behaviour. However, the question is whether that 'talking-behaving' (world I) is conducive to 'new behaviour-behaving' (world II) or simply remains an information interchange between brains (and some hearts). Understanding and planning for behaving is not behaving[11].

Another point of 'conflict' usually comes from one-to-one interactions aimed at change. For example, is coaching (world I) successful? Of course it can be, depending on quality, etc. Far be it from me to say that the one-to-one quality interactions between individual and coach are useless or that they will not result in substantial behavioural change in the coached individual. But as a social infector, coaching does not rank very high as a mechanism for social change as it is hardly scalable. I would not discourage coaching for managers and leaders and it can be a good use of time or resources. However, unless you have the budget to coach 90% of the corporate population (surely a nirvanic scenario for some), I don't see how this is going to change the culture of the organization anytime soon.

---

[11] Organizations spend more time preparing for doing than actually doing. We should remember the riddle: Five frogs are sitting on a log. Four decide to jump off. How many are left on the log? Five, because there is a difference between deciding and doing.

World I and world II are co-existing worlds. And in order for them to benefit from each other, they need to be linked and work together. But before that can happen, you need to make sure that your expectations from each world are correct.

In the example of the safety culture, there is no suggestion whatsoever that you stop any safety training or any awareness and sensitization campaigns. Nor does it suggest that you avoid any strong declaration from senior management about the inexcusable state of safety in the firm. But all this in itself does not have the power to change the organizational culture unless individuals actually exhibit concrete safety behaviours which are mimicked and copied by others in a way that becomes the norm and permanently changes 'the way we do things here'. What is intellectually acquired and emotionally hosted through training and awareness can fade at the speed of light unless it is translated into behaviours which are socially infected and scaled up.

> *What is intellectually acquired and emotionally hosted through training and awareness can fade at the speed of light unless it is translated into behaviours which are socially infected and scaled up.*

Similar arguments apply to the other examples. A process-improving system of training such as Lean Six Sigma[12] (LSS) may have its place in the organization's world I. However, when specific behaviours impairing continuous improvement are identified (which hopefully is a clear aim of the exercise), the only way to then change the culture to one

---

[12] Under the LSS umbrella there are some variations. I am using it here in a generic way to describe continuous improvement programmes, substantially based on training, directed by specific role-holders (trainers, Green/Black belts, etc.)

defined by continuous improvement 'as a way of living' is large-scale behavioural change, not large-scale training.

Same for the case of the value system in need of 'deployment'. Please do not stop the CEO or leaders at any level from articulating loud and clear what the values are, and why and how these values will lead to success. And please, use any traditional, web 2.0, or social media communication system to make sure that these values are explained explicitly in all the corners of your empire. However, if you really want to be remembered for more than your posters, your videos, your PowerPoints, your workshops and your contribution to the unstoppable sales growth of Post-its, please do me a favour and think 'infection' and 'epidemic'. For that, you need to add world II 'activism' to the mix and find a way to spread the behaviours associated with the values so that they become 'the culture'. You may have your Homo Sapiens 'engaged', but you need your Homo Imitans to make it real[13].

The following real-life case highlights very common challenges seen again and again in post M&A or re-structuring situations. It shows how difficult it is to leave world I territory and the risks of not trying seriously (or not knowing how to do it).

---

[13] People always say, "Let's communicate the objectives and their rationale, let intelligent and well-paid people digest and 'apply' these, let them interpret a pre-cooked and communicated set of behaviours (for example, pre-defined in a new vision for the firm) and then our people will behave accordingly. Behaviours will happen as a consequence of the communication about behaviours..." Really? Behaviours, the currency of world II, cannot be disseminated or made scalable in world I.

## I reorganize ergo sum

A reorganization has taken place. A new structure amalgamating old divisions is in place and now the ways of doing must change. The Big Consulting Company has left (well, not quite, they never do) and there is a myriad of PowerPoints and fresh materials articulating the new structure, the new operating model and the new processes and systems in extreme detail.

Senior management cascades this information down through all the layers of the organization (from VPs to directors to managers) in a series of workshops. It's all very rational, sophisticated and legitimized by the enormous budget used to reach this point.

**(1) The 'small' detail of how people are actually going to work together in the new regime...is not in 'the slides'**

A key component for successful change is that people not only understand the new structure (they are now de facto part of it) or the new processes (they all make sense on paper), but also that they actually behave differently. Suddenly, they have to share information with people who they have not worked with before. They can no longer draft their business plan in the cosy isolation of their office with the assistants of their three loyal lieutenants. Now, they have to 'co-develop it' (sic) with a dozen of inter-connected 'stakeholders' who didn't need to know about each other before (or if they did, they pretty much ignored each other without the sky falling down). There is nothing in the colossal stack of PowerPoints left behind by the Big Consulting Company that even touches on explaining, suggesting or helping with how people are going to behave differently. Why? Because the Big Consulting Company operates in world I and in world I, the availability of the information is an end in itself. After all, if new B is better than old A, Homo Sapiens will do B. 'OK, and if not, we'll train them.'

**(2) So they make an attempt to define which new behaviours are needed**

Their management team has become acutely aware of 'the small detail' mentioned above and now develops a series of exercises to define the kind of behaviours that may be needed.

The output of the work done during a few off-sites states that behaviours need to be (and here a long list of familiar things is mentioned): well-understood, interiorized, made 'your own', applied by people empowered to do so, not imposed. They need to be logical, sensible, credible, ethical, good, positive, etc. And they plan to leave it to managers to figure out what those behaviours may be because they do not want to be seen as dictating. Towards the end of the last session a perceptive member of the team points out: *"However, when you put all those things together and multiply them by 1,000, we still wouldn't have any guarantee that behaviour communicated equals behaviour made real, i.e. behavioural change."* The team agrees to follow up on this in the next session.

**(3) But just when you are getting somewhere, somebody says that another thing is needed 'first'**

Your HR people decide that behaviours need something else first. People first need to change their mindset or their attitude, or behaviours 'obviously' won't happen. (Incidentally, The Big Consulting Company also did not leave behind any PowerPoints on how to change a mindset.)

I have a problem with this. In my previous life as a practicing psychiatrist, I never saw a mindset or an attitude, let alone treated one. So when people say to me that we need to change our mindset, I look very puzzled and humbly ask, *"What's that?"* I have seen behaviours, lots of them, but never a mindset. I suspect that a mindset or an attitude is a label that we can use when describing a cluster of behaviours that we see. If we say that our neighbour has something against foreigners or women ('bad attitude'), it may be because of the things he says or does. I can see/hear those, but not his attitude.

This argument causes long debates at the leadership team meetings. Everybody agrees about the need to change the mindset (none of them having read this book or *Viral Change*™), but because nobody actually knows how to do this, the 'mindset' is left pending.

**(4) The team then decides that for behaviours to be 'real', they need to be reinforced (gratified, acknowledged, rewarded) or they won't stick**

Agreed! Any behaviour that has no reinforcement, whether in your external world (it is physically or psychologically rewarded) or somewhere in the intimacy of your brain (it is psychologically consistent with what you may call your values, beliefs or moral system), will tend to fade.

Given the nature of the reorganization (driven by cost-cutting, consolidation and 'new dynamics between stakeholders'), the management team now decides that it is actually up to them to define which behaviours are needed and that they cannot leave these open to multiple interpretations. A new list of behaviours, renamed 'leadership behaviours' is created and it reads:

| | |
|---|---|
| Learning from each other | Customer focus |
| Being inclusive | Empower others |
| Taking ownership | Being open |
| Do teamwork | Sense of urgency |

Problem is, none of those eight 'things' are behaviours of any sort, since they can be interpreted in as many ways as there are people on the payroll.

Nonetheless, to ensure these 'behaviours' are reinforced, they agreed to add them to the new performance appraisal system. This way, they said, it will be clear to managers that these behaviours are not only required, but an official part of their performance evaluation, with its compensation implications.

The adding of 'behaviours' to the performance management system (performance appraisal) is the default position in many organizations that think that the listing of such behaviours next to the goals and objectives solves the problem.

## One year later...

One year later, post-reorganization (and a few million dollars and Post-its lighter) an internal employee satisfaction survey highlights some problems: lack of clarity of the new structure, lack of clarity of responsibilities, persistence of coexisting cultures (described as 'the consolidation never took place, we are still working as before') and pervasive communication problems. How the story continued from there is not relevant. The journey of management trial and error, intuitive grasping of the need for behaviours, the quick fix of performance management, the incredible waste of managerial time and reorganization-but-only-on-paper are incredibly common in today's corporate life.

The management team never managed to leave the safer paths of world I so skilfully mapped out by The Big Consulting Company. They wanted to explore beyond that map, but they didn't have a good toolkit. They thought of changing mindsets, but didn't know how. They retreated further into world I with a list of well-intentioned aims written down in HR documents. They didn't change the culture and their people were confused even after one year.

This story is real (the company a subsidiary of a Fortune 500 company) and dozens if not hundreds of similar stories are taking place every day in corporate life. I, for one, sympathize more and more with revolutions.

## Formal and informal conversations and the two worlds

Why could information not travel through the social networks of world II? It could, it does so all the time. Those nodes in the social network (remember, that's you) are not mute. They talk and pass information between them. It is called conversation. Conversations are to a social organism (the organization, the firm, the social group) what chemical reactions are to the biological organism. They represent the difference between life and death. There are formal and informal conversations. Formal conversations mainly (but not exclusively) use world I organizational devices such as meetings, teams, committees, forums, conferences, etc. By definition those devices are there to provide borders (objectives, deadlines, topics, styles, desired outcomes...) so that what happens in those conversations has a purpose. Good management needs this kind of framed conversations and a great deal of the efficiency of the organization depends upon their smooth functioning.

75% of what is written, taught, learnt and praised in Best Practice Management is about framed conversations. 75% of what keeps the organization alive (or what could kill it) does not take place in those kinds of conversations, but in informal ones.

> Conversations are to a social organism what chemical reactions are to the biological organism. They represent the difference between life and death.

The organization needs both conversations. A healthy social organism is one with a good balance between the two. When framed and formal conversations completely dominate life, the environment becomes progressively predictable, stiff and bureaucratic. Trying to domesticate all conversations politburo style is not a good idea, but it provides management with an illusion of control that is very appealing...if this is the kind of leadership you want. The other extreme, complete de-formalization of conversations, would not provide any valid structure for any efficiency of any sort. But balance is truly a fine-line concept. Most of our organizations are imbalanced towards the framed conversations, because that's what we have management toolkits for.

Informal conversations not only use world II structures (the social network), but they are also their real oxygen. Cut their air supply a bit and bear the consequences.

Ideas travel through both the social network of world II and the formal communication channels of world I. When ideas hit the highly connected nodes in world II, they may spread faster and in

79

a viral way. However, the viral spread of ideas or viral communication alone does not equal change.

A word of caution. In the social media era, it is now fashionable to add the word 'viral' to anything of some scale to make a big thing of it. I will comment on this in chapter 4.2 when addressing influence.

Ideas spreading through the informal conversations of social networks could be viral (or not) in similar ways, depending on the structure of the network and the proprieties of the hubs and nodes[14]. The ideas also have their own laws depending, among other things, on their 'stickiness' and the kind of reaction they generate[15]. In this respect, even when using world II highways, these ideas have all the characteristics of world I currencies and their associated lifecycle. Send the same ideas again and again and receptors may switch off, both in world I and world II.

If, like me, you are in the business of change—i.e. transforming organizations so that they are a fabric of conversations that create individual and collective wealth (my definition, not necessarily yours) while learning how to use 'world II technology' (my goal as well) in the process—you will need behaviours, not ideas. All ideas are welcome, but the travelling of ideas (viral or not) is not change.

---

[14] Rumours travel via informal social networks and as such adopt some of their properties. At some point, loosely connected gossip suffers a threshold change and 'a new truth' emerges of a size no longer easy to control. Rumours, positive or negative, can only be 'caught' before their threshold change transition. At that stage, a world I communication could re-address their content by a counter-campaign. The only way for management to pick up the rumours before the point of no return, is to listen to the organizational chatter. The best way to do this is to be part of it. Unfortunately, a great deal of world-I trained managers still dismiss the importance of the untamed informal social networks, rejecting it as 'un-focused' or 'non-purpose' stuff. Socially-inept managers discover their blindness all too often too late and at their own cost.

[15] Seth Godin, a generator of endless ideas, has written extensively about the viral nature of some of those ideas. See: http://sethgodin.typepad.com/

Let me also mention two other components. They are of importance to both worlds, as they provide a natural bridge between them. The first one is stories. As you will see in chapter 4.4, they are the true accelerator of change. Or, as I have called them before, the true WMDs. The second component is leadership and I will deal with it separately in chapter 4.5. Leadership has a dual role. In world I, it serves as a reference, as agenda setting, as commanding (in different degrees). Formal leadership sits here. In world II, leadership is completely distributed amongst the individuals with high connectivity and influence. The formal leadership needs to operate backstage and it needs to learn how to do it. Both stories and leadership deserve their own special attention.

## Summary

In the following table, I have summarized the two worlds' characteristics.

I want to end this conversation about the worlds the same way I started and that is by reminding you of the mother of all problems in the change management business: the mixing up of both worlds and their possibilities and outcomes. In a nutshell, communication (world I) is <u>not</u> change (world II). Behaviours (world II) <u>cannot</u> be changed by presenting them (world I).

The business of change (processes, goal-directed initiatives, adoption of a technology, a culture of safety, innovation, collaboration, customer centrism, etc.) is a world II business (with all the aid possible from world I) and is a world of social infections, not of broadcasting. If you are a leader, you should be in the infection business, not in the broadcasting business. Because of the (behavioural) infection mechanism, world II is easily scalable. Viral Change™ orchestrates the infection so that the desired goal(s) is (are) achieved by a true epidemic. More on this later.

81

| World I | World II |
|---|---|
| **Communication** | **Behaviours** |
| Currency: Information | Currency: Action |
| Facts, information, knowledge<br>Vision, goals and objectives<br>Intentions, declarations<br>Directions and guidelines<br>Methods, tricks<br>Rational appeal, 'a logic' | What people do or don't do (actions)<br>Visible<br>Reinforced or not<br>Acceptable, unacceptable<br>Increase frequency or fade<br>Consequences of behaviours dictate<br>their life |
| **Packaged**<br>Presented, verbal, written<br>PowerPoint world<br>Traditional or social media<br>(video, audio) | **Exhibited**<br>Displayed, demonstrated, lived<br>Associated to a (cultural) context |
| Passed on, cascaded (down),<br>distributed<br>Linear, algorithmic pathways<br>(Big issues, big programmes)<br>Big is beautiful | Copied, imitated, followed<br>Heuristic<br>Non-linear<br>(Small intervention, big impact)<br>Small is beautiful |
| Quality, quantity of information<br>From origin to destination(s)<br>Emission to receiver | Mechanisms of influence<br>(Hierarchical, peer-to-peer, 'people<br>like us', friends, friends of friends)<br>Social contagion<br>Conformity mechanisms<br>From origin to critical mass |
| Information channels<br>Vehicles<br>Email dominance<br>(flow, block, saturation) | Social network<br>Social diffusion<br>(receptive/resistant/not affected) |
| 'Stock economy'<br>(empty/full recipients)<br>Destination and receiver model<br>Success is state of container plus<br>number of them (depleted, filled in) | 'Connect economy'<br>(layers and networks)<br>Infection and epidemic model<br>Success is magnitude and stability of<br>the social infection |
| Big Splash, 'tsunami' | 'Butterfly effect' |

82

| PUSH | PULL |
|---|---|
| Hierarchy primed | Heterarchy driven |
| Organization: plumbing system | Organization: network, organism |
| Effectiveness based upon repetition ('communicate, communicate, communicate') Predictable patterns | Effectiveness based upon viral spread ('small fires, different places, whole mountain on fire') |
| **Maths of attrition** Large targets → small impacts ('lost in translation' metaphor) Effectiveness decreases down the pipes | **Maths of build-up/scale-up** Small number of people → large critical mass Effectiveness increases through network spread |
| Ideas conveyed Advocacy | Ideas infected as actions Activism |
| 'Communication packages' primary factual | Information by-product = stories, primarily experiential |
| Traditional hierarchical leadership: top-down agenda setting and/or command-and-control (depending on levels of control exercised) | Unconventional: (1) Formal world I leadership→ backstage leadership (2) World II leadership→ Distributed |
| Cascaded-down, stepwise change management: Big initiative x all management layers x communication channels = Traditional Change Management (gate/stage) | Viral: Small set of behaviours x small number of people x networks of influence = Viral Change™ |
| **Awareness and sensitization** **'Stimulation, Motivation'** **Education** **Rational/emotional appeal** **Training** | **Behavioural change** **Ways of doing** **Culture building** **New social norms** **Culture change** |
| Famous inhabitants: Homo Sapiens | Famous inhabitants: Homo Imitans |

# 4

# The five disciplines of Viral Change™

We can now unpack the requirements for world II. Where world I required information, a sender-receiver system, formal channels to cascade it down, 'spaces' (formal communication systems, team meetings, workshops, etc.), communication packages and the top-down leadership dictating the action, world II requires a clear focus on behaviours, the use of social copying and imitation mechanisms and the informal networks of the organization. It also needs stories and a different form of leadership. I have already mentioned some of these components before in different degrees. These five world II ingredients form the basis of social infections, both inside the firm and in the macro-social world.

85

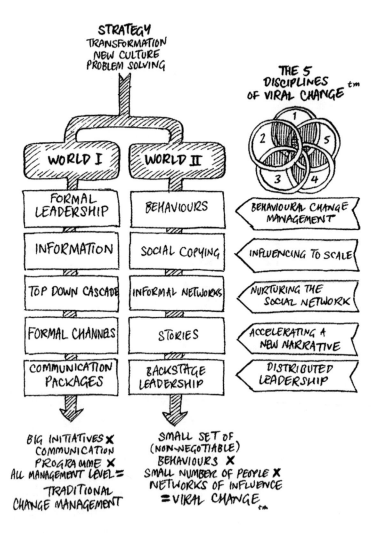

Confronted with the execution of a strategy (problem solving, culture building or any other aim), we are always offered a choice of routes: world I and/or world II. As we know, traditional management's default position is world I.

In the following chapters, I will address each of the world II components on their own. Each of them relates to disciplines in the social and/or network sciences and all of them contain a fair amount of counter-intuitive principles. Mastering the combination of these components or disciplines is the basis for Viral Change™. As the graph on the previous page summarizes, the art of social infection requires:

## (1) Obsessive focus on behaviours

The first discipline is behavioural change management which is well-anchored in traditional behavioural sciences. I am still surprised to see how the management world remains filled with folk psychology and half-baked behavioural answers, eagerly embraced by people in search of quick fixes. Invalidated behavioural concepts are widespread and anybody in 'management' or 'HR' seems to be a de facto expert in the matter. I'm advocating for the application of some standards, like those needed to master accounting or running a production line.

When it comes to 'people', it seems anything goes. The results are things such as ludicrous incentive schemes which reward exactly the opposite of what they intend to promote or extraordinarily complex competence frameworks that seem copied word-for-word from the latest management book on the shelves. Chapter 4.1 will explore key concepts about behaviours in the context of social infection of the viral change type. As it will be impossible to summarize the whole discipline of Behavioural Change Management in one chapter, I will focus on a few key concepts that are crucial or simply not well understood.

## (2) Choosing influence that can scale up.

The second discipline of Viral Change™ is influencing. However, this is not about just any kind of influence, it's about 'scalable' influence. Or in other words, it's about how to create a fast build-up of the social infection. There is a new 'industry of influence' that promises to teach tricks and shortcuts, sometimes with poor or no scientific basis. It tends to be thrown in the same basket as 'motivating people' or 'inspiring them'. 'How to influence people' often appears in 'training packages' that promise to teach you skills in achieving goals, managing your own boss, getting a raise or simply being in control. Becoming an 'influencer' now seems to be part of the expected portfolio of politically accepted goals.

> • • •
> Very often, influencing gets trivialized and reduced to the 'tools' and 'how to'. Often it's limited to listing vague requisites which would work equally well for 'being a good manager' as for 'navigating through life'.
> • • •

Very often, influencing gets trivialized and reduced to the 'tools' and 'how to'. Often it's limited to listing vague requisites which would work equally well for 'being a good manager' as for 'navigating through life'. In those 'packages', people are asked to 'change their minds' or their 'mindset' (remember, that thing I still can't find?). They make it sound as logical and easy as changing the oil in your car. Or they are asked to 'request and clarify responsibilities and reward appropriately'. It's hardly something to disagree with, but it makes you wonder why the other thousand things you could do to be an influencer are not listed. In chapter 4.2, I'll share which aspects of influence are relevant for social infections and which ones are good for nice conversations and bullet points in training programmes.

### (3) Taking care of informal social networks

It is no longer a question of 'acknowledging' that informal networks exist. The real issue is now mastering them! Today, we know more and more about how (social, digital or other) networks work. We have come a long way in just a few years. We went from networks as pretty pictures on PowerPoint to networks as 'a real thing', an organizational fabric that we need to nurture.

This area of the 'organizational theory', formal versus informal networks, is one that best represents the 'toolkit imbalance' managers face today. Most of our training, experience and Best-Practice-brainwashing have been focused on aspects of the organizational life which are necessary, but not sufficient for organizational growth. Managers are well-versed in the formality of teams and 'by design structures', the land of formal conversations. However, we're not that well-adept when it comes to the territory of informal conversations: the part of the organization where informal social networks are in control and often have the answer to critical things such as innovation, idea generation, problem solving, spontaneous collaboration, etc. The third discipline of Viral Change™ is nurturing the social network, seeing it as 'the asset' that needs special care and monitoring of its health, amongst other things. More on this in chapter 4.3.

### (4) Stories: creating a new narrative

Stories are quite memorable, especially when compared with the average life cycle of a bullet point. Stories are a wonderful mechanism of social reinforcement. When spread, they create an immediate sense of reality, of progress or achievement. Mastering story-capturing, story-developing and story-telling is fundamental for the orchestration of social infections. This area is 'a specialty' in its own right and I will provide some highlights relevant to our social infection goals in chapter 4.4. The fourth discipline of Viral Change™ is not storytelling per se, but the acceleration of the creation of a new narrative for the (changing) organization. By this, I mean that every day we need to build on our story, bring a new brick, however small, to the new house, in the form of 'this is happening', 'we are moving', 'we have achieved x', etc. The more we do this, the faster the social infection will spread.

It's often argued that stories are not 'new' in corporate life and that's true. However, how have we used those stories until now? The 'new narrative' (which I sometimes like to call the 'new logic of the organization', once the behavioural change has started and the new culture is emerging) must be the protagonist, not the individuals and their ranks. If I could, I would scrap all the 'employee-of-the-month' schemes in favour of a 'story-of-the-week' programme.

## (5) 'Backstage' leadership

The fifth discipline of Viral Change™ is mastering distributed leadership. This is a new model of leadership which is far more complex, powerful and influential than the traditional leadership-of-the-organization-chart. When you have peer-to-peer conversations, engagement and joint actions going on across the organization; when highly influential and connected people are at the front of the behavioural, social and cultural change; when, suddenly, the richness of influence not described or articulated in the organization chart has been uncovered, liberated and promoted and when the formal leadership of the organization takes a backstage position in favour of 'a thousand leaders in action', a new dimension of (collective and distributed) leadership appears and elevates the organization to a higher level of possibilities. This is not necessarily an easy ride for command-and-control leaders. But there is no choice: social infections are hardly the result of command-and-control. I will address this fifth discipline in chapter 4.5.

The five disciplines are the pillars for the orchestration of social infections. Unfortunately, they are full of counterintuitive stuff which will not be picked up by a world-I-aficionado's approach to change. My recommendation is to get professional advice in those cases where there is no in-house expertise. I make no apologies for sounding 'commercial'. I have seen the disasters that happen when DIY behaviours/social sciences meet change management. If you suddenly have difficulty breathing and chest pain when you climb the stairs at home after that incredibly difficult day at the office, you have several choices: you could do some yoga, go on a diet, listen to those stress management tapes or you could go and see a doctor. Even if I sound biased due to my professional background, I feel that you should do the latter...now. Yet, I am amazed at how often 'management' chooses the DIY pathway when it comes to management of change.

## 'We are doing this already'

Imagine the following dialogue. I have it often and it's usually between a tired me and a cheerful, bright, up-and-coming Head of Organizational Development.

Behaviours? Yes, of course we focus on behaviours; we have them listed in the value system. Influence? You bet! We know how it works. Our Head of Sales is very charismatic, he can move and shake beyond his division. He's a true influencer and we'll get him on board for your Viral Change™, of course. Social networks? Oh yes, we have lots of virtual teams working very well and collaborating across affiliates. Yes, we have networks (said like 'we have electricity'). Stories? Sure! We have been sending them out in our monthly in-house newsletter. How we built the new plant in Kazakhstan in record time is an amazing story! Nobody has ever done it! And we also post this kind of stories on the intranet. Backstage leadership? Well, delegation and empowerment are two of our core values and the top

91

management team has stressed this many times in their Town Halls. Incidentally, since March, in any Town Hall there is a presentation not only by the top team, but also by some of their people, a good example of that backstage that you mention. So, yes, we have been doing this Viral Change™ for a long time.

At this point in the conversation I usually pretend I have an urgent call coming through on my iPhone and I secretly reach for the Prozac.

> *When we put together all that we know about change management programmes, the track record is far from impressive. Generally speaking, about 70% of initiatives fail to deliver on the expectations.*

Viral Change™ has this wonderful characteristic of familiarity. It's similar to the 'do I know you?' at a party when meeting somebody for the first time and feeling that it is not the first time. This is good and bad.

It is good because managers recognize elements of Viral Change™ which makes a lot of sense. Actually, 'it makes sense' is the most frequent feedback received when introducing Viral Change™ for the first time. The bad side is that it makes some managers feel as if 'they are already doing all that'. The trouble with this is that it may or may not be true. Many viral-change-that-we-are-already-doing elements are based upon the wrong behaviours (poorly articulated is usually the main problem), the wrong influencers (choosing an 'established population' like the talent pool is usually the biggest mistake) and/or the wrong informality of networks (creating formal teams of champions is the biggest flaw here).

## How to fail expensively: don't leave the calm shores of world I

It should be clear by now that while world I is a conveyor of important and vital messages that play an imperative role in raising awareness, educating, establishing rules of the game and engaging minds and hearts, it is world II where the real cultural change takes place. And that cultural change can only take the shape of an infection, a behavioural infection that creates new norms (ways of doing, ways of supporting new processes, style of dealing with customers, etc.) That is why the concept of social infection is so important.

My insistence on the shortcomings of world I in creating social change do not come from a dogmatic position. On the contrary. I have seen traditional change management programmes fail and many well-intentioned efforts to 'convince' and 'engage' with 'communication tools' fall by the wayside. I have also seen the incredible waste of energy and money involved in all this. Basically, I have seen enough to question why on earth people continue to do the same. Perhaps this also rings some bells for you.

There is also plenty of depressing data. When we put together all that we know about change management programmes (those surrounding an IT implementation, those aiming at a broader cultural change or those aiming for transformation), the track record is far from impressive. Generally speaking, about 70% of the initiatives fail to deliver on the expectations. This is a big number by any account, but management has come to think of it as something more or less inevitable. Imagine for a second that 70% of airplanes crashed, 70% of bridges fell down, 70% of buildings collapsed or, simply, that 70% of the time your corporate IT system was down. Dreadful thoughts, no doubt. Well, this is the equivalent in change management.

93

There are plenty of sources to support this figure. A recent summary[1] offers some highlights worth showing here:

| | |
|---|---|
| McKinsey (various) | 75% failure |
| Bain and Company | 70% failure (90% for cultural change) |
| Hammer & Champy, 1993 | 70% failure for business process reengineering programmes |
| Patrick Morley | 75% failure for total quality management programmes |
| Miller, 2002 | 70% failure |
| Computer Weekly, 2003, review of IT change programmes | 16% success 35% behind schedule 59% over budget 54% under-delivered |
| The Standish Group, 2003 | 66% of IT projects totally abandoned or failed against measures |
| UK Labour government | 26 billion pounds sterling lost in failed projects |
| KPMG, 10 year survey | 28% of M&A result in enhanced shareholder value 36% reduced shareholder value |

Addressing this colossal waste of time and money (not to mention the frustration, finger-pointing and overall damage to the health of the organization), is obviously important, but it needs to be done with an open mind. Post hoc blame is thrown in any possible direction, but many of the arguments are far from convincing.

---

[1] Warrilow, S. 2010. Change management: The horror of it all. *ProjectSmart*. (http://www.projectsmart.co.uk/change-management-the-horror-of-it-all.html) [Accessed May 2010].
See also: Keller, S., C. Aiken. 2008. *The inconvenient truth about change management*. McKinsey and Company.

In my experience, in large organizations, the leadership at the top is often under pressure from the board to use a well-known Big Consulting Company to provide some mental comfort to the board members. That leads to a sort of groupthink, turning a blind eye to the published failure data and it ends up in the repetition of a standard process, 100% delivered in pristine world I clothes and with a 30% maximum probability of success. The classical big three arguments coming from post hoc reviews to explain failure look like this:

(1) *"The strategy wasn't well-defined."* Not in my experience. People spend a lot of time not only mapping the goals and objectives, but also the processes and interventions. If anything, people have a myriad of documents showing what needs to be done and why. You may or may not agree with the strategy, but on the whole, chances are, it has been well-defined, even though it is fashionable to say otherwise.

(2) *"The stakeholders were not involved."* Not in my experience. Legions of project teams, users' teams, specification teams and implementations teams are in operation. They involve, if anything, too many people and often try to reach an impossible consensus.

(3) *"The technology was flawed."* Not in my experience. The available technology is extremely versatile and able to perform at a high level of sophistication. If anything, the problem is that technology is often promoted as a 'solution', taking over everything else. 75% of the issues come from 'people and organization' and only 25% from technology. However, we spend 75% of the time and resources on fixing the technology (including upgrading to a more expensive system that will deliver 'this time') and only 25% on people and organizational issues.

These three are the main usual suspects to justify failure. But other arguments are just as familiar. For example, people are resistant to change. This one usually comes up when things start

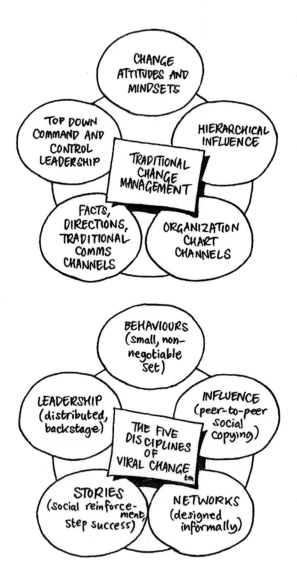

looking gloomy and it is one of the several myths of change management that I have debunked in my book, *Viral Change™*. Others quote a lack of resources or management not being a very good role model. I have already made some comments about the possible overestimation of the importance of the role modelling at the top. Whilst in an extreme scenario (when top management is severely disconnected with the reality or exhibits behaviours greatly different from what the programme needs) this bad role modelling is likely to be significant, in the majority of cases one cannot seriously attribute many of the failures to the behaviour of top management. It is a cheap argument that may be very good at settling some anxieties, but it's not a serious one.

## Summary of the five disciplines

The graphs on the previous page illustrate the differences between the five disciplines of Viral Change™ and the components of traditional change management. The differences are self-explanatory and comparing them is helpful in understanding what needs to be done for large-scale social infections. When you put the ingredients that traditional management of change provides next to those for Viral Change™, you'll see it's a completely different recipe!

# 4.1

# It's behaviours!

Behaviours are wonderful things! They are powerful, they are explicit and they provoke many emotions. However, for many people today behaviours are still 'secondary citizens', only understood 'as a result' of other things such as values, beliefs or thinking.

These are people who, very often truly genuinely, say that changing behaviours means little unless the mindset or the attitudes have changed. They would say you can change behaviours, but it will be just superficial, not for real, just a game of pretend. Your (real) thinking will not have changed. Mindsets and attitudes... You know how I feel about those!

In many parts of the world, 'behaviours' still get bad press. They seem to be mentally associated with 'forcing people' to do something. In English, 'to behave' means to behave well, to conform to the norm, to stick to the rules. In psychiatry, behavioural therapy has long been labelled as a sort of superficial approach, not comparable with the more 'serious' and 'deep' therapies such as psychoanalysis or psychotherapy, which are based upon understanding and insights.

> • • •
> Large-scale change? Bypass the individual 'understanding', the 'state of readiness', the 'intellectual awareness'. Behaviours x influence x networks will give you the scale-up statistics you need.
> • • •

These stereotypes won't go away soon. I don't have much room to digress here and I know a discussion about this could go on for hours, perhaps even days or months...but I do believe we need to elaborate a bit on this before we move on. People, particularly the ones who associate behaviours with carrots and sticks, have a hard time understanding the potential value and pragmatism of focusing on behaviours.

This view of behaviours as the poor, secondary, visible representation of more noble bodies such as mind, mindset, cognition, value systems, etc. is well-maintained by many Homo Sapiens professions for very good reasons. We all tend to attribute all motivation for our actions to the essence of Sapiens. The opposite would mean accepting that we are less in control than we think we are and that our free will is less free than we think.

There are at least two possible positions here to address this dilemma from the behavioural sciences' perspective. One is the 'behavioural-fundamentalist' view. This view takes the stand that we have a black box called 'mind', filled with spirit, will, cognition, mindsets, attitudes, etc. This black box has a very rich life inside of it, but, unfortunately, we can't see any of those things. Fortunately, we can see behaviours and we know what to do with them. Besides, the contents of the black box do not matter, as long as we can reinforce (or block) outputs or behaviours. Period. It is as simple as that.

The second position is the 'behavioural-pragmatic' track. This approach seems to say very similar things, but the clear distinction is at the end of the argument. This position acknowledges all those 'good things' going on inside the black box. It would not tend to deny or dismiss them, but will focus on the visible manifestations because that is the only practical thing to do. So far they're both the same. But here is the fundamental distinction: this position would have no problem with trying to understand or extrapolate 'the thinking behind' or 'the frame of mind' or 'the cognitive status' of individuals changing or not changing behaviours. However, they would also insist that what needs to be done is largely independent from this understanding.

Very often, to the horror of the cognition-lovers who need to 'understand' what's happening 'inside the box' (mind, cognition, brain, soul), it is 'afterwards' that the behavioural-pragmatics would try to make sense of the 'mental state'. Let me explain. Imagine behavioural change on some scale. That would involve defining specific behaviours and a (complex or simple) system of reinforcement. The behavioural-pragmatic approach would craft that infection without the need for personality tests for all individuals in order to 'explain' their potential readiness or resistance to change, or their ability to intellectually absorb the thinking behind the change.

Statistically, the success of the change largely depends on the strength and ability of the reinforcement system, the mechanisms of social influence and the structure of the (informal) social network. Some people will change quickly, some slowly, some will maintain those behaviours, some won't, etc. It is unlikely that there is any correlation between the 'cognitive understanding' and the results of the change. And besides, it would be very impractical to have everyone complete a personality test!

Imagine this: a revolution that needed to understand upfront the correlation between the personality of the revolutionaries and the outcome of the revolution; a revolution wanting to know the differences in adoption of the revolution depending on some cognitive and mental capacity of people. Or needing some survey on 'change readiness'. I am not trying to trivialize the importance of 'knowing', but the scaling up of 'acting' is very much independent from it. And that's the very significant distinction of the behavioural-pragmatic approach. Large-scale change? Bypass the individual 'understanding', the 'state of readiness', the 'intellectual awareness', the measure of 'emotional engagement', the degree of 'personal internalization', etc. Behaviours x influence x networks will give you the scale-up statistics you need. Remember: cogito is a bonus.

A great deal of modern management thinking has been influenced by a poor understanding, poor grasp and poor execution of behavioural sciences, which seem to stay stuck at the very superficial level of the 'carrot and the stick'. Performance appraisal systems, sales management incentives, bonus schemes...they all look somewhat (or a lot) like carrots. A few years ago, I conducted an informal review of about a dozen sales management incentive schemes in several pharmaceutical companies. Only one made sense from a behavioural perspective. All the others were completely flawed and at least half of them had outcomes that were the opposite of what the scheme had intended to reward. All of them seemed to have been designed by a (well-paid) quantum physicist.

The problem is that behavioural-sciences-carrot-and-stick models seem cheap to apply. Everybody seems to know how. But they'll also need to bear the consequences, of course.

102

Behavioural change management is neutral, blind, amoral. The user of behavioural sciences, however, may be purpose-driven, have a clear vision and choose a moral path. He may also be stupid.

To reward high-risk, invisible, short-term, virtual market investments (those 'vehicles' brought to us by the City of London or Wall Street; vehicles which have no consistency and would belong better in Monte Carlo or Las Vegas) and to do it with massive amounts of money is simply stupid. Obviously not for the recipient of the reward, but for the community at large that suffers the consequences.

> ⦿ ⦿ ⦿
> **Behaviours create cultures, not the other way around. Focusing on behaviours is the only way of spreading social infections at any kind of scale.**
> ⦿ ⦿ ⦿

The really good thing that has happened in the last years to real behavioural sciences is their 'discovery' by economists. Historically, economics was based on the rationality of the individual. You know, given a choice, people will maximize its utility. This was even written on the frontispiece of economics as a discipline. Well, at least until behavioural economics came along and added the graffiti: 'sometimes'. This 'sometimes' or 'maybe' was enough to start challenging all basic assumptions. Behavioural economics today look at things from the perspective of the behaviours of the individuals, who frequently exhibit 'non-utilitarian' behaviours, irrational ones that do not fit the theory. Behavioural economics do not take the simplistic carrot-and-stick approach. These people know that there is a complexity to, even competition between, carrots. They also know that sticks sometimes don't work.

Let me state the following to be crystal clear: in Viral Change™ we take a 'behavioural-pragmatic' approach and we are pretty conscious of the choice made. The key reason for this choice is one word: scalability. As you may know by now, we are in the business of social infections! We, practitioners of Viral Change™, believe deeply that behaviours create cultures, not the other way around. Focusing on behaviours is the only way of spreading social infections at any kind of scale.

## What are behaviours?

The currency of world II is behaviours and to create a social infection, inside the firm or the macro-social world, we need a particular concept of behaviours that will allow their orchestrated social spread through networks of influence (Viral Change™). These are the five criteria, or perhaps five tests that they need to pass[1]:

| 1 | Recognizable units of action | Concrete things that people do or don't do. A complex routine of several actions cannot be called 'a behaviour'. |
| 2 | Than can be attributed to an agent | Remember, 'an agent' is you and me (a manager, the CEO, employees with names and surnames). 'The behaviour of the market' is a figure of speech . The market doesn't have a behaviour. |
| 3 | That have unequivocal meaning | There must be little or no room for interpretation of what the behaviour is or is not. |
| 4 | Able to be reinforced | Any behaviour is reinforce-able, but by this I mean that it has to pass the test that that particular behaviour can be recognized and rewarded by somebody. |

---

[1] These were expressed in a slightly different way in my book *Viral Change*. Here, I have emphasized the need to pass the tests for the purposes of orchestrating a social infection.

| | | |
|---|---|---|
| | 'Measurable' | People constantly confuse measure with outcome. The behaviour can be measured in multiple ways such as their frequency for example. If that behaviour leads to an increase in sales, that is the outcome. Increased sales are not a measure of the behaviour. |
| 5 | It will create a good story | Stories could easily be associated with the practice of the behaviour. The test is a simple 'imagine' test. Imagine that behaviours X, Y, Z were spread a thousand times today. What kind of stories would we hear? |

The most important of these tests is number 3: does this behaviour have unequivocal meaning? In my book, *Viral Change*™, I described three levels of behaviours: macromolecular (high level, such as 'collaboration'), molecular (a medium level description, such as 'sharing information between A and B') and atomic (the most concrete, such as 'send a one-page report to B every week'). The closer we can get to the atomic level, the better our position will be to spread behaviours and generate the desired social contagion.

'Behaviours' such as 'live the brand', 'be sympathetic, or 'be customer-driven' are miles away from actually being a behaviour. They would not pass the number 3 test! 'Participate in meetings' starts to look like a behaviour. But still, your concept of participation may be nodding at the presenter or taking notes. My concept may be to give an opinion or view, or to actively say something. Always asking the question 'would there be a better way to do this?' is pretty atomic. Either you do it or you don't. It's not always possible to come up with a good atomic translation of behaviours, but it should still always be our aim.

In many cases, it is a good idea to describe several concrete scenarios that show what the behaviour is about. This allows for many atomic 'translations', making sure that the interpretation is as unequivocal as possible. On page 107 is a real example of the behaviour 'agility' (a label of behaviour which, if left as such, would not pass test 3) described further. This is not a universal definition of agility, but the behaviour 'used' in a particular Viral Change™ programme[2].

In this case, the definitions were less 'atomic' than they should be, but in each of the five described scenarios there were key behaviours that the organization had no problem in recognizing: don't wait for the next meeting if you can make a decision now, don't wait for a reply to your request for input in order to do something, stop going to so many meetings, ask the question *"why are we doing this the long way?"*, find a barrier and break it. These are the real atomic ones.

> 'Behaviours' such as 'live the brand', 'be sympathetic' or 'be customer-driven' are miles away from actually being a behaviour.

Following the 'agility' example is another example, this time of the behaviour 'challenge toxic attitudes'[3] in the context of a Viral Change™ programme focused on safety in a global oil and gas company[4].

You can see that both examples represent different formats of articulation and definitions, each of them tailored to the needs of their population.

---

[2] With thanks to Pfizer (www.pfizer.com) for the permission to reproduce it here in a slightly modified way.

[3] Despite my reservations about the use of concepts such as 'mindset' or 'attitudes', I have no problem using them if they are then quickly translated into tangible behaviours. It is almost impossible not to use those concepts. The key is to translate them efficiently.

[4] With thanks to Saipem (www.saipem.it) for their permission to reproduce.

## Agility

**Make decisions in 'real time'** when possible without waiting for a formal meeting or a pre-scheduled calendar event (e.g. next cycle planning or team meeting)

**Define a realistic timeline and act upon it** if you are empowered to do so: no reply to a request for input is to be taken as approved

**Trust others** to represent you so that we avoid over-inclusiveness in meetings. Think hard about who needs to be involved

**Challenge processes which are out of sync** with business needs. Within the law and agreed standards, such as the company's code of conduct, take the fastest and shortest route

**Uncover the barriers** that prevent you from doing a successful job and act to overcome them, gaining support from others

## Comments

Behind this behaviour lies the desire to act fast, the willingness to make decisions, to be smarter at prioritizing and not being only reactive to others' agenda. Agility is not about bypassing standards or making unsound judgements for the sake of speed. However, it may entail making decisions without all the facts, and therefore taking more risks than before.

Confronted with a decision and a process to make it, you may want to think of what you would do if it were your own (small!) business: would you pick up the phone? Gather people to discuss your idea, but only those essential for the decision to be made.

Defining realistic timelines, sticking to them and going ahead even when some people have not answered your request for input, entails making an effort to understand responsibilities, the role of others and their time constraints. However, we need to avoid a culture of delays and deferral to the next meeting, or the next agenda, when everybody is involved.

Agility as a behaviour goes against complacency and does not allow anyone to hide behind 'we have too many processes' (how many would be acceptable?)

## Challenging toxic attitudes

*'Safety matters'*. This behaviour is about addressing and confronting behaviours—often small ones—that may not carry a safety risk by themselves, but demonstrate negative 'toxic attitudes' and are possible triggers of high-impact incidents. If people are cynical or dismissive about safety, this will affect the way they work and will create more hazards for everyone. These contribute heavily to a culture which opposes the goal of 'safety as primary concern'. From all possible triggers, three are chosen: dismissing or undermining the importance of safety; expressions of defeatism; and a culture of blame and excuses.

| Behaviour | When/where this is most appropriate | What the champion should do | It's not about |
|---|---|---|---|
| **Challenge dismissive attitudes:** Confront attitudes and intervene in conversations that **dismiss the importance of health & safety** or that portray the health & safety priority in a cynical way | Conversations where safety priorities are dismissed as 'nice talk' or 'the official line', versus the 'reality' of operational targets. Out of work situations are also important, e.g. driving without seat belts | Take a stand against dismissive comments: *"I disagree with you. It may just be 'nice talk' to you, but for me it's important because...Maybe others here agree, but chose not to say so".* This includes challenging non-verbal signals | Creating a conflict about different views, but leaving it 'open', without resolution |
| **Challenge defeatism:** Address **signals of defeatism** such as *"We can't change things around here"*, *"It won't make a difference"*, *"Managers don't care"* or *"We tried it last year and it didn't work"*. | Informal or semi-formal conversations where these signals appear | Take a stand against defeatist comments. Identify cynics and defeatists in the organization and aim to turn them into believers. Explain why safety matters. Use stories to remind people that death and injury result from poor safety practices | Challenging aggressively |
| **Challenge blame and excuses:** Confront people who simply **blame others** for poor safety or **make excuses,** e.g. *"That's ok in X, but not here in Y"*, *"Accidents will always happen"* | In any circumstances when this happens | Invite others to find/bring solutions, address the problem or its causes. Make people understand that all incidents are preventable. Give examples, tell stories | Not accepting that people have responsibilities and should be accountable for them |

## Why a small set?

I have repeatedly alluded to a 'small set of behaviours'. Why a small set? Because behaviours are such powerful tools at the core of many interconnected things. Many big problems can be understood as the failure of a small number of behaviours, repeated several times. The other way around is also true. A small set of behaviours can create a big cultural change.

Behaviours are also interconnected. They are bound to be 'good for several things in one'. On the next page is an example of a behaviour ('intervene in an unsafe situation', in the context of a Viral Change™ safety programme) and how the practicing of that behaviour has an impact on other behaviours. In this case, 'intervening' (the primary behaviour) is not only good for safety itself, but it is also boosting accountability, innovation, recognition, collaboration and leadership itself.

It is almost impossible to talk about a behaviour in isolation. They will always be linked and interdependent. So whilst it is important to choose a small set and focus the Viral Change™ spread on them, it is equally important to be conscious of the extended consequences of boosting those behaviours.

Viral Change™ acts as glue in the organization. You may be focusing on 'innovation', for example, but the extended consequences of spreading innovative behaviours will go beyond 'the innovation project', spreading perhaps to other initiatives such as organizational effectiveness or customer-centrism.

These intended and extended consequences need to be thought through strategically before starting. In the outside macro-social world, a health campaign around a particular health issue, smoking, for example, should focus on (a) the behaviours around smoking in a target population (intended) and, perhaps, (b) the change in behaviours of health workers dealing with that target population.

## Uncovering behaviours in 10 ways

'Where' can you get behaviours? And how do you do it? Let's start with the first one. It may seem unnecessary to stress again that it is not until we have real behaviours in front of us that we are ready to craft the social infection. Nothing else will do. It is not processes or values, or credos, or beliefs. We need a good translation of those things into behaviours.

Within the organization, the origins of the 'need for change' may be diverse. But whatever they are, they need to be translated into the (underlying) behaviours. And once this is done, there are the famous two routes of world I and world II...and you know which one to use for social contagion purposes. The graph on page 112 represents these choices again.

Staying in the organizational territory, I want to share with you the 10 possible ways to use for uncovering behaviours needed for change. Uncovering them is the first step. Step two is choosing which ones will be 'non-negotiable'. This is an even smaller set that, by choice, will become the focus of the behavioural change.

I have artificially divided these 10 ways into three groups:
(A)  Uncovering behaviours from existing data
(B)  New focus
(C)  Simulation of new behaviours in reality.

All 10 ways need some skills and perhaps external facilitation. In my consulting work, I usually choose a combination of several of them, never just one single one.

## (A) Uncovering behaviours from existing data

1.  ***Past positive and negative experiences.*** Digging in the learning from the past, perhaps by choosing several projects with positive and negative outcomes, may be a good first port of call to start uncovering the behavioural fabric 'underneath' that led to the success and/or failure.

2.  ***Positive Deviance.*** In any organization there are people who manage to get things done and achieve positive outcomes by doing things in an unconventional or different way[5]. These 'deviants' may or may not be favoured by management who usually dismiss them as mavericks. The organization is always wasting tremendous insights by ignoring its internal deviance. Positive deviance is a great source of insight about needed behaviours.

---

[5] See chapter 11 of my book: *Viral Change: The alternative to slow, painful and unsuccessful management of change in organizations* (meetingminds, 2008)

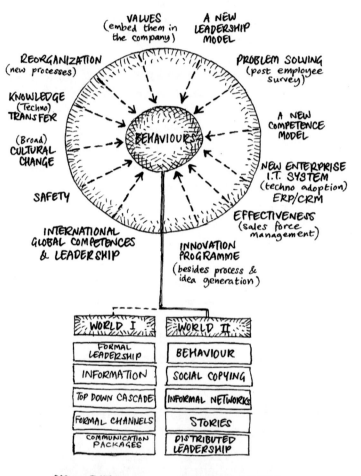

VALUES
(embed them in
the company)

A NEW
LEADERSHIP
MODEL

REORGANIZATION
(new processes)

PROBLEM SOLVING
(post employee
survey)

KNOWLEDGE
(Techno)
TRANSFER

A NEW
COMPETENCE
MODEL

(Broad)
CULTURAL
CHANGE

BEHAVIOURS

NEW ENTERPRISE
I.T. SYSTEM
(techno adoption)
ERP/CRM

SAFETY

EFFECTIVENESS
(sales force
management)

INTERNATIONAL
GLOBAL COMPETENCES
& LEADERSHIP

INNOVATION
PROGRAMME
(besides process &
idea generation)

| WORLD I | WORLD II |
| --- | --- |
| FORMAL LEADERSHIP | BEHAVIOUR |
| INFORMATION | SOCIAL COPYING |
| TOP DOWN CASCADE | INFORMAL NETWORKS |
| FORMAL CHANNELS | STORIES |
| COMMUNICATION PACKAGES | DISTRIBUTED LEADERSHIP |

BIG INITIATIVES X
COMMUNICATION PROGRAMME X
ALL MANAGEMENT LEVELS =
TRADITIONAL
CHANGE MANAGEMENT

SMALL SET OF (NON-
NEGOTIABLE) BEHAVIOURS X
SMALL NUMBER OF PEOPLE X
NETWORKS OF INFLUENCE =
VIRAL CHANGE™

3. *Organizational survey data.* Many large organizations have employee satisfaction surveys and/or exit interviews. They may be a good source of uncovering key behaviours (positive or negative). My experience is that these surveys are not necessarily behaviours-driven, so a good deal of 'translation' may be needed, but the often rich data cannot be ignored. More interesting for me are 'stay interviews' where we, more or less literally, ask people *"Why are you still here?"*[6] They are a tremendous source of insight into the hidden organizational fabric of the firm.

4. *Existing value framework.* An obvious first port of call is also the value system that the organization may have. These values may or may not already have been 'translated' into behaviours. If they have been, we can't take those translations at face value. In my experience, many of those 'behavioural definitions' of values would not pass test number 3. Strict behavioural definitions are needed. On top of this, it may be that the behaviours needed for a specific 'change project' are not exactly the same as the ones articulated in the company's mission statement. Although you can expect some overlap, the kind of behavioural fabric that may be needed for a particular change focus may be different (in scope or emphasis) from the declared 'generic behaviours' of the organization.

## (B) New Focus

5. *Project specific.* Take the new project focus (safety, broad cultural change, sales force effectiveness, innovation, a customer-centric organization, etc.) and 'go backwards' from there, uncovering the kind of behaviours that could lead to success or failure.

---

[6] See my article *Why are you still here?* in the section 'Search Ideas Lab' of www.thechalfontproject.com

113

6. *Take 'universal' or 'researched' behaviours*. Although these are not strictly speaking universal, Viral Change™ has some researched and applied areas where, across the board, specific sets of behaviours seem to be pretty common. This is the only way out of the ten suggested here where I am referring to proprietary data, based on our research and execution experience. We have Viral Change™ 'solutions in areas such as 'culture of innovation', 'culture of safety', 'internationalization' (of management skills) and many others.

7. *Branding of the organization*. Branding is a good platform from which to extract behaviours. Many organizations embark upon this kind of exercise, but then remain at the level of descriptions listing the qualities, 'experience' and 'personality' of the (organizational) brand, or even the behaviours expected. But this is where it all stops. The existence of a change focus, a strategic need to change (for example, any of the reasons listed in the graph on page 110) is a good platform for a branding exercise to visualize 'the new organization' or the new culture when those changes are in place. By doing so, we are bound to find behaviours very soon and, as such, will uncover the ones we need for our world II social infection.

## (C) Simulation of new behaviours in reality

8. *Success and failure scripts*. This is literally about writing scripts that would lead to success (however you define this) and/or failure and then about extracting the behaviours behind that success/failure. It is a visualization exercise[7]. When I facilitate them within the context of our Viral Change™ programmes, I use both scripts, 'written' in parallel by two independent groups of leaders, comparing notes at the end and extracting the common behaviours.

---

[7] In management consulting jargon sometimes called 'visioning'.

9. **Simulate a new 'operating model'.** Usually a reorganization or M&A requires new processes. New processes require new behaviours, not just the rational understanding of what the new processes look like! Splitting the new operating model into components allows us to uncover which new (or not that new) behaviours are needed. The 'standard' operating model we use (which we call Project Anatomy™) includes planning, decision making, resource allocation, priority setting, accountabilities reporting and knowledge transfer. Simulating how those will work under 'the new regime' is a way of extracting the (new?) behaviours needed to support those new processes.

10. **'Who needs to know' vs. 'Who does what'.** Most organizational structures are based upon a 'who does what' model. The division of labour, corporate pipes and the command-and-control system dictate 'the way we *do* things'. But a real alternative model in this knowledge economy would be to structure 'the way we do things' in terms of who needs to know what. Knowledge flow and action flow are not the same. By simulating a new structure under the 'who needs to know' question, one discovers a complete new world of possibilities, including behaviours that were perhaps hidden. This isn't a difficult exercise, but a very valuable one.

The best method to get to the bottom of which behaviours are needed is to use a combination of ways and a combination of mechanisms. These are four that we use:

1. **Field observations are extremely valuable.** Traditionally, 'the world of management' does not have good observational and interpretative skills in its toolkit. In the day-to-day management of organizations a lot is taken at face value, without further (or any) reflection. To be able to get under the skin of cultural dynamics and observe real behaviours requires skills belonging more to anthropology than to

Harvard's strategic courses. Employing independent people with that observational and interpretative capacity is smart.

2. **Focus group validations.** If conducted well, these are excellent sources of validation for preliminary sets of behaviours that management groups may have drafted. Checking for understanding and meaning and testing them in front of selected groups of employees always pays off.

3. **Behavioural audit.** There are ways to have a good sense of the real behavioural fabric of the organization by auditing the existence of some sets of behaviours. This audit, when done online, can reach a relatively large number of people (answering anonymously) in a short period of time. Our own tool is mainly designed to flag relative differences between behaviours as a way to validate data coming from other sources, such as management teams.

4. **Senior management uncovering.** Leaders are responsible for the behavioural fabric of the organization. Therefore, they are a logical part of uncovering the (new) behaviours that may be needed for a particular change focus. In-depth exercises with these groups are standard in our approach as a way to ensure their engagement. But the outcomes of these relatively inward-looking set-ups need to be validated by other means.

## Non-negotiable behaviours and a magic word: choice

The uncovering of and search for behaviours may present us with a rich collection. Now, we need to exercise a crucial prerogative that 'management' has and that isn't always completely pleasant: the choice. There may be, say, 10 crucial possible behaviours that have been proposed by management, validated by various people and that are consistent with our external advice. They are all plausible candidates. They all make sense. But we need to halve them. Although there is no dogmatic number, just imagine the spread of them around the organization and the potential difficulty of explaining them (world I) and endorsing and practicing them (world II).

You may be disappointed when I say that there is no scientific method for choosing the ones which from then on will be called 'non-negotiable' to stress their importance. Nor would I recommend the traditional prioritization system based on maximum impact and degree of control, for example. You have just decided that all of them may have great impact. The leadership team needs to make a decision and determine the ones to focus on based upon a technique as simple as imagining: imagining those behaviours multiplied a thousand times every week across the organization and imagining the kind of organizational culture that would result from that. Obviously, there will be a combination of factors in their brain: impact, personal closeness, etc. It doesn't matter. They still need to choose, so that the initial infection at least focuses on the spread of that small set. Remember my previous comment about the interdependence of behaviours. That may help in making the choice!

> *Imagine those behaviours multiplied a thousand times every week across the organization and imagine the kind of organizational culture that would result from that.*

## Articulating behaviours

There are three fundamental models of articulation in our world of social infections and Viral Change™:

### A. Behaviours as world II currency

This is the detailed articulation needed for the currency 'behaviour' to behave properly. This level of detail is required when the highly connected, highly influential people ('champions': see next chapters) are asked for help. They will 'practice' those non-negotiable behaviours, engaging other people to do the same. The examples mentioned before (agility, safety) are representative of this. At first glance there is too much information contained in each of them. But this is done on purpose to allow for good understanding and to achieve as unequivocal a meaning as possible.

### B. Behaviours as world I expressions of direction

Yes, you need to 'show' the behaviours world I-style. However, 'showing' behaviours doesn't need the same level of articulation here. On the contrary, that would be counterproductive. A communication campaign needs a simple version of behaviours, well-articulated and well-presented, using whatever media appropriate to the culture. Traditional communication techniques (to ensure that the message is solid and easy to receive and understand) are crucial in this world. Visualizations are also very important.

> There is nothing better than a behaviour that doesn't need or doesn't have a definition, but a set of stories.

### C. Stories

There is nothing better than a behaviour that doesn't need or doesn't have a definition, but a set of stories. "*Do you know what we mean by accountability around here? John spotted a basic error in our plans to deliver the service to the customer. It was late on a Friday and the service was due to be delivered to the customer on Monday. The error had nothing to do with him or his department, so he could not do much personally. So, John called a couple of colleagues who he thought would know more about the root of the problem. It turned out to be a bigger problem than they thought. They had to work overnight to solve it, getting hold of some external IT people who needed to fix something urgently, as the internal IT people were unavailable over the weekend. They had to pay for some crucial expenses using their own company credit card, although they were not supposed to do this for this kind of expenditure. By mid-afternoon on Sunday, all was fixed and ready for the customer. The delivery team could not believe that all could have been fixed in 24 hours by people whose expertise and responsibilities had nothing to do with the problem. It was great. You know, my son, this is an example of what accountability looks like here."*

Try to beat that definition! Note that I have managed to describe the components of the behaviour without explaining what the service was, what the problem was about, what the industry was or the set-up, etc. Whatever it was, it was first considered a problem, then a bigger one and it was fixed by unconventional means by people who were not required to do so according to their job description. They 'took' responsibility. (Note that the English expression of 'taking' responsibility often implies 'having' it. A fine linguistic nuance.)

Finally, let us remember that behaviours are uncovered and articulated in world I, lived and spread in world II and then sent back to world I in the form of stories. This is the real circle of life

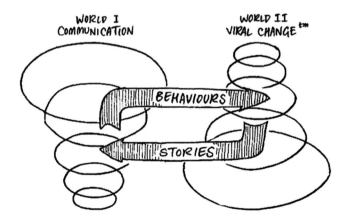

of change in behavioural terms. This is how Viral Change™ closes the loop between the two worlds.

## Behaviours and airtime

What gets reinforced (rewarded, recognized, gratified), increases in frequency. What is not, fades. This is your PhD in psychology in a sentence. At a social level, the most simple reinforcement mechanism of behaviours is airtime. And that means having the behaviours present and visible, and spending time talking about them or doing something about them.

The best example of the importance of airtime that I have seen in one of our Viral Change™ programmes was in a sales force transformation within a large pharmaceutical company.

Before Viral Change™, sales reviews between the district manager and sales managers were done quickly, one-on-one, sometimes on the phone (virtual teams), sometimes over a quick coffee in a service station on the highway and always with spreadsheets and numbers. Only occasionally, and then often only at the end of the session, the district manager would enter into more qualitative insights. They simply had 'no time' to do that on a routine basis. Their formal district meetings were a mirror of this. First thing on the agenda was always something that looked like a spreadsheet, felt like a spreadsheet and actually was a spreadsheet with 'the data', i.e. the sales numbers. One after another the salesmen would parade around explaining the ups and downs of the bars and pie charts.

One of the identified behaviours that the Viral Change™ programme wanted to spread at epidemic levels was 'moving up the customer'. They wanted to focus on obtaining and understanding customer insights and they wanted to put the customer first in the day-to-day business (as opposed to having the customer as a sort of 'afterthought' after sales numbers had been discussed). This simple change, multiplied a hundred times, was thought to be a good desirable drive for a new culture. You bet it was and it happened very quickly.

One particular sales team was miles ahead of the rest in their reports on how frequently they started any business conversation with this theme. You may think that this should be just natural, but in the context of that particular company (and many others I have worked with) this was a significant departure from the norm. And it was surprisingly fast, happening only 2-3 months after the start of the programme!

> ◦ ◦ ◦
>
> **What gets reinforced (rewarded, recognized, gratified) increases in frequency. What is not, fades. At a social level, the most simple reinforcement mechanism of behaviours is airtime.**
>
> ◦ ◦ ◦

How did this happen? Was anything different in the 'mindset' of the people involved? Well, as you may gather, I could not find their mindsets so I looked at behaviours. Soon I discovered that the district manager lived very close to one of her team managers. This team manager used to take a train every day to reach the large hospital where she was based most of the time with some of her team members. Every day, the district manager gave this sales woman a ride to the station, about 20 minutes away. For some reason, this district manager had 'clicked' very well with the need to shift the emphasis to 'customer conversations' and this is what they talked about every single day for 20 minutes. So, the behaviour was reinforced for 20 minutes every day, week after week.

And the impact of that simple chat was overwhelmingly greater than anything else in the rest of the sales force. They talked about it, it then occupied their minds and it was what the team manager repeated unconsciously with her team. And, seemingly overnight, it simply became the norm to start any conversation

**121**

with 'the customer', not with the sales figures. When spread across the board, they got a culture change of great magnitude. By the way, that district also did extremely well in sales numbers. I would not dare to claim that it was a result of the behavioural change, but I must admit that I am tempted.

## Don't do that

Giving airtime to X reinforces X. If X is a negative behaviour or a negative behavioural pattern, X gets reinforced, even if the intention is to stress 'don't do that'. I am a collector of 'don't do that' signs from public and private places[8] as a way of understanding what behaviours are likely to be around.

You can see some picture examples on the previous page. The one at the top left is from an airport. It contains almost apocalyptic warnings about abusing staff. What it actually tells me is that abuse surely must be quite common around there or they would not have bothered to put up the (dozens of) posters.

The top right image is from a hospital where one is warned in all corridors about the 'zero tolerance' policy regarding violence to staff. Those corridors must have been very violent at some point. The bottom left is equally apocalyptic and also from a hospital where abuse of nurses may have been a sort of sport, to say the least, given the size of the letters.

The bottom right picture, once more from a hospital, educates us about the detrimental effects of duck faeces in the garden ('Duck faeces cause infections and pollution'). This clearly shows us that there must be lots of ducks and lots of faeces around, because otherwise why would they bother with this unsolicited education about the physiological habits of the animals?

---

[8] If you have 'don't-do-that' pictures, please send me a message through www.thechalfontproject.com. They'll be graciously received and acknowledged.

All these posters have been created by world I 'communication consultants' and with world I intentions. They are intrinsically flawed in behavioural terms since they will not contribute to the extinction of the problem/behaviour and may probably even exacerbate them. So, be careful what you give airtime to.

Just in case you're wondering how to approach these posters differently, here is my alternative to the UK airport poster:

> Thank you for supporting our security staff who are working hard to get you through fast and hassle-free, despite the system's inconveniences. And thanks to your understanding, we were able to decrease the waiting time by 10 minutes. Your smiles where a bonus (particularly for the early morning shift)!

What the new copy is now 'saying', is that this is a place of tolerance to inconvenience, sympathy to the staff and smiles as a bonus. What you promote is what you get.

In the next chapters we will see how the other Viral Change™ pillars (social copying, internal informal networks, stories and distributed leadership) use behaviours. They are nothing without the strong presence of behaviours. Put behaviours first on your agenda and you're on the right track.

# 4.2

# Scalable influence

During 2009, the advertising agency DDB in Stockholm created a campaign for Volkswagen in which the car company sponsored a competition to find ideas that would make people change behaviours...by making something more fun. Not surprisingly they called it 'The Fun Theory'[1].

The three original experiments were fascinating (see pictures on the next page). In one of them, the stairs of an underground station, next to an escalator, were converted overnight into a giant piano keyboard. The proper notes would play when people stepped on the keys/steps. The idea was to make more people use the stairs instead of the escalator, because the stairs would

---

[1] You can see the submissions and the winner at www.thefuntheory.com

be more fun. Sure enough, 66% more people than normal used the 'piano stairs'. In a second experiment, a 'bottomless' bin was installed in a park. It was fitted with invisible receptors and a sound system so that when anybody dropped anything inside the bin, it would sound as if the item was falling deeper and deeper. Well, 72 kilos of rubbish were collected in a single day, 41 kilos more than in the 'normal' bin nearby. In a third experiment, a public recycling bottle bank was fitted with a dashboard and flashing lights similar to an arcade game. Throwing bottles through the holes produced different sounds and different scores on the flashing dashboard. In one evening, 100 people used that bottle bank compared to only 2 at the 'normal' one nearby.

These experiments are wonderful examples of many things, not only of 'making things fun changes behaviour'. But powerful as they are, the key questions for us in the business of social infections are: what happens after the first day/week/month? And how sustainable is this behavioural change?

In the case of the bin in the park, how many similar bins would you need to make it scalable? And for how long? And if at some point, all the bins did the same, would the effect fade?[2] Or have

---

[2] There are many other things that a behavioural scientist would ask and/or recommend. For instance, the reinforcement power of the 'sound from the depth' would multiply exponentially if the sound would not follow every piece throw in, but only selected pieces in a random way. In technical terms it is called 'reinforcement of variable ratio' and it is far more powerful than any other reinforcement. This is also what's behind slot machines. Interestingly, the winner was Kevin Richardson's idea: Rewarding Speed Limit Signs. He described the idea as 'Can we get more people to obey the speed limit by making it fun to do?' The idea was to capture on camera the people who stuck to the speed limit. Their registration numbers would then be recorded from the photos and entered into a lottery. Winners would receive cash prizes and were notified by post. Better still, the winning pot would come from the people who were caught speeding. And it did. The system achieved a 22% reduction in overall speed across the board. It all makes sense from the behavioural sciences' perspective because it is banking on (1) reward of positive [vs. punish the transgressors] and (2) random possibility of reward, as lottery intrinsically is. This is sustainable in behavioural terms.

we simply proven that people can do things differently when confronted with new, fun circumstances? To trigger new behaviours is relatively easy. Sustaining them is the key to real behavioural change.

Many formal change programmes (both in the corporate world and the macro-social one) have a short honeymoon of adoption, perhaps filled with enthusiasm, good intentions and high energy levels, but then they progressively fade. The initial 'change' activity is neither sustainable nor scalable. We are on the whole very good at producing the noise, bringing the bells and whistles, even a full orchestra...in short, at creating a 'Big Splash'-world I-push situation. But we are far less careful about ensuring a continuation or follow up of that 'change'. In the business of change (transformation, public initiative, culture, etc.) the names of the game are sustainability and scalability. They are not the same, but they travel together in a package deal.

> ● ● ●
>
> **Many formal change programmes have a short honeymoon of adoption, then progressively fade. The initial 'change' activity is neither sustainable nor scalable.**
>
> ● ● ●

In Viral Change™, we look at all the available influence mechanisms in the organization/society to find the ones that can orchestrate social copying that is both scalable and sustainable. Don't get me wrong, it's great that your team is completely on board, has fully embraced the change rationale, is emotionally engaged and has changed behaviours. You now all do things very differently and you feel very good about it! Congratulations to your 15 team members! But how are you going to infect the other 1,500 or 15,000 people in the organization? In recent years, some people have come up with an answer to these scale-up questions: stick the word 'viral' in front of everything. From advertising agencies to marketing gurus, 'viral' has been gaining ground as an alternative way to spread things, from ideas to songs and video clips. The blogosphere is full of links to this 'viral song', that 'viral video' or the 'viral campaign'. In many cases the word 'viral' has become synonymous with massive, large and fast.

No video or song is 'viral' until it is spread like an infection. There is no such a thing as a 'viral' anything. There may be different characteristics in the piece of world I information that may make it more suitable for a viral spread, but even a very suitable and potentially viral element is not viral until it is spread via a viral mechanism.

> *In recent years, some people have come up with an answer to these scale-up questions: stick the word 'viral' in front of everything.*

In a study of almost 7,000 online news articles from *The New York Times*, researchers from the Wharton School in Philadelphia, USA[3], found some strong similarities between the stories that were 'more viral'. They found there was a pattern. Content that was shared more, was usually 'practical and useful, surprising, affect-laden and positively valenced'. Also, 'articles that evoked more awe, anger and anxiety, and less sadness' were more likely to be emailed.

I can't say that I am overwhelmed by the findings. I am also not sure whether they are using the term 'viral' as a synonymous to email-able or emailed. I think the obvious conclusion is that there must be some characteristics that make some stories, ideas or even actions more viral than others. But you will still need a viral mechanism to achieve that.

---

[3] Berger, J., K.L. Milkman, 2009. Social transmission, emotion and the virality of online content. *SSRN Working paper* (http://ssrn.com/abstract=1528077)

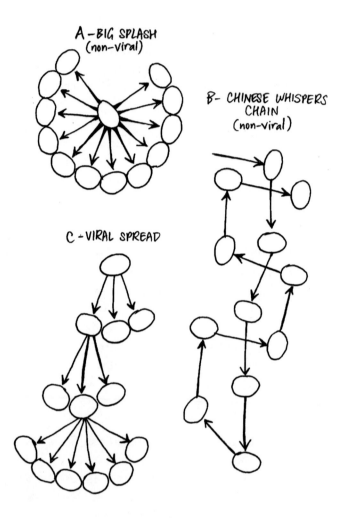

A – BIG SPLASH
(non-viral)

B – CHINESE WHISPERS
CHAIN
(non-viral)

C – VIRAL SPREAD

So, not all that is called 'viral' is viral. 50,000 downloads of a YouTube video in one hour is certainly an achievement, but not necessarily a viral achievement. Unless we know what the mechanism behind a certain phenomenon was, the word 'viral' could be misleading or simply a synonym for massive. Picture this. A front page news article prompts people to go to YouTube to see a video clip (something funny, extraordinary, curious, unexpected or appealing) and hundreds or thousands of people do so. That produces a massive peak of downloads. So far, so good. But the peak is not viral, not yet anyway. It only becomes viral if I send you an email with the link, suggesting you go to YouTube AND asking you to send the link to your friends. The level of infection goes up when you do send the link to your friends AND ask them to send it to their friends, etc.

In the graph on the previous page, A represents a Big Splash that may have been called viral, but it isn't. As represented, its scalability is zero, because it is simply a 'multiple of pairs'. B is a simplified Chinese whispers chain. Its scalability is poor and it also is not viral. C may look a bit modest compared with A, but it is viral: some interaction triggers others in a multiplying effect. Its scalability is only limited by the characteristics of the network.

## Models of social infection

There are three basic models of (scalable) social infection, equally applicable in the organizational world and the macro-social world (see the graph on the next page).

(1) The first model is the one I call **'Zero model'**. In epidemiology, the 'zero patient' is where the epidemic starts. Therefore, it means that the Zero model of social infection requires an origin, a trigger or initiator. There may be more than one and these triggers receive different names depending on the disciplinary hat you wear. This is the world of opinion leaders, influencers, champions, activists, etc. In other words, recognizable people or

groups of people with the ability to exercise their personal influence and trigger engagement around them.

(2) I call the second model the **'Orphan model'** because, unlike the Zero model, it doesn't seem to have an obvious trigger, certainly not in the form of identifiable opinion leaders or influencers of some kind. In this model, we notice the trend of a social infection once it becomes visible.

(3) I call the third model the **'Splash model'**. Here, the social phenomenon seems to appear 'as a result' of a rather broad world I system, perhaps dominating the media or part of it, perhaps as a result of a sudden massive 'push' from a Facebook- or YouTube-like event. Sometimes a Web 2.0 campaign or a large, perhaps persistent social media initiative (concerted advertising campaign?) seems to be at 'the origin' of the new social phenomenon.

There is also a fourth model which in reality is a combination model in which we can find elements of the other three. But it still leads to a new 'established' social norm. I'd like you to keep in mind at all times that these models of social infection are equally valid for the business organization and macro-social change.

## The Zero model

The Zero model is popular by definition. It counts on the presence (and identification) of influential people or influencers, both in society and the organization.

In the macro-social world, this model dominates disciplines such as market research, market trends and 'applied sociology'. Not surprisingly the quest has always been to find those particular people or groups whose influence can be 'used' for market(ing) purposes. For example, in their book, *The Influentials*[4], the authors describe individuals in the American society who are likely to exercise high influence on others. Their demographics include middle-aged, middle/upper class, college educated, married with children, homeowners, employed and executive or professional. Beyond demographics, the authors claim that the influentials are above all (1) 'activists' (attending community meetings and political events, as well as volunteering), (2) well-connected people and (3) ...err, influentials (others tend to look to them for advice).

The name of the game in this type of sociological efforts is predictive value. Pollsters, market researchers and sociologists love this. In the Clinton-campaign, Mark Penn[5] gained prominence with his creative segmenting of societal layers to predict voting (one of them being the famous 'soccer moms'). The idea is always to match segments with their particular influence, which will then lead to your desired action.

'Consumer-to-consumer' models have been very popular for many years and form the basis for many 'viral marketing' campaigns. These well-documented models of market(ing) influence[6] have a lot to teach us about macro- or micro-social change. Which does not mean to apply every single 'technique' used. There are people who have trouble accepting that understanding how a marketing campaign on diapers works, has the potential to teach us how cultural change can be created. As soon as you wear a Social Infector hat, the cross-learning is no longer 'a problem', it becomes a necessity.

---

[4] Keller, E., J. Berry. 2003. *The Influentials*. New York: Free Press.

[5] Penn, M., E.K. Zalesne. 2007. *Microtrends: The small forces behind tomorrow's big changes*. New York: Twelve.

[6] Earls, M. 2009. *Herd: How to change mass behaviour by harnessing our true nature*. Chichester, UK: John Wiley & Sons Ltd.

Inside the organization, there are many coexisting types of influence and influentials. Understanding and identifying them is one of the key elements of 'social intelligence', a well-needed competence for leaders and managers. Unfortunately, many leaders and managers only have just a vague idea of the richness and variety of influence that surround them, and most don't know how to harness this richness or how to treat each of the types differently. The graph on the following page gives some examples of those types.

> Inside the organization, there are many coexisting types of influence and influentials. Understanding and identifying them is one of the key elements of 'social intelligence'.

I tend to ask my clients to attach specific names to the different Post-its. It often starts as a 'trivial exercise'. However, very soon they find many 'aha'-moments and a much welcome understanding of the richness (of influence and therefore possibilities) around them.

Different kinds of influencers may be suited for different aims. In a high-tech R&D organization, for example, top leaders may have a great deal of hierarchical influence, but some of their employees may be stronger than them in scientific or technical authority and influence. For our purposes of scaling up with the aim of cultural and social change in mind, we need to understand which types within our 'portfolio of influencers' would be more suited to produce a faster and more robust spread of behaviours – since this is the currency we want to use in world II.

In recent years, successful authors such as Malcolm Gladwell[7] have popularized the idea of categorizing influencers into types

---

[7] Gladwell, M. 2002. *The tipping point: How little things can make a big difference.* New York: Back Bay Books.

such as 'mavens' or information specialists, who people rely upon for information; 'connectors' or people who link us with others; and 'salesmen' or persuaders. These terms found fertile ground in popular publications and have now been more or less incorporated into the socio-jargon.

This typology is intuitive and makes sense, which is why it is popular. But it is not entirely relevant to the crafting of large-scale social infections inside the organization or in the outside world. Many people with a high degree of influence would score

136

high (or low!) in more than one of those categories, making the typology a bit misleading[8]. What's more, in large-scale mode the following two criteria are more relevant:

## (1) Connectivity – high social capital

Highly connected people within the network of the organization have greater opportunities to influence, in a positive or negative way. Connectivity and high influence are two different things, but inside the organization they are difficult to separate. In pragmatic terms, connectivity becomes a proxy for influence.

> Highly connected people owe their connectivity not so much to their hierarchical position, but to their high social capital; that is, the depth and breadth of their rich relationships.

Highly connected people owe their connectivity not so much to their hierarchical position, but to their high social capital; that is, the depth and breadth of their rich relationships. By definition, highly connected people are unlikely to be 'silent' or 'invisible'. But a great deal of their connectivity has to do with their informal social networks.

Network sciences are no longer just something on the resume of the 'techies'. It has become vital in observing and interpreting any social reality, including the one where people spend most of their life: the organization. It tells us that:

---

[8] Van den Bulte, C., S. Wuyts. 2009. Leveraging customer networks. In Kleindorfer, P.R., Y. Wind, R.E. Gunther. 2009. *The network challenge: Strategy, profit and risk in an interlinked world.* Chapter 14. Upper Saddle River, NJ: Wharton School Publishing.

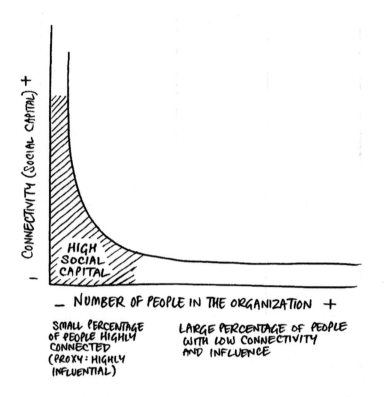

CONNECTIVITY (SOCIAL CAPITAL) + / −

HIGH SOCIAL CAPITAL

− NUMBER OF PEOPLE IN THE ORGANIZATION +

SMALL PERCENTAGE OF PEOPLE HIGHLY CONNECTED (PROXY: HIGHLY INFLUENTIAL)

LARGE PERCENTAGE OF PEOPLE WITH LOW CONNECTIVITY AND INFLUENCE

(a) the organization looks like a network, smells like a network and 'behaves' like a network.

(b) the organization is composed of a fabric of clusters of connections: some small, some big (some of the small ones have a theory of their own: 'small world theory'[9]) .

(c) some nodes are very well-connected, others are not.

(d) the connectivity inside the network follows a power law (logarithmic) distribution in which a relatively small number of nodes have high connectivity and the majority of nodes have low connectivity. It is not democratic and it is not equalitarian.

---

[9] Watts, D.J. 2003. *Small Worlds: The dynamics of networks between order and randomness (Princeton Studies in Complexity)*. New Jersey: Princeton University Press.

(e) the organization chart is utterly useless in telling us anything about the above. In fact, the correlation between the managerial labels in the boxes and connectivity is usually very poor. Some bosses (high hierarchical power in the organization chart) may in fact have low connectivity (which is why many people cannot name the composition of top management teams). And some highly connected nodes only appear on page 23 of the organization chart's stack of PowerPoints.

If connectivity is a reasonable proxy for influence, a relatively small minority is bound to have a great degree of influence and the large majority would not have a lot of influence at all. In the world of network influence, inside and outside the firm, the power law is the true law of power. If you get the highly connected, highly influential individuals on board, you'll be able to say: *"Never was so much owed by so many to so few."*

## (2) 'Social GPS':

Connectivity is great, but it has to be relevant to the social infection. So, it matters a lot 'where' (in the network) these highly connected individuals are. I call it their 'social GPS'. When aiming for a social infection, it's no use to have your best connected people in a cluster on the periphery of the network[10]. Intuitively, you'd say that's very obvious, but surprisingly it is very often overlooked. However, in my experience in the organizational territory, highly connected people tend to be very 'central' and 'relevant' as well.

In the Framingham study and its subsequent analyses by Christakis and Fowler[11] (spread of obesity, drinking, etc. See

---

[10] Kitsak, M., et al. 2010. Identifying influential spreaders in complex networks. *Available at http://www.scribd.com/*.

[11] Christakis, N.A., J.H. Fowler. 2009. *Connected: The surprising power of our social networks and how they shape our lives.* NY: Little, Brown and Company.

Annex), a particular 'social GPS' stood out: friends, and in more concrete terms 'a friend of a friend'. That 'position' in the network had greater influence than the 'sibling' or 'spouse' position. These findings have yet to be 'explained', but are consistent with empirical evidence about how far influence can reach (it tends to dilute or fade after going through a few 'layers' of your immediate social network).

> So, it matters a lot 'where' (in the network) these highly connected individuals are. I call it their 'social GPS'.

What's more, there is a special type of 'social GPS' coordinates that matters: the links between clusters. The influence potential will increase enormously if the highly connected-highly influential individual is not only social-capital-rich within its own network, but acts as a bridge between networks or sub-clusters. Think of those individuals you may know who seem to have a great ability to tap into sub-cultures of the company, to link between divisions that don't talk to each other that much, to cut across language or ethnic barriers, etc.

These two criteria (degree of connectivity and 'social GPS') are far more important than any other influence typology, particularly when the goal is large-scale change. Finding these individuals and engaging them is key to the success of Viral Change™. Viral Change™ has 'zero model inside'.

## The Orphan model

In recent years, people have challenged the importance of the influencers' role in the macro-social field. It is not difficult to understand why. For most macro-social phenomena, particularly in the formation of (social) fashions or some social movements, it is hard to see how the whole thing was triggered by anybody in particular. With no apparent command-and-control centre, these phenomena seem to appear out of the blue. It's not clear when it started, let alone who triggered it. A lot of consumer behaviours follow this pattern (although it may be 'induced' by marketing or advertising campaigns, which is model 3 or the 'Splash model'). Examples of these phenomena are easy to find: the spread of fashion, some music trends, healthy eating, jogging as a 'movement', digital social networks such as Facebook, as well as the epidemics of obesity, suicide, violence in the streets, etc. Section 3 in the Annex is rich in references to orphan models.

All these are basic examples of social phenomena without a clear 'initiator'. It does not mean that people do not attribute these phenomena to some precursor, but usually there is not a lot of convincing evidence of a clear cause-effect. You could easily suspect that multiple factors have contributed, not a single initiator. To me, this does not mean that the macro-social-influencer is dead. But some avant-garde voices insist that the role of the influencer/opinion leader has been overestimated[12].

This position has been held and widely articulated by Duncan Watts, a well-known thought leader and an influencer himself! Ever since Malcolm Gladwell became the popular face of 'the influencers' from his pulpit at *The New Yorker magazine* Duncan Watts has been overtly critical of *The Tipping Point*. Watts is right in saying that many social phenomena occur through imitation (music to my ears). In the macro-social world of mass marketing, he is right in pointing out that he can't find the influencers anymore (just like I can't find mindsets). The truth is that the death of the influencer may have been grossly exaggerated – even if playing 'where is Waldo the Influencer?' is getting harder and harder in our 24/7 consumer society.

---

[12] Thompson, C. Is the Tipping Point toast? *Fast Company*. January 2008.
Bentley, A., M. Earls. 2008. Forget influentials, herd-like copying is how brands spread. *Admap*. 43 (499): 19-22.
Watts, D.J., P.S. Dodds. 2007. Influentials, networks and public opinion formation. *Journal of Consumer Research*. 34 (4): 441-458.

## The Splash model

The internet has become The Big Initiator of many things. But even this cyber-Goliath needs some extra mechanisms to sustain what has been initiated. The instant digital ability to reach millions of people constitutes an obvious source of massive mobilization of ideas and behaviours.

> Since the aim of Viral Change™ is large-scale, fast spread of behaviours leading to social change, we in Viral Change™ always explore the spectrum of influencers inside the organization, or in the macro-social world for that matter.

The relevance of a social media splash—from the massive, global advertising campaigns to subtle (and not so subtle) use of YouTube or Facebook—can't be underestimated. Once the triggers (in whatever 'format') manage to create a critical mass of individuals establishing 'a new norm', and this initial critical mass is then copied by others, the potential scale-up is logarithmic. Whether the initial peak will cease existence as such (fad), or will establish new social norms (fashion) will depend on the availability and robustness of social reinforcement mechanisms. From those, social proof ('most people are using X') is a very powerful one.

Splash models can create social infections, but somehow they still follow world I maths. The difference is that, due to the sheer scale of a social media splash and its ability to reach millions in one go, the numbers at the end of the tunnel are still potentially vast.

One can easily imagine that a combination of mechanisms is not only possible, but very well present in reality. At a mature point of any social infection, it is probably impossible to dissect all the

142

mechanisms that have contributed to it. As with many things, this frustrates some (academics), while others (practitioners, including me) take a more relaxed stance.

## The Viral Change™ way

In terms of scalable influence, Viral Change™ is mainly a Zero model in which we combine, craft and orchestrate:

a. the power of a relatively small set of non-negotiable behaviours
b. the enrolment of a relatively small group of highly influential individuals
c. their informal conversations with people and joint actions and commitments to make those behaviours real
d. the power of the massive distribution of leadership resulting from these
e. the continuous social reinforcement of achievements and changes via stories

Why the Zero Model for Viral Change™? I hope it is obvious. In the business of creating social infections inside the organization, I can hardly wait for critical masses to appear out of nowhere (Orphan model) or for Big Splashes to be organized inside the firm. Since the aim of Viral Change™ is large-scale, fast spread of behaviours leading to social change (in whatever form it has been pre-defined), we in Viral Change™ always explore the spectrum of influencers inside the organization, or the macro-social world for that matter. It's therefore not surprising that a great deal of thought goes into profiling those individuals, identifying them and asking them for help. Usually this is a community described as 'champions'.

The core principles of connectivity and social GPS should not only be respected, but it should be given the heaviest weight. The refining of that profile is more culture-specific. There may be add-ons depending on variables such as maturity of the organization, high levels of 'knowledge authority' (in R&D or hi-tech organizations) or other intrinsic structural issues such as geographical dispersion. But Viral Change™ will never compromise on the clarity and homogeneity of the profile.

There is nothing more disastrous than a profile of champions that compromises on so many variables and possibilities that it makes the community very heterogeneous and lacking any identity at all. Here is a Very Bad Idea in Viral Change™ management: using an existing population or community and converting it into change champions. A few examples of terrible choices are: those on the path of Key Talent ('it would be good for their development'), low(er) layer(s) of management ('we empower managers'), or multi-disciplinary teams already working as such ('we give them the extra remit of making change happen'). 'Key talent' may be very key, but they are not necessarily well-connected with the right GPS. Managers should be managers and manage. Multi-disciplinary people are good for cross-fertilization of ideas and 'representation', but there is nothing in this category that ensures connectivity or social GPS.

> A community of Viral Change™ champions is never a bunch of lieutenants asked by their generals to do a bit of their work.

A community of Viral Change™ champions is never a bunch of lieutenants asked by their generals to do a bit of their work. Yet, I see these errors more frequently than I would like, lead by people who 'know about these things' and who are stuck in old hierarchical models. Believe me, it doesn't work.

Champions are asked to help the organization in its efforts to shape a particular culture through the spreads of behaviours, or to embed values translated into behaviours in real time in the organization, or to support the development of new processes or ways of doing things by spreading behaviours and engaging others to do the same.

Who are these others? 'People like them'. 'People like me' refers to people I can easily relate to because 'we use the same language' and perhaps we have the same worries or other similarities. These are people I tend to trust because I am 'one of them' or they are 'one of us'. I have mentioned before that the 'people like me' category ranks high in the annual Edelman barometer as a source of trust within the organization (to receive or assess corporate information on strategy, future, etc.). In the macro-social world, many principles of the 'people like me' type also apply. We are talking about 'horizontal reciprocated influence of people like us', to use the geography of the organization chart. People in their natural network of connections.

> 'People like me' refers to people I can easily relate to because 'we use the same language' and perhaps we have the same worries or other similarities. These are people I tend to trust because I am 'one of them' or they are 'one of us'.

I tend to use the term 'peer-to-peer influence' in a broad sense in my own Viral Change™ practice, but one needs to qualify the expression because (among other things):

(a) It doesn't translate well. To quote an English dictionary, a peer is 'a person who is of equal standing with another in a group'. In other languages, this is often translated as 'equals' (close), comrade (maybe), friend (why?) or even 'a person in your entourage'. In the Anglo-Saxon business world, peers are interpreted as people of your level or ranking on the corporate ladder. If we say that the VP of Sales will talk to his peers, we assume that he is going to talk to the VP of Marketing, the VP of Production and perhaps the Director of External Affairs, all members of the top executive committee, having in common that they report to the CEO. Strictly speaking it is not exactly the 'same level' as in 'all level 4 managers of the company', but it tends to identify a layer or layers with some proximity and relatively similar position in the company. This is not rocket science in the English speaking world, but it is far from clear in other environments.

(b) The term has a strong presence in the computer and IT fields, most of the time abbreviated as P2P, where it means 'computer systems which are connected to each other via the Internet (and in which) files can be shared directly between systems on the network without the need of a central server'. In other words, each computer on a P2P network becomes a file server as well as a client. Some people take this beyond the simple technical and utilitarian collaboration between computers to extend the concept to the alliance of technology and people for the purposes of global cooperation in a decentralized and non-authoritarian way[13].

## Champions and Viral Change™

Unlike many other 'champions' that one can find in organizations ( brand champions, product champions, innovation champions...) Viral Change™ champions have a very specific role: exhibit and role model the key non-negotiable behaviours, as well as engage with peers (informal conversations, joint commitments, engaging others).

---

[13] The wonderful Peer to Peer Foundation initiated in The Netherlands is a good example of this and a rich source of information, ideas and references coming from a variety of disciplines. See http://blog.p2pfoundation.net/

Exhibiting and role modelling the non-negotiable behaviours is easy to understand. There is no point in having champions who don't exhibit the key behaviours at the core of the change that we want to see. Because of their connectivity, social GPS and trust within their peer group, a fair amount of imitation and social copying will follow. But this may still be a bit passive, or not enough, or not fast enough.

Viral Change™ champions do more than that. They engage with peers in informal conversations about the change goals and the associated behaviours. They start by endorsing them[14]. However, what I have described so far only amounts to a good conversation, a good transmission of information and endorsement. This simply constitutes good advocacy. But advocacy is not enough to create a social infection. Advocacy still belongs to world I, even if the channels have been changed from the hierarchical 'top-down' pipes to the outside-the-organization-chart informal networks.

The moment of truth comes when the champion invites peers to do something concrete, to go beyond understanding and endorsement, to actually 'practice' the behaviours. They will look at potential situations where those behaviours are crucial and perhaps they will agree to tackle a particular angle of their working life where that behaviour is not present or blocked by something else. This joint engagement translated into day-to-day reality is essential to 'orchestrated social change', i.e. Viral Change™.

How does it start? Well, it may happen on a one-to-one basis or perhaps within a small group of people in the immediate

---

[14] I am frequently asked the question: *"What if the champions do not like the change ideas or the behaviours that have been crafted? Or what if the whole thing is simply not credible to them?"* My answer is simple: then you have a problem. If you can't convince the internal engine of distributed leadership, your community of highly connected, highly influential, social-capital-rich people, why would you bother going in that direction? My advice then would be to stop, rethink and reboot.

147

network circle of the champions[15]. This initial duo or trio will agree to engage other people, who in turn will engage yet other people, etc. I am now describing activism. Viral Change™ is activism, not 'simple' advocacy or communication.

## Understanding activism

Activism is a misunderstood term. Where I live, in England, we often see political party 'activists' going door to door, offering leaflets and information about the party manifesto. To me, many of them would not qualify as 'activist' until they engage me in a

---

[15] Highly connected, highly influential champion-activists with high social capital (these are several ways to describe this population) create a preferential attachment effect. New people coming on board will tend to attach themselves to these hubs, whose larg(er) networks then get larger. This is the equivalent of the Matthew effect and the network version of 'the rich get richer'. The Matthew effect takes its name from the bible quote: "For to all those who have, more will be given, and they will have an abundance; but from those who have nothing, even what they have will be taken away." Matthew 25:29, New Revised Standard Version.

specific conversation about voting. Up to that point, they are simply advocates or perhaps just leaflet deliverers. Yes, I know I am strict.

The conventional meaning of 'activism' in those electoral times is equivalent to 'being active', which of course includes folding leaflets and stuffing envelopes. In the more sophisticated digital campaigns of the Obama era, we see a similar dilution of the activism concept. In that instance, it's driven by what Micah White calls 'clicktivism'[16]: an obsession with measuring the number of emails sent in the campaign, the number of people visiting a web site, the number of clicks.... He believes that this is killing real activism.

● ● ●

---

[16] White, M. Clicktivism is ruining leftist activism. *The Guardian*. August 12, 2010.
Morozov, E. 2011. *The net delusion: the dark side of internet freedom.* Cambridge: Public Affairs. Gladwell, M. Small change: why the revolution will not be tweeted. The New Yorker. October 4, 2010.
Digital activism does not mean the number of 'Like' clicks on a Facebook page or seeing the same thing pop up over and over. As Evgeny Morozov points out, the group Save the Children of Africa, which has 1.7 million members, spent several years raising the princely sum of $12,000! This unquestionable fact is dismissed by critics of Morozov's position saying that a bad example of Facebook activism does not make digital activism irrelevant (see www.meta-activism.org and Mary C. Joyce's writings).The place of social media in large-scale (macro-social) change may have been largely overestimated. At some point, according to 'experts', the Iranian anti-government movement, was on the brink of becoming a true revolution...through twitter. Twitter activity on the Iranian issues during the peak days of street demonstrations was clearly colossal. But a small detail was overlooked. Most of this activity took place outside of Iran, as Iran only has a very small community of twitter-aficionados. Is this the modern version of Karl Marx's prediction that the railway would destroy India's cast system? Digital-social activism is just beginning to take a prominent position in the macro-social world, so we are bound to see many inconsistencies (effective-ineffective, success-fiasco) for a while.

● ● ●

# 4.3

# Informal networks

The network is THE asset! The network is the organization. If you want to understand or create social infections, network knowledge is indispensable. Years ago, I remember seeing lots of 'pretty pictures' in presentations reminding us that 'it looks like a network, so it must be a network' (opinion leaders, connections of individuals inside the organization, the web, etc.). But that was where it all stopped. It was a way of talking, of describing things. And after the presentation, life went on like before: hierarchical organization, top-down leadership, etc. The disconnect between the network images and the daily reality was big.

Today, doing the exact same thing would not make sense. The knowledge about networks has grown exponentially over the years. And with this growth, networks have become increasingly popular.

A great deal of that expanded knowledge about networks has come from a better understanding of how the mother of all networks, the internet, works. It is probably not completely sound to extrapolate and simply apply what we know about the web to other macro- and micro-social structures, but some fundamentals about networks and the power of the connectivity are truly similar and enlightening.

> ❋ ❋ ❋
> **Within the organization, we have transitioned from team-work to net-work, effectively from a 'teamocracy' to a 'networkracy'.**
> ❋ ❋ ❋

Macro- and micro-social structures are 'networkracies' in which unlikely fellow travellers can get together: political campaign and smoke cessation dynamics, biological epidemics and idea infections, marketing fads and herd behaviour in the financial markets, riots and physical fires on mountains, collective exuberance on the religious TV channels and crowd behaviour, centre-less terrorist organizations and dispersed social groups, etc. These are not completely different worlds. On the contrary, the similarities are significant.

Within the organization, we have transitioned from team-work to net-work, effectively from a 'teamocracy' to a 'networkracy'. Indeed, the ability to 'ride the network'[1] may matter more than the perennial creation of new team structures.

I have referred to some fundamental laws of social networks in the previous chapter. In particular how understanding the distribution of connectivity within the social network allows us to understand how a small group of individuals within the

---

[1] Herrero, L. 2007. *New Leaders Wanted: Now Hiring!* UK: meetingminds.

organization is relatively well connected whilst the majority has a lower level of connectivity. It follows a power law distribution (see the graph on page 138 of the previous chapter). I have also referred to the importance of the social GPS, i.e. the position within the network. Here in this chapter, I will focus on two more aspects of the networks: (1) their functionality in general and (2) the place and role of informal networks and their informal conversations. Nurturing informal social networks is one of the five disciplines supporting Viral Change™.

## Ten functionalities of the internal social network

The richness of the social network is only understood when one looks at the variety of functions that an internal social network in the organization performs. Some of these functions may seem obvious, but when you combine them, people start realizing how important it is to nurture the network and ensure that it is healthy.

> A common mistake is to equate connectivity with collaboration. People may be connected (socially, digitally or both), but that does not mean that they cooperate or collaborate.

Much has been written about the healthy and functional team, but the healthy and functional network, a more crucial element of the life of the organization, has been seemingly 'forgotten'. Those organizations that understand the need to have a network-centric approach (inside the organization, between organizations, with suppliers and customers, etc.) have a distinctive competitive advantage. The language of networks has been growing in presence and prominence for a long time. But we need to go beyond the language and embrace a new understanding, a new conceptual model and its real life

153

implications both in day-to-day management and in change management itself.

**1. The social network provides connectivity.** But connectivity is not necessarily collaboration. This seems obvious, but perhaps it should not be. Sure, the social network connects, but the common mistake is to equate connectivity with collaboration. People may be connected (socially, digitally or both), but that does not mean that they cooperate or collaborate[2]. It should not need more explanation. However, many (technological and/or structural) systems are created to link people with each other, assuming that this will then create collaboration. The ability to be connected is a precondition for collaboration, but if the behavioural DNA of the firm is not consistent with collaboration, the connection in itself will not create it.

**2. The social network provides a vehicle for information traffic and communication.** World I activity also takes place throughout the network (informal passing of information, gossip, rumours). As I have insisted before, this spread of information may or may not be viral. And it will definitely not lead to change, unless the information currency is converted into behaviours.

**3. The social network is a vehicle for clustering.** It provides us with solicited or unsolicited groupings or affiliations. The notes at the bottom of your Amazon order ('people who bought this, also bought this') remind you that, whether you like it or not, you are in a cluster of potentially like-minded people (an idea-preference group)[3]. The social network is cartography at its best, locating us in social coordinates. These 'points on the map' may

---

[2] Turkle, S. 2011. *Alone together: Why we expect more from technology and less from each other*. New York: Basic Books.
Also see footnote on page 149 on 'clicktivism'.

[3] Valdis Krebs, social network analysis practitioner, has wonderful examples of this clustering (applied to US politics amongst other things) on his website: http://www.orgnet.com/divided.html

be intentional and conscious or, as in the case of your Amazon purchase, created de facto by your own choice. I am amazed at how little we use this 'feature' in our building of digital platforms inside the organizations: people who did X also did Y; who achieved A, also achieved B; those who were successful in spreading behaviour N, also did well in M; etc.

**4. The social network is a listening tool.** Giving and receiving feedback, sometimes almost instantly, is possible thanks to the connectivity of the social network. The organization doesn't have the opportunity for a constant feed-back loop anywhere else. Most of the traditional ones are static and take place when people meet: at the next sales convention, the monthly meeting, etc. Nothing compares to the scale and power of the permanent loop that is the social network.

**5. The social network is a 24/7 Q&A system.** It does not close down for weekends, holidays or casual Fridays. It allows for 'Houston, we have a problem' on a permanent basis. Social networks of great fluidity, particularly if supported by friendly technical platforms (think Facebook inside the firm), constitute an environment where a question could be asked at any time and an answer would come. This is nothing 'new' in the macro-social network of the internet, where it is very common to use 'groups' and 'users' communities' to launch a question, even if you do not know anybody in the group. Amazingly, people respond and dialogues take place. Software firms such as Microsoft are very aware of this, encouraging the use of 'groups' for asking your (technical) questions. Imagine this fluidity inside the firm. What an amazing idea! But most organizations are lagging hopelessly behind in this area.

**6. The social network is crowd-sourcing territory.** It allows you to systematically tap into intellectual capital wherever it is, whatever their rank, hierarchy or geography. Ideas could come in big numbers and get qualified instantly. Idea generation and qualification is possible at the speed of light because of the social network characteristics. This is so crucial, that I even dare to say that idea generation systems that are not based on the 24/7 use of the social network, are missing the point and have become pre-historical. For example, sending in suggestion forms via email to an innovation committee is like using a bicycle when you should be using a Ferrari.

**7. The social network is an obvious creator of social capital.** Social capital is defined as your quantity and quality of relationships. The social network allows the coexistence of strong ties (close connections and relationships) and weak ties (looser and 'remote' relationships). Both can happily coexist, thanks to the social network, which acts as a constant relationship builder. Domesticate the network and the overall social capital of the firm will go down quickly. Tame conversations and your organization will be weaker in ideas and innovation.

**8. The social network is a host for innovation**. Linked to the above, innovations come from the seeking of unpredictable answers. The teamocracies are predictable environments. Teams are not very good for innovation, networks are. The health of your weak ties (where unpredictability comes from) dictates your capacity for innovation. The social network as a host for conversations is a host for innovation at the same time.

**9. The social network is the highway for storytelling**. Stories are the main reinforcement vehicle for social infections (see chapter 4.4) and these stories travel mainly via the informal conversations. In Viral Change™, we purposely capture stories and broadcast them in world I, but for every story, life starts in the connectivity of the social network.

**10. The social network 'makes sense' (provides meaning)**. Complex phenomena within the organizations—from dynamics of power to collective intelligence, employee climate and engagement—can't be understood without reference to the

156

totality of the social organism, that is, the network. Individual psychology in all its richness is unable to explain life in the organization, let alone social infections.

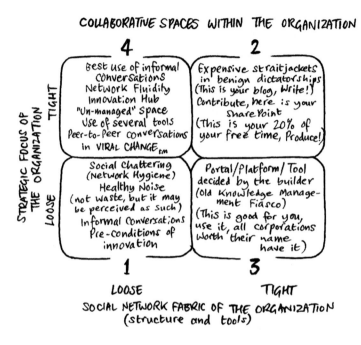

COLLABORATIVE SPACES WITHIN THE ORGANIZATION

## Nurturing vs. domesticating the network

The graph above illustrates the four basic collaborative spaces within the organization and their pros and cons.

**The loose-loose space.** This space [1] is characterized by loose strategic focus or under-specified objectives for network interactions, plus a loose structure of network conversations. It has traditionally been seen by management as 'waste' (people not doing their jobs, just spending their time 'chattering') However, a good dose of chatter fuels the social network and keeps it healthy. Organizations with little or no room for informal, un-focused conversations become very stiff. Social chatter and 'noise' are part of a living organism like the modern organization. Obviously, if all business life took place in this loose-loose quadrant, there would be no business life! But the old days of managers creating standard operating procedures prescribing that the internal email and the web are provided for business use only, are gone...or are they?

There is another old stereotype in folk-management land which is actually a mirror opposite of the 'waste' invoked by many. Here loose-loose lovers claim that loose-loose is where innovation happens. This is far from real. Loose-loose spaces are vital for the network health, as mentioned above. Loose-loose is the rainforest of the organization, the provider of a great deal of the oxygen (and sanity), but it does not work well as a conduit for innovation. It is a myth that innovative companies live in loose-loose territory where there is almost no structure and anything goes. Innovation has a far better chance in the tight-loose environment (see below) where some high level directions have been framed and then a real degree of freedom and informality is allowed.

**The tight-tight space**. This is space [2] and focuses on the domestication of the network: blog this, write that, use your 'free time' on this topic, collaborate, but only on pre-determined topics or 'discussions', everything else is considered pretty much a waste. It is an unhealthy and expensive straitjacket. Conversations in captivity do not breed new ideas.

**The loose-tight space** [3] is a more benign environment, more open to network conversations with high(er) degrees of freedom. However, it tends to allow only a few vehicles or possibilities. It may look good in principle (great portal or intranet, sophisticated SharePoint, good internal chat rooms), but it is usually too orchestrated, particularly when a technological platform has been built 'for everybody'.

**The tight-loose environment** [4] is the one that produces the best network results. The strategic focus of the conversations is

**158**

clear here, but there is a significant degree of freedom in the dynamics of these conversations and in the choice and use of several tools. There is also no pre-determined obsession with how useful (outcomes, measures, return on investment) the space would be. Most innovative companies are abundant in tight-loose quadrants. Viral Change™ champions navigate in this territory. The strategic imperative is set (what are the goals of change, the non-negotiable behaviours, what is needed from them, etc.), but the peer-to-peer conversations and interactions are informal.

These four spaces may overlap or indeed co-exist within the organization. It is important to understand where Viral Change™ is going to live and the consequences of the different spaces in facilitating or impeding the peer-to-peer activity.

## Viral Change™ champions' engagement space

Let me translate these four network spaces into four potential models of Viral Change™ champions' engagement.

**(A) 'Let's do viral'.** I mentioned that the loose-loose territory was needed for the overall healthy breathing of the organization. It's not good for innovation, because it lacks focus and it's not good for Viral Change™ champions' activity either, because the mandates and objectives are blurred (and most likely behaviours would be absent or poorly articulated).

I see many managers in organizations suddenly converted to the 'grassroots' concept, advocating the need for un-structured conversations and mistakenly thinking that Viral Change™ champions should be completely 'loose'. No wonder some of the managers of those managers fear Viral Change™, as this kind of lack of control is a recipe for chaos!

159

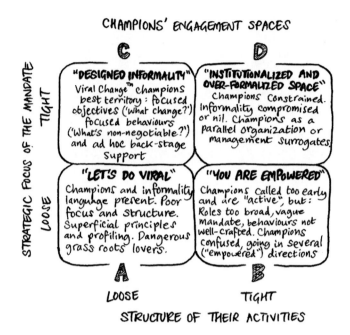

CHAMPIONS' ENGAGEMENT SPACES

**STRATEGIC FOCUS OF THE MANDATE**

**C** — "DESIGNED INFORMALITY"
Viral Change™ champions best territory: focused objectives ('what change?') focused behaviours ('What's non-negotiable?') and ad hoc back-stage support

**D** — "INSTITUTIONALIZED AND OVER-FORMALIZED SPACE"
Champions constrained. Informality compromised or nil. Champions as a parallel organization or management surrogates

**A** — "LET'S DO VIRAL"
Champions and informality language present. Poor focus and structure. Superficial principles and profiling. Dangerous grass roots lovers.

**B** — "YOU ARE EMPOWERED"
Champions called too early and are "active", but: Roles too broad, vague mandate, behaviours not well-crafted. Champions confused, going in several ("empowered") directions

TIGHT / LOOSE (vertical axis)

LOOSE — TIGHT

STRUCTURE OF THEIR ACTIVITIES

It is theoretically possible to use this space as a change engine of some sort, banking on the 'emergent properties' of both networks and conversations. In plain English: hoping that a 'constraints-free environment' will generate good engagement of people and voluntarism.

In the business of social infections I can't just close my eyes and hope that good things will happen. The Zero model requires focus and structure, even if the structure is minimal. This 'let's do viral' space is full of people who love the 'viral' aspects of things, but who stopped at that word in their intellectual efforts to actually change anything. Loose-loose is not good champions/activism territory.

**(B) 'You are empowered'.** The loose-tight space is a slightly less dangerous one, but it's full of problems. With the growth of Viral Change™ initiatives across the world, I find more and more situations of viral-change-like projects which could be described

160

as well-intentioned efforts with misinformed ideas, uncooked plans and strategies full of holes. There is also a fair amount of over-enthusiasm in some cases. Sometimes, it feels to me as if the champions have been called to arms too early when the decision to go to war has not been fully made yet and the ammunition is still in production.

In this space, the tight is tight ('we have champions', 'we are having a champions' conference', 'we have created the network', 'meetings are taking place'), but the loose is also really loose. Management seems a bit naive here, thinking that the champions' community will completely figure out by themselves what to do, including the 'translation into behaviours' (a thousand versions will come up) and the modus operandi (people will easily revert to meetings and formal conversations with lots of PowerPoints).

> I call the methodology 'designed informality' because it operates in a very informal way, but it's all well-orchestrated and designed in terms of how to support the community.

If the previous loose-loose space was grassroots lovers' territory, this loose-tight one is empowerment lovers' land. Not surprisingly, many new communities of so-called 'empowered' champions called in to help with half-baked strategies feel a bit confused. Rescue from this kind of situation is possible, if it's caught at the peak of early over-enthusiasm.

**(C) 'Designed Informality'.** The tight-loose model is, as I have mentioned before, the natural territory for Viral Change™ champions' engagement. The organization first says thanks to them! Then it provides them with goals and a sense of the behaviours needed, a sense of pathways and some 'training' on what works and what doesn't, a structure to support them from

161

the background, but a lot of freedom as to their engagement with peers and the establishment of joint commitments. I call the methodology 'designed informality' because it looks, feels and operates in a very informal way, but it's all well-orchestrated and well-designed in terms of how to support the community.

**(D) 'Institutionalized'.** Finally, the worst engagement space is the tight-tight. Here the organization has formalized and corporate-sized the champions' activity. It is peer-to-peer and informality wearing straitjackets. Obviously it doesn't work! In any Viral Change™ programme there is always a risk that the formal structures (management) will swallow the informality of the peer-to-peer conversations. This institutionalization takes place whenever there is an attempt to convert the champions' community into a team (or teams) or to formalize and 'command-control' their mandate ('let's give them objectives and Key Performance Indicators').

In the worst case of institutionalization, Viral Change™ is converted into a formal, visible, corporate initiative where spontaneity is killed, champions' voluntarism compromised and informal conversations domesticated.

Understanding how networks work, what some of their fundamental laws are, what degree of informality of the social network is required and what the risks are of trying to create a social infection in the wrong collaborative space, are some of the elements of this third discipline of Viral Change™.

# 4·4

# Accelerating a new narrative

Organizations have their own narrative. That narrative is the host of their identity. And every business has one: the business that started at the kitchen table, in a garage or with a single idea; the company that grew from a small family firm to a big corporation; the organization that discovered the cure for something.

Within their broad narrative there are stories. Heroic stories, struggle stories, sad stories, success stories, war stories, disaster stories, etc. It is difficult to understand the dynamics of many organizations without paying attention to their stories. In my work as an organizational consultant, I find that in some cases those stories may not be entirely obvious at first glance. For me, it is always a sign of deeper mutual understanding of the organization when stories pop up in conversations or simply accumulate in your observations and evaluation. Things become real when stories are on the table. Until then there may be a myriad of mission statements and strategic intentions on paper. The narrative (which includes language) provides the organizational logic.

Anthropology has paid good attention to stories for obvious reasons. 'Stories of origin' are common in subcultures: the ancestors who crossed the river and established here, the descendants of migrants coming from afar, the ones who could be traced back to the big war between A and B. Those narratives provide the meaning, the identity cards, the sense of belonging, the qualification as a distinctive tribe worth the visit by the anthropologist.

However, a good anthropologist knows that in more cases than people care to admit, scratching the historical surface may be disappointing when more prosaic facts (or the lack thereof) hide below that surface. There may not have been an obvious river crossing, no real trace of that migration or no evidence of 'The War', but the stories are strong and hold up. Not because they are true or not, but because they provide the glue for traditions, belonging and a sense of identity.

Entire belief systems provide Homo Sapiens with meaning based upon stories. The main world religions are a good demonstration of this. And their 'books'[1] are rich storytelling sources for that kind of glue. Homo Sapiens tells the stories that explain how Homo Imitans has worked and still works.

---

[1] Christianity, Judaism and Muslim religions are often called 'book religions' because the narrative of their beliefs is written down.

Stories also provide bedtime comfort for children, making some sense of it all at the end of the day. It seems as if Small Homo Sapiens needs the reassurance of a little meaning before night as an antidote to some meaning-less travels during sleep. Once upon a time... and the imagination is put to work. There is a logic to it, after all. Then, all is OK.

There have been numerous attempts at classifying the type of stories that Homo Sapiens creates and how the characters have transformed in the course of history to produce a finite number of plots. Greek tragedy still comes back today, every day, even if the characters wear suits, sit in government or have boardroom jobs. Psychology has been digging into the archaeology of the mind to see it can find universal stories[2]. The history of literature itself is a perennial permutation of characters, places and spaces. Novels or screenplays repeat the permutations. The difference between the ones that excel and the rest that do not, resides in the ability to use new clothing and new landscapes. A Greek aphorism says 'nothing new under the sun'. Homo Sapiens' task is re-creation. Homo Sapiens is at his best when he (re-)creates a story, whether it's a three-hundred-page narrative or short poem. Even poems without plot are a story in the mind of the writer and the reader, united in a little journey which may last only a few seconds.

> Homo Sapiens is at its best when he creates a story, whether it's a three-hundred-page narrative or a short poem.

Stories are so close to us, human beings, that they hardly need an introduction to stress their value. But the organizational

---

[2] The work of Carl Jung on archetypes, the writings of Joseph Campbell (*The hero with a thousand faces*) or the modern attempt to classify universal plots by Christopher Booker (*The seven basic plots*) are examples of Homo Sapiens narrative by people who did not have the word 'anthropology' on their business cards.

world in particular has been so busy with facts, figures and bullet points that it is only recently that storytelling has come up on the radar screen and people started paying concerted attention. Storytelling is indeed one aspect of the five disciplines of Viral Change™, but it is a particular aspect of storytelling that we need to master.

## Stories and self-belief

Change of any kind disrupts the status quo and with that, it disrupts the narrative that was associated with the status quo. An organization may have been very successful in the past under old market conditions, but they have now completely changed. Its old narrative of success—perhaps based upon heroic, caring and paternalistic behaviours of the family owners—is suddenly thrown upside down because the heroic family members need to be replaced by 'professional managers', bringing with them a new market narrative full of war terminology: kill the competition, win the battle, be faster than the enemy and so on. A new chapter of their own version of War and Peace is written and suddenly the old stories not only sound unsuitable, but forgettable.

> In each phase of organizational transitions, people tend to hang on to their known narratives and the narratives hang on to them.

In each phase of organizational transitions, people tend to hang on to their known narratives (after all, they're the ones that provide the meaning). And the narratives hang on to them, without letting them go. As a result, there may be a lack of belief in the new future or in the ability of the organization to move forward. The beliefs of those narratives kick off and become vocal: we will never be like X, we are too small/too big, it is too early/too late, we don't have the money or the scale, we don't have the skills, we are not that kind of people, not here in Spain/India, we are a dinosaur, we are too slow, we want to do too many things, we will never succeed, not in a million years, not us, we are what we are.

Those beliefs are strong beacons and often stand in the way of moving fast and changing. They do not move easily under 'the

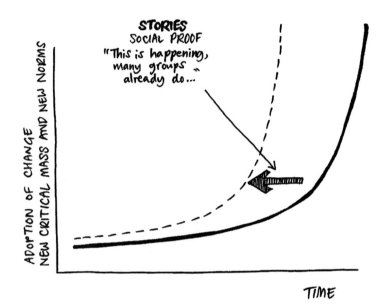

promise of change' (or success or a new future). They need to experience success and change to believe in success and change. It is a vicious circle. Stories have a key role. They accelerate the building of a new narrative. Little signs of achievement, change, broken barriers or recognition by others go a long way toward accelerating the belief in new possibilities. And little movements in those solid self-beliefs go a long way toward starting to believe in the real possibilities of success, whether you are small or big, early or late, have the money, scale or skills or don't, are in Spain or in India, a dinosaur or a gazelle. In the above graph you can see how a traditional curve of adoption gets modified by stories. They accelerate the visibility of changes. Stories are certainly the Weapons of Mass Diffusion (WMD). Stories of success generated in world II need to be captured and disseminated in world I as soon as they occur so that the organization starts seeing positive signs as early as possible.

Let me make three qualifications:

**(1) Engage world I.** The stories will also travel through the informal social networks of world II, but this is not enough to create social change. World I hosts the hierarchical system of managerial influence and that system is often the one in greater need of 'changing their beliefs'. Use traditional or less traditional communication channels to close the loop with world I. Yes, there will be some attrition, but you need the management system to move forward in their own curve of adoption of 'new possibilities'.

**(2) As early as possible.** There is no point in waiting until all the evidence of massive change and success is right in front of people! Social infections need all the 'little evidences' they can gather to accelerate the new narrative, the collective self-belief system. The best way I can describe this for you is as an orchestrated bombardment of the message 'it is happening, it is happening, it is happening...' 'Those guys in the North have shrunk their decision time for X by 50%, what a great example of accountability! It is happening!' 'Legal in HQ now responds to your queries from the field within 48 hours! This is how they have translated the customer-centrism behaviour! It is happening!' 'People from A and B now get together informally over a coffee on Monday mornings to share their latest insights from the field. Since then, we've had no more complaints from customers on 'us not being a single company'. Well, that is an example of collaboration. It is happening!'

**(3) The less heroic the story, the better.** You may have heard and 'lived' those stories travelling through the corridors of the organization where somebody somewhere has achieved extraordinary success in almost heroic circumstances. There was that impossible situation where some things were about to go extremely wrong with great impact for everybody. And those guys moved heaven and earth, putting their own health at risk, putting the company's interest above everything else, including their family and achieving the impossible. Their efforts saved us 50 million dollars. And, yes, you'll see them on the cover of the internal magazine shaking hands with the President.

> Heroic stories produce an unintended negative impact: people switch off.

These heroic stories (the one above may be an exaggeration, but there may be dozens of less heroic ones floating around you) produce an unintended negative impact: people switch off. People find it difficult to relate to the circumstances, the magnitude of the problem or the size of the financial achievement, and so their brains say: "Not me"[3]. And 'not me' is a good trigger for deviating attention away from the story to pretty much anything else that's around. Corporate Hercules is a long way away from day-to-day me.

The story may be rich; the achievements worth all the praise and recognition and the amount of effort and commitment shown commendable, so, yes, the President should shake hands with those people! But to bank on this as a model of social infection is like using the example of crossing the Atlantic solo as a model of resilience, or planting the flag on top of Everest as a model of the 'will to win'. Which, incidentally, is what many organizations do when they bring the sports narrative into the organizational

---

[3] There is no contradiction between this and my example of accountability-behaviour described before. The key difference is precisely in the 'people-like-me' component. The listener in the accountability story could think: "*I could do that, it is a good example.*" Here he says 'not me', that is, I don't have access to those budgets, I am not in those situations, etc.

life[4]. But day-to-day me would say: "*I want to see 'people like me' doing things that 'I could do' (imitate), that feel real, that I can relate to and happened in ordinary circumstances.*"

A good way to sensitize people to stories is to bring their own ones to life. Here is a list of possible prompts:

- You heard or saw…
- What happened?
- How did it end up?
- Why do you remember it?
- Is this an example of…?
- Did it make you (think/do something different)?
- Did/will you share it? Why?

To qualify a story as good or bad makes little sense unless we explain what it was good or bad for. For the purposes of social infections—which have behaviours as world II currency and 'peer-to-peer' scalable influence as main conduit—good stories have these characteristics:

- They are memorable. This seems obvious, but it's not! Note: this criterion rules out most bullet-point narratives, as well as any PowerPoint-generated ones.
- It is 'transferable'. People feel 'it could happen to me or to my team'. Not necessarily in the same way and under the same circumstances, which could be very different from yours, but with a similar plot and outcomes.

---

[4] Sport heroes and celebrities are in great demand in the corporate circuit of 'motivational speeches'. They provide excellent entertainment which may or may not be followed by organizational impact. I want to be very upfront about my negative bias towards the sports analogies in 'the business of the organization'. I'm genetically unable to understand why heroic American sports coaches reach prominent status in business books or management education. Instead, I would suggest you find as many 'people-like-you' as possible as a model of anything that you think should be modelled by your management team or your organization. One 'people-like-me' story of resilience, commitment, ethics or leadership is worth fifty Everest climbers and a few trans-Atlantic solo travellers.

- It prompts emotions. Here you could argue that anything does that! But I mean that the story seems to have an immediate association with an emotional state: sadness, fun, anger...
- It is easy to tell others. That rules out Homeric-sized ones.
- The story itself is (or becomes) more powerful than the protagonists. Eventually people may remember the story more than the names of people, the identity of the characters or the plot (which is why so many versions of a good story tend to pop up with a different cast).
- The story can be directly associated with a behaviour or behaviours. Whether within the organization or in a macro-social change, the story is a good representation of a non-negotiable behaviour in a Viral Change™ way. Let's make it explicit: 'this is a good example of what accountability is in this organization'. Remember my comments earlier in the chapter about behaviours: it doesn't get any better than having a story as definition of a behaviour.

It is not always possible to match all criteria, but in the business of Viral Change™ we focus the fourth discipline of 'accelerating a new narrative' on stories as close to these ones as possible in terms of their architecture. And the epic is not at the top of the list.

● ● ●

# 4.5

# Leaders outside the charts

The short table on the following page contains parallel descriptions referring to the same person. The left profile tells us about Maria's GPS in the organization chart: the hat she is wearing, what her performance is compared to others, who her boss is, how many people report to her, what kind of team membership she has and what the company's managerial succession plan entails for her.

The right-hand profile tells us about Maria's GPS in the social network of the organization: her potential informal influence, positive or negative, something about her 'ways of doing', her priorities and also a bit about her connectivity outside the formal job and work.

### Maria Smith

| | |
|---|---|
| Manager, Customer Services | Well-connected, highly trusted |
| Performance grade 4 (contributor) | High influence amongst other supervisors of Customer Services |
| Supervises team of 4 | Department |
| Reports to Section Head | Rejected offer to relocate. |
| Member of Customer initiative Task Force | Sceptical of our modernization efforts |
| Member new CRM project team | 'Does her own thing', but gets |
| Talent Management: grade 3 (four year succession plan path) | things done. Her team loves her. Active in company-sponsored |
| 5 years with the company | community initiatives |

Management attention is usually on the left hand side. When the right hand side is taken into consideration, you find a spectrum: those who have no idea whatsoever about anything in the box; those who regard that content as a 'curiosity'; those who don't want to know because 'they don't do politics'; those who are aware and perceptive, but don't know what to do with it and those who fully integrate that right-hand side into their 'social intelligence'. Of course, you'll find combinations of any of the above as well.

The left-hand side tells us about what kind of managerial authority we may count on to create social change. The right-hand side tells us about the true potential of Maria Smith as a change agent, as an informal influential leader amongst her peers. Viral Change™ will need to count on Maria beyond her managerial hat, because she is highly trusted and seems influential with others. She seems connected and involved.

Maria's boss is bothered by her scepticism. In truth, although never articulated as such, this trait is preventing Maria from climbing the managerial ladder faster. But her scepticism may be useful. If we could get Maria on board and manage to switch her opinion from the sceptic 'the opportunity is nowhere' to the promising 'the opportunity is now here' (just one space difference!), then we have a highly connected, highly influential and trusted person who can engage with many in a convincing and effective way. Maria is a natural leader in need of a good social infection as much as a good social infection is in need of a Maria.

As I have repeated many times, connectivity, influence and trust generation are the key characteristics of the viral leader who is a leader not because of the box he occupies on the organization chart, but because of his social GPS. We need these people for social infections. We need the 'people like me/one of us': able to engage with others and to engage them to engage others, etc. What happens in the process of 'calling' these individuals for help?

(1) Help! First of all the leader, CEO or senior leader of the organization, or social engineer in an NGO or in government needs to start with a simple, very humble word: help! We need you. And the most candid of explanations. We need you because you command trust and influence and we need that to be able to change things here. By the way, this is also the most simple answer to their possible question 'why me?'

(2) My experience is that if you profile and identify these people properly, they will be flattered to be asked. Or at least, most of the time. Often I get responses such as, *"About time that the organization asked me to do something beyond my routine job"* or *"I didn't expect this candour"* or *"Tell me more about it!"*

(3) These individuals usually don't want to feel that they are alone. It is important to give them a feeling of belonging to a group of colleagues or fellow citizens with similar characteristics. And it's also important to let them know that you will be calling them all together at some point.

175

(4) That sense of belonging gets reinforced when all of them, say, belonging to a part of the organization where Viral Change™ is going to be implemented, get together for the first time, physically if possible. This is the 'engagement phase' in a Viral Change™ map, as described later.

> If you can't 'convince' your highly connected, highly influential, perhaps highly trusted pool of natural leaders, why would you bother doing anything at all? You have a significant problem!

(5) People ask all the time, "*What is in it for these people? Why would they do this?*" If your appeal is correct, if it makes sense, if the formal leadership is humble enough to acknowledge that there are more powerful forces of influence around in the organization, the community of agents is mainly self-reinforced. People are actively participating in the orchestrated engagement because they feel they are contributing to a good cause. Within the business organization this cause may be the shaping of a new culture, the embedding of a new way of doing things or an overall transformation. In the macro-social world it may be the social change that is needed, the effectiveness of a health campaign or a social entrepreneurship focus. These are simple examples. Remember, we are not talking about 'any people' here, but about a particular profile of individuals who would at the very least be well-connected and used to the interaction with others, even if perhaps in some cases that is simply 'passive' interaction.

(6) "*What happens if they don't like it?*" I am asked this question again and again and it never ceases to surprise me. The answer is: then you have a big problem. If you can't 'convince' your highly connected, highly influential, perhaps highly trusted pool of natural leaders at the core of the informal conversation fabric of the organization, why would you bother doing anything at all?

If that's the case, you have a significant problem with your strategy and vision, you are presiding over a time bomb and you'd better stop everything you are doing and reflect upon the disconnect between your world I aims and the reality of your world II reception.

## Backstage leadership

Assuming that the above is not the case, the formal leadership role is backstage leadership. It is about obsessively focusing on supporting the community of agents or champions without the normal visibility of a world I leader. The word 'supporting' needs to be translated into your own reality[1].

Informal conversations need space. Facilitating that space is a matter of providing both physical and psychological space. Working years ago on a Viral Change™ programme that involved a large and geographically dispersed sales force, I learnt that many champions' needs were far more prosaic, down to earth and 'unsophisticated' than we had anticipated. We had expected to be asked by the champions to provide coaching skills or something of that sort. What they wanted was permission to use their small discretionary budget to pay for coffee meetings with colleagues at service stations on highways. Don't assume what support is, ask what can be done to support them as agents and suspend all judgments. The first line of responses may include something like: *"Nothing, thanks for asking. But I just want to make sure that it is OK with you that I do such and such."*

In another programme, which had very marginal involvement from my team, the leaders of the organization decided that it would be good for the community of champions to receive

---

[1] *"A leader is best when people barely know that he exists, not so good when people obey and acclaim him, worst when they despise him. But of a good leader, who talks little, when his work is done, his aim fulfilled, they will say, 'We did this ourselves.'"* Laozi, founder of Taoism.

177

leadership development training. This way they would be 'compensated' for their efforts and the process would facilitate their progression up the career ladder. Borrowing from physics (where theories are sometimes classified as 'right theories', 'wrong theories' and 'not even wrong theories'), the above idea was not even a bad idea. It was the equivalent of providing biochemistry lessons to a cook in the hope that his increased understanding of the chemical reactions and enzymatic whereabouts of the ingredients would make him a better cook, or perhaps, secretly, an incredibly grateful cook. Thanks, but no thanks. The world of highly paid HR and OD people is full of individuals who 'know what is good for others' and who decide what is going to make you happy. They have never asked you, but, hey, that doesn't prevent them from 'knowing'.

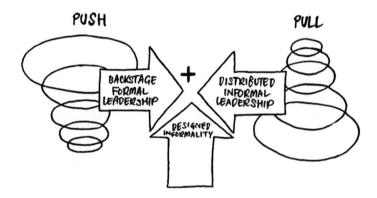

Whilst the kind of support that's needed has to be crafted case by case, it's pretty universally clear what that kind of support is not:

- It is not about the crazy mixing of world I incentives and world II aims as in the above not-even-bad idea.

- It is not about having formal discussions with the champions to report on progress over an excel spreadsheet.
- It is not about creating key performance indicators for them around the number of people they talk to a week.
- It is not about saying, *"I'll give you 15% free time to do this!"* or the incredibly 'encouraging', *"Do this by all means, as long as you also do your job."* Over the years, I have come across those management behaviours more than you would think. However, I also found similarly high levels of unexpected resilience in change agents putting up with them and still willing to volunteer for the common good!
- It is not about giving them a bonus.
- It is not about creating a beauty parade of champions at the next all-company annual convention.

Distributed leadership is the richest engine of change that organizations or macro-social structures have. It is not always understood as such. For example, it took many years for people to understand the concept of 'distributed intelligence', that is, the ability to maximize knowledge spread across boundaries and geographies and still make sense of the whole. Security Services and Intelligence Agencies (should) have understood the counterintuitive proposition that a 'centralized intelligence system' is more prone to groupthink than a distributed system of constantly challenged assumptions. But of course, the skills to handle this are different from the strict centralized command-and-control.

> **Distributed leadership is the richest engine of change that organizations or macro-social structures have. It is not always understood as such.**

In leadership, we are still behind because we still have a leadership concept that is mainly top-down. Even people who intellectually grasp the idea that there is more to leadership than the top to bottom dynamics, still use expressions such as 'leaders at the top' or needing to have 'the top leadership' on board. Leadership seems inevitably linked to some kind of physical or psychological height!

Rebalancing leadership is an important piece of Viral Change™. My recommendation is always a universal 'suspended judgement' when confronted with the (often very strong) assumption that 'our leadership will never get this' or something similar.

People 'don't know what they don't know' and need some space and education to understand the alternatives to the default positions they have lived with for many years. I have been told many times, *"Viral Change™ is different"*. Yes, it is. And that is why it works so well.

# 5

# Viral Change™ in action

Viral Change™ can be described as the orchestration of the five elements discussed in the previous chapters, the elements behind the five disciplines. Viral Change™ is at the same time:

(a) a process of designing and engineering the combined power of behaviours, scalable influence, informal social networks, success stories and formal leadership's move to backstage. As I said before, I call this process one of designed informality to stress the combination of 'design' (this is not about just having the five elements present, they must also be connected) and the 'invisibility' of any sort of 'formal change programme'.

UNIQUE ADDED VALUE OF VIRAL CHANGE™
ABOVE CHANGE OBJECTIVES THEMSELVES

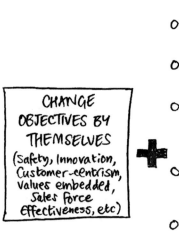

CHANGE
OBJECTIVES BY
THEMSELVES
(Safety, Innovation,
Customer-centrism,
values embedded,
Sales force
effectiveness, etc)

+

○ EMPLOYEE ENGAGEMENT. People at
all levels de facto architects of
change (triggered and shaped by
champions)

○ DISTRIBUTED LEADERSHIP. New
engine of leadership added to
the formal systems

○ RE-INVENTION OF INTERNAL
COMMUNICATIONS. Becoming the
master story tellers

○ New emphasis on INFORMAL
CONVERSATIONS brings breathing
space to the traditional, more
formal organization (networks
become important)

○ BREAKING TRANS-CULTURAL BARRIERS.
World II behaviours cut across
cultures better than any other
currency

○ NEW 'BEHAVIOURAL DNA' of the
organization in place

○ SELF-BELIEF IN URGENCY AND ABILITY
TO CHANGE. Experiencing the pace
of change (faster) and having a
finger on the pulse

○ CHANGE READINESS [change-ability]
Once VIRAL CHANGE™ is live, a new
way of life starts (state of
continuous change)

(b) an implementation of change focused on achieving predetermined objectives; a careful roll-out of the 'designed informality' described above, supported in the background by a small 'project team' able to help the community of champions in whatever form is appropriate to the organization.

(c) a way of life in the organization. The application of the principles above makes Viral Change™ not just a methodology and a process, but also a way of life, a unique concept of the organization, a concept of management and leadership in itself with the distinctive accent of:

- **Behavioural focus:** translating as much as you can into visible behaviours
- **Peer-to-peer influence:** banking on the power of the connected/influential people regardless of their social GPS on the organization chart
- **Informal networks:** switching emphasis towards the informal conversations versus the formality of teams and meetings
- **Stories:** putting storytelling at the core of accelerating the new narrative that the 'new' organization needs
- **Distributed leadership:** exercising the richness of 'leadership outside the charts', not at the expense of formal leadership, but by giving the latter a backstage support role

When Viral Change™ is live in an organization, there are expected and intended outcomes (the focus of the change intention itself), but also extended consequences. To an external observer they may be rightly called 'unintended consequences'.

We call them extended, because there is extended intention built into Viral Change™, an inevitable extension of the value beyond the focus of change itself. Examples of these 'extended consequences' of Viral Change™ have been summarized in the graph on the previous page.

It is not surprising that Viral Change™ sits in different 'places' in the organization and in the minds of management and leaders, depending on what model of change has been identified with the plans. Let me share my own classification of these models:

(1) **'Destination' Change.** Organizational change here is seen as going from A to arrive at B. Most formal change processes live here. That is why they have specifications, steps, milestones and metrics. Most 'change management methods' available in the organizational development supermarket are (more or less) linear processes in search of an 'application'. They are largely destination models.

(2) **'Journey' Change.** Here organizational change is like a journey. The emphasis here is on the experience, learning and 'mind and soul' transformations taking place during the journey from A to B. Usually the journey lovers do not dismiss the importance of B as a destination, but they think that the real value of the change lies on the dynamics of the expedition[1].

(3) **'State and Being' Change.** Change here may include destinations and journey, as above, but is primarily 'a state of being', that is, the normal way of life. In other words,

> (i) not something that starts in A and needs to go to B, so that when B is reached it is 'done'.
>
> (ii) not a journey (from A to B), even if the journey is rich, insightful and 'mind changing', as it's still time-dependent on reaching B.

---

[1] Journey Change attracts both passionate followers and dismissive bystanders. The 'journey language' is seen by many people in management of organizations or macro-social initiatives as a bit of New Age contamination. The more method- and process-oriented the manager's mind is, the more 'results focused' he'll be. And the more the manager is a lover of project management tools, the more antibodies he'll have against journeys and experiences. On the other side of the spectrum, there are individuals who genuinely feel that involving thousands of people in focus groups or in an 'appreciative inquiry' approach (for example) is in itself of greater value than what the destination will bring. These are extreme caricatures of respectable positions. But of course, there are also many things in the middle.

184

(iii) it's a way of life and state of being that includes all of the above (change as permanent state) where 'B' is a transitional point only signposted to check whether some destinations were reached (extremely important achievement in itself). Then the journey continues on to the C and D of this world.

Viral Change™ is philosophically very close to (3), which is why I have said before that one of its characteristics is that it is/becomes a 'way of life' or 'way of doing'. But it is clearly also a method to implement change (model 1) and a parallel way of experiencing a journey (model 2).

Let me give you an example. Suppose Viral Change™ lives in an organization focused on creating 'a culture of collaboration'[2]. There will be a process to orchestrate the five elements and disciplines described before, and a clear idea of what 'achieving collaboration' will look like. That is well within the destination model.

The process of identifying the champions, exposing management to the 'backstage leadership' principles and extracting and broadcasting stories of success may in itself constitute an eye-opening experience for many people, regardless of the 'objective of collaboration' itself. This is well within the journey model.

Once the champions' community is in action, formal leaders have learned to support those informal leaders in a 'backstage manner' and both formal and informal 'leadership tracks' coexist and leverage each other, you have gone beyond the journey and destination. Then, informal conversations are rich, focused and agile; employees are largely engaged with each other (triggered

---

[2] Let's assume for the example that 'collaboration' has been identified as the core behaviour (to be translated further) which will need to be spread by the power of the peer-to-peer activity of the champions.

and shaped by the champions' community) and collaboration and co-operation behaviours (as observed in many ways) have become the new visible DNA of the organization. In other words, it has become the sum of all 'good experiences and insights'. It is a distinctively 'new way of doing' (culture), a new live ethos (belief system) and therefore 'a state'.

I started this talk about these models by saying that it would not be surprising to see Viral Change™ in different positions in the minds of management and leaders. Indeed, in some cases the focus of the intended change can even be described with one word: safety or innovation, for example. In other cases, the target is far broader such as 'the creation of a new culture'. There is no difference in the Viral Change™ approach other than the different degrees of complexity, mainly (but not only) driven by the behavioural fabric that needs to be created. For example, in one case, everything revolves around 'safety behaviour', whilst in the other extreme we may be playing with a rich portfolio of behaviours targeted at different outcomes such as increasing effectiveness, better decision making, more costumer-centrism, etc.

> Viral Change™ leads towards a distinctively 'new way of doing' (culture), a new live ethos (belief system) and therefore 'a state'.

The following are some live examples of Viral Change™ within the borders of an organization:

- Overall corporate transformation: creating a 'one culture' in the M&A context
- Rescue efforts when technology implementation was unsuccessful due to no obvious change of behaviours
- Sales force effectiveness – broad cultural change
- Safety in the workplace: beyond training and communication, creating true behavioural change

186

- Post-leadership development or team building: implementing values and behaviours across the organization
- Globalization: companies 'going global', redefining the new 'international manager or leader' and embedding the new behaviour across cultures and geographies
- Collaborative culture: transitioning from individualistic and silo culture to cross-collaboration and collective intelligence
- Cost reduction and rationalization: eliminating processes and barriers, creating a new agile culture with diminished resources and new behaviours
- Organizational branding: defining non-negotiable behaviours that need to be applied to the organization's interfaces with stakeholders
- Transforming the organization into a true customer-centred one: the new behaviours spread globally and a new customer-centred culture (and competency) being shaped
- Employee engagement: redefining engagement by creating a new culture of collaboration, ownership and accountability through new behaviours spread virally
- Fast alignment across divisions/affiliates after M&A

## A roadmap

To orchestrate Viral Change™ is to take care of all its components in their own merit and at the same time 'design a journey' where each of them will come to life at the right time, in the right place and at their own degree of maturity (i.e. no half-baked ideas!)

In our own praxis as organizational architects of Viral Change™, we use the roadmap described in the graph on the following page. In each phase, the joint efforts between the client and us have a different focus. As in any journey, the map is not an end in

187

itself, but a tool[3] to orchestrate the combination of skills (the client's and ours), ingredients of Viral Change™ (behaviours, influence, social network, stories and leadership) and pace or sequence of events. Although the roadmap is visually sequential, the reality is less so, with frequent overlap between phases. It is important to have clarity of the outcomes achieved (needed to achieve) at each phase as a way to signpost the joint efforts[4]. These are highlights of activities usually hosted by each phase.

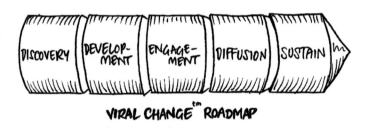

VIRAL CHANGE™ ROADMAP

---

[3] This is unlike many 'change management processes' and 'methods' on the market which seem to demand that the business needs and the change focus fit into them, not the other way around. The well-known saying, 'when the only thing you have is a hammer, everything looks like a nail', reigns handsomely in Change Management Land. 'Here is a method, here are the phases, here is how many project teams and work streams, here is how long, here is how much. Now, tell me, what is your problem?'

[4] The Change Management industry has contributed to a conceptual and linguistic mess by creating blurred borders between otherwise very different things. Many people still confuse 'outcomes' with 'deliveries' and 'activities'. A one-day workshop with a management team is an activity. A management team well informed about X at the end of the workshop is an outcome. A facilitator facilitating the workshop is a delivery by the facilitator. Mix them up and you'll have dangerous confusion. It is business converted into busy-ness. The objectives of a change programme (or training for that matter) should not be defined in terms of its activity (number of workshops) or the delivery people (numbers of consultants or trainers), but in terms of the desired outcomes.

188

### Discovery phase

Principal desired outcome: a full change strategy blueprint in place. To do this, we need the following elements:

- **'Visioning':** What kind of culture to shape? This may or may not be clear a priori.
- **Behaviours:** Uncovering and articulating ('non-negotiable') behaviours, as described in chapter 4.1.
- **Mapping influence:** What kind of champion or influencer do we need? Understanding the possibilities in the organization or the (macro-) social environment.
- **Model of infection:** What kind of social 'infection' do we want? What kind of networks? What kind of pace? In the mountain analogy that I have used before, where are the mountains for the fires?
- **Leading:** Internal Project team and accountabilities. Who is going to do what? What is the best composition? Working together with external help[5].

### Development phase

Principal desired outcome: all things in place and 'project managed', ready to call in the champions.

- **Stakeholder management:** Constituencies need to be educated and onboard.
- **Champions' pool:** Profiling and identification of champions takes place. Champions called in to help afterwards.

---

[5] It would be absurd to promulgate that every Viral Change™ project, journey or way of life would need my organization or its Associated Practices (accredited to facilitate and use the trademark), but I strongly caution you—as I have hinted at before several times —not to be taken in by folk versions using folk-psychology and folk-project management. Ask for professional help if you need it, for the whole process, parts of it or as a reality check. Not everybody using spreadsheets is an accountant, not all HR people are behavioural experts, not all people who 'know about virtual teams' understand informal networks, not all internal communications people are storytellers, not all the empowerment language in leadership programmes empowers.

189

- **Top-down, non-viral framework:** Non-viral internal corporate communication plan ready to support Viral Change™. Sign off on plan and create materials (This is about having world I ready to support world II).
- **Project Management:** Pre-champions first conference. Everything in place to get the champions together for the first time.

### Engagement phase

Principal desired outcome: a community of motivated and informed champions has been formed. Management at all levels is engaged in supporting.

- **Champions' first conference:** Day 1 of social infection is live. Champions leave with a clear understanding of roles and expectations. A highly motivated community is born.
- **Backstage leadership:** Further and parallel management engagement and support. Closing the loop again with managers who have champions in their organization chart: champions do NOT report to their managers as champions.

### Diffusion phase

Principal desired outcome: new behaviours spread and visible changes in place (at a different pace). Progress is tracked. Stories of success are broadcasted to the organization.

- **Champions in action:** Peer-to-peer engagements taking place in real life.
- **Non-viral communication campaign:** Traditional communication campaign operating in the background in world I mode.
- **Management support:** ongoing feedback and engagement with the formal leadership.
- **New critical masses:** 'New ways' become visible.
- **Stories:** Created, gathered and broadcasted.

- **Champions' community supported:** Social interactions between champions, shared learning and mutual reinforcement[6].
- **Tracking progress:** Behaviour audits and dashboards[7].
- **Review points:** Re-directions, behavioural focus. Understanding pace of progress in terms of behaviours becoming visible at a different pace.

### Sustain phase

Principal desired outcome: changes are stable in a desired way. Aspects of the strategy may be re-directed. Viral Change™ is becoming (has become) a 'way of life'.

- **Adjustments and re-focus:** Geography, sectors, functions, new behaviours.
- **Tracking progress:** Further audits or refinement of the scoreboard.
- **Review points:** All levels.
- **Extended learning:** 'Extended' impact of Viral Change™ explored, e.g. distributed leadership model now in action.
- **'Viral Change™ inside':** viral change and distributed leadership as way of life.

## The diffusion of scalable influence in Viral Change™

The pace of change usually follows a (social) network-driven, diffusion progress as expressed in the figure on the next page. The initial engagement of 'people like me' is followed by a period of not so visible changes. At some threshold point, new behaviours start to become visible and embedded, and stories of success are captured and highlighted.

---

[6] This is vital and will require a good exploration of smart ways to support the community. Face-to-face meetings and 'Facebook-for-champions' are not mutually exclusive.

[7] How to do this, needs to be agreed upon in advance. A common misconception of Viral Change™ is that measuring progress will be difficult. However, there are many ways to obtain evidence of behaviours being embedded in the culture.

This period can be accelerated by increasing the number of good stories (see chapter 4.4). Once some new (cultural) norms start to appear and become normal in the initial critical mass, a second threshold point appears. Other groups 'join in' because they 'see it' and accept it as a 'new way of doing things'.

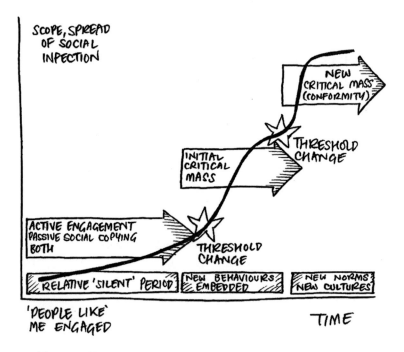

### The Viral Change™ Manifesto

The following is a manifesto or list of statements about Viral Change™ in organizations. If you've been following along until now, I doubt that anything here would be new to you, but I have compiled them as a quick overview. (Apologies for the list in bullet point style. In the next edition I'll try to use stories!)

## The Viral Change™ Manifesto
## (The organization)

### Behaviours and change

1. There is no change unless there is behavioural change. Communication is not change.
2. Sustainable behavioural change does not occur as a by-product of processes and systems change, or new (collaborative?) technology implementation.
3. If a desired behaviour (collaboration, for example) is not part of the behavioural DNA of the firm, a change in collaborative processes and systems will not create that behaviour. The behaviour needs to be 'installed' first, in order to sustain the new change in processes and systems.
4. Change behaviours, get culture, not the other way around.
5. Only a small set of new behaviours is needed to create high impact sustainable change.
6. Desired behaviours need to be reinforced (reward, attention, 'air time', personal gratification, money…). Behaviours that are not reinforced, fade. Be careful what you reinforce, you might get it (if you want teamwork, don't a give bonus for individual contributions!)

### The concept of the organization

7. The organization is a living, social network, not a top-down plumbing system: strategy from the top, actions at the bottom.
8. In this network, connectedness is unequal. A relatively small number of people are highly connected; a large number is less connected. Connectedness follows a power law distribution, not a Bell curve.
9. Those highly connected tend to increase their connections. They have high potential for influence.

### Viral Change™ model

10. If the small number of highly connected, highly influential people are 'on board', their endorsement and role modelling

will be more powerful than any top-down, management-led command-and-control system of change.

11. Identifying these people and working with them is the key focus of Viral Change™. If you can't convince and engage this group, why would you even bother?

12. Behaviours spread via social copying and imitation, creating true 'social phase transitions' where new behaviours, new ways of doing, become established and routine.

13. Small set of behaviours x highly connected/influential people/people trusted = critical mass. Critical mass x critical mass = social threshold change = established change.

14. Change is an infection. Biological infections, idea-infections (including social fashions) and behavioural infections (including negative ones such as street violence) travel in similar ways.

### Viral Change™ process

15. Top leadership needs to reach out to highly connected and influential people ('champions', 'agents', 'activists'). The keyword is 'Help!'

16. Champions engage colleagues in informal conversations. Peer-to-peer engagement is in; group indoctrination via 200 PowerPoints is out.

17. Conversations are not an end in itself. They need to lead to joint commitment to action. Advocacy is not enough. Activism is needed.

18. Colleagues engaged by champions eventually engage in similar conversations (and actions) with other colleagues in their networks.

19. Stories of success or barriers are recorded and spread. Stories are the messengers in Viral Change™. They increase the organization's self-belief and therefore the pace of change rapidly.

20. Management and leadership role in Viral Change™ is backstage supporting the champions, not front-lining the informal conversations and 'managing' the informal social networks.

### Viral Change™ vs. traditional models of change management

21. Traditional change management (big set of initiatives x all management levels x cascaded down and replicated

communication systems = change) has a poor track record. It is based upon a linear model ('big change requires big initiatives) and a top-down 'plumbing system' concept of the organization (CEO→VPs→Directors→Managers→Staff). Viral Change™ is 180 degrees different.

22. World I, 'Push', 'Big Splash' initiatives have limitations in their effectiveness. A percentage of people will pay attention. A percentage of those will consider change. And only a percentage of the latter will effectively change.

23. World II, 'Pull', Viral Change™ process starts with a small group of activists engaging other small groups. When critical masses appear, social threshold changes appear and a percentage of other people will imitate and 'conform' with new norms.

24. Big Splash ('Push') and Viral Change™ ('Pull') follow inverted mathematics: Splash= More→less; Viral Change™ = Less→more.

25. Push and Pull work together very well, provided clarity of expectations for each. Push-communication programmes are needed to support pull-Viral Change™. Stories bridge the two worlds.

### Viral Change™ (extended consequences)
### Challenging and shifting traditional managerial practices

26. Top-down hierarchical leadership as single model → Distributed leadership (the champions' informal/formal community is not even in bottom-up mode, but in a multi-centric one).

27. Top-down, all layers/levels communication ('tsunami change') → small, well-designed, well-spread behavioural changes ('butterfly model').

28. Traditional performance segmentation and categorization of people (achievers, contributors, key talent, low performers...) → Connectivity/behavioural roles (highly connected, highly influential, sceptical, deviant, champion...).

29. Emphasis on teams ('collaboration by design', 'teamocracy', small worlds with strong ties) → emphasis on networks (spontaneous collaboration, invisible connections).

30. Formal, visible, structured 'change management programme' → 'designed informality', high degree of invisibility.

## Three examples of Viral Change™ solutions[8]

The following graphs are three representations of a solutions-driven approach to an organizational challenge following the Viral Change™ Principles. The graphs are self-explanatory, but allow me to point out some obvious points[9].

Though the focus is different (innovation in the first, safety in the second and values/leadership in the third), in all three cases the value creation results from the combined power of structures, processes and behaviours. For example, an innovation strategy will need, after the articulation of the strategy itself:

*The crafting of a micro-social or a macro-social infection follows similar rules. Leave each world, I and II, their own roles and make sure the combination adds exponential value.*

(1) a process of idea generation and qualification. Many 'innovation vendors' sell this in the form of a digital mechanism that allows tapping into the collective brain of the organization. Unfortunately, in the absence of an organizational DNA truly geared towards innovation, the presence of a process in itself is a waste. Collaborative and 'innovation software' installed into non-collaborative, non-innovative organizations results in an under-use of the process, great frustration and a negative precedent for anything else brought in afterwards to try and fix the problem.

---

[8] As practiced by Viral Change companies, part of the Global Viral Change Network (www.viralchange.com)

[9] In the graphs, *Innovactions* refers to an awareness and training seminar that my firm provides.

(2) some sort of awareness and communication campaign that allows the organization to know the why of the strategy and the objectives of having 'innovation' as a focus. As we have explained in chapter 2, top-down communication systems do not create change per se, have the maths of attrition within and are not sufficient to create any stable culture. However, they have a place in the process in the context of a broad approach that includes world II.

So far, (1) and (2) are world I approaches. The world II approach is one:

(3) where innovation behaviours need to be uncovered and articulated; influence needs to be mastered so that those behaviours are spread through informal social networks; stories of innovation success are created and devolved to world I for broadcasting of their 'social proof' and a (formal) backstage leadership and an (informal) distributed leadership is in place to support the social infection.

The second illustration on safety and the third on the deployment of a new value system and/or leadership model across the organization follow the same principles. All example graphs are provided here as an illustration of mapping of 'solutions' via the Viral Change™ approach. The crafting of a micro-social or a macro-social infection follows similar rules. Leave each world, I and II, their own roles and make sure the combination adds exponential value. Implementing a safety culture, mentioned before in this book, follows similar patterns for combining world I and II ways. A solution based exclusively on world I ways is a waste, as it does not create a culture. On the other hand, in some cases, behavioural and social change may need a functional process to facilitate the implementation. Innovation and safety are chosen here because they are good examples of these cases. But many Viral Change™ approaches on culture shaping do not need a specific, de novo, process to be 'implemented'. A viral change approach to shape a culture of

197

collaboration, increased effectiveness or customer-centrism is likely to have two tracks: world II Viral Change™ supported by a world I communication and awareness campaign.

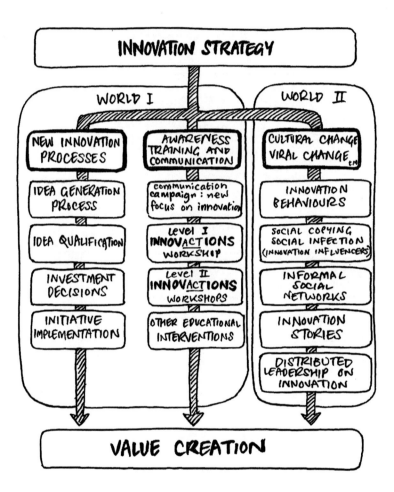

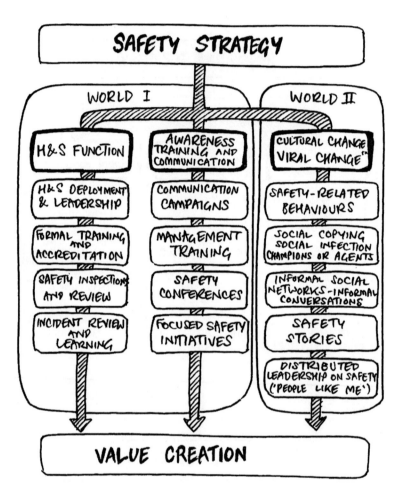

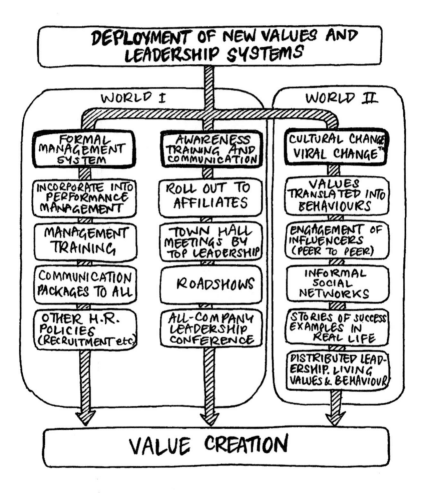

# 6

# The art of social infection

In previous chapters, I have described our incredible ability to imitate, how social copying travels through the informal networks of the organization and (the components of) Viral Change™ in action. And I have used 'the organization' as the model for all this, because this is where my experience as a practitioner is. I have made no distinction between kinds of organizations, because the basis is the same: Where there is a group of individuals linked by common goals, structured in formal and informal clusters of connections (whether you call them teams or informal networks), there is organized activity, i.e. 'an organization'. Whether it's public or private, geographically dispersed or not, an NGO or a publically traded company: it is an organization. There may be cultural differences

203

and differences in ethos, purpose and ways of doing, but Homo Imitans will be there with his ability to copy.

In this chapter, I am climbing a step higher to invite you to see the commonalities between the social infections I am predicating in the organization and the macro-social infections outside the firm. The 'macro' is very artificial and mainly used to point towards social changes in society, good or bad. The principles and disciplines of Viral Change™ are equally relevant. Indeed, the main premise of this book, stressed from the beginning, is that the more we see the commonalities, the more 'business' can learn from 'social change' and the more 'social change' can learn from 'business', the better we can craft meaningful changes and help the advance of meaningful organizations and a meaningful society.

> The more we see the commonalities, the more 'business' can learn from 'social change' and the more 'social change' can learn from 'business', the better we can help the advance of meaningful organizations and a meaningful society.

By going up the scale and looking at things from a macro perspective now, I hope you will feel inspired to go up and down as many times as needed to become a social infector. If you are engaged in health campaigns for example, it would be very useful for you to look at how Viral Change™ works inside an organization, because it may give you some insights that you were not expecting and that could be translated into the work you do. If, however, you are a manager or leader within a firm, you'll also find it very useful to look at Viral Change™ from the macro-social perspective to open your mind to other possibilities of action.

204

'Macro' and 'micro' have a lot in common. People forget that there is a main reason for this: both are populated by Homo Imitans.

As I have mentioned several times, scalability is the name of the game. There is no such thing as a social movement within a team or even within many teams. Viral Change™ deals with scalable influence and scalable change. That is why the world of executive coaching, team building or leadership development of a 'Key talent' population within the firm does not enter this territory.

> These tsunamis reach television screens, news bulletins, billboards and cities with no plan whatsoever for a pull mechanism of any kind.

The following are empirical rules for the designing and orchestrating of social infections. Most of them, but not all, have appeared in the previous pages in different ways. But don't see this as a duplication, see it as a helicopter view to provide a generic framework that could be applied to both 'macro' and 'micro', although the spirit of this chapter, as I have mentioned, sits more on the 'macro' level.

Confronted with a situation that requires scalable social change, you immediately need to look at a world I and world II intervention, plus the 'plus'… You would be surprised how many 'social initiatives' of any kind are solely predicated on the basis of a world I push.

To say the least, there is a tremendous naivety amongst many public initiative leaders. They hope that a massive, well-funded and well-publicized world I communication and awareness campaign will do the trick and create behavioural or social change at a scale.

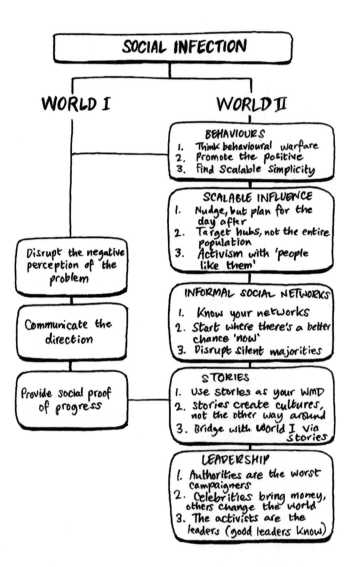

These tsunamis reach television screens, news bulletins, billboards and cities with no plan whatsoever for a pull mechanism of any kind to take advantage of it and start the spread in real life. I would include here the world I apocalyptic, threatening 'initiatives' based upon the fear of punishment[1].

Think of yourself as a social designer and ask, *"How much of world I and world II do we have here (or do we need to have here)?"* The graph with the key rules on the previous page provides a summary for you. Let's explore this a bit further.

## World I

### (1) Disrupt the negative perception of the problem (if it started with a problem)

Most teenagers do not go around binge drinking and making a fool of themselves on a Friday night, only regaining conscience the following day. And yet television screens and newspapers are full of stories about this. It is a social phenomenon/problem of many Western cities. The perception we have, is that teenagers do this in alarming proportions. After all, this is why politicians intervene with new drinking regulations and why police are instructed to act as well. The perception of a massive problem is in our brains. But there is no 'massive problem'. Most teenagers (or college students) do not follow that pattern. Disrupting a wrong perception is step number one. Tell the world, *"Actually, we do NOT have a problem of colossal magnitude."*

Remember, what gets airtime gets reinforced. Do you also remember my examples of signs in chapter 3? The signs that

---

[1] The current UK government is moving to scrap the anti-social behaviour orders (ASBOs). The previous government created this system of punishment and apocalyptic warnings to people displaying anti-social behaviour. ASBOs actually were ill-informed and made little sense from the behavioural and social sciences perspective.

claimed 'we have a tremendous problem of abuse here, please do not abuse'? Ok, this is not what they wanted to say, but this is what they ended up saying. In the area of disrupting the negative, nobody has been smarter than the policy makers of the state of Montana, USA. They actually mastered saying, *"We do NOT have a problem, thank you. On the contrary, a high percentage of people do Y (as opposed to X)."* The health campaign they orchestrated 'declared' 81% of the citizens of Montana alcohol free. It also claimed that most college students consume no more than 4 alcoholic drinks per week and that 70% of teens do not smoke[2]. As a result, the situation improved even further...because the norm (to conform with) had changed. Similarly, the state also ran campaigns about littering in their parks. The perception was that everybody littered, but that wasn't actually the case. They publicized the figures and the amount of littering decreased even further.

An area where the 'highlighted reality' is negative because of its very nature is Health and Safety, especially Safety. Most safety programmes focus on the number of incidents, accidents, near misses, fatalities, etc. and on how to avoid them. This is only natural. But for every accident that occurs, there are hundreds if not thousands of safe acts. You want an epidemic of safe acts, not an epidemic of avoidance of accidents. These two are not the same. Sure, you want to have both. Understood! But a bit of disruption of the perception will do you good. Tell your world that most of the time you are safe, and you'll increase your safety rates (whilst still training people to avoid accidents).

In my organizational world, I very often see the curious phenomenon of massive generalizations (usually negative) that have become the shared perception, and which have little or no grounds. 'Teams don't work here', 'communication is our biggest problem', 'the champions are not doing their job', etc. I then

---

[2] Perkins, H.W. 2002. Social norms and the prevention of alcohol misuse in collegiate contexts. *Journal of studies on alcohol. Supplement.* (14):164-72.

need to painstakingly trace the origins of these new plagues to often find that the opposite is actually true. How come? Because these plagues have virally spread from a very concrete or small problem of origin to a large-scale legitimization of a false truth. Disrupting that perception is the first step in addressing the reality. As in the Montana examples, just the highlighting and the broadcasting of the opposite (real and positive) has positive consequences, maybe even of great magnitude.

## (2) Communicate the new direction

This is where the non-viral communication, top-down, splash campaign sits. Remember that we said there is an implicit attrition in their mathematics, but you still need to communicate to the audience (group, society, organization...) what the desired outcomes are and the cost (monetary, social, political) of not achieving them.

## (3) Provide the new social proof

Gather the success stories (as described in chapter 4.4) and provide the social (legitimization) proof of progress, even if it's small. Do not wait for the big achievements, because the movement has already started, the revolution is on its way, we have started to decrease the number of people affected with X, we are winning this battle, more and more teenagers are choosing not to drink, violence has started to disappear in those neighbourhoods, etc. Be ethical, don't lie, but don't wait for the Big Truth.

There are numerous other things that must be crafted on the world I side of social infections, but I am focusing here on the key generic drivers, not the specifics of a situation. Later on, I will share a couple of examples where I have included other world I components for very good reasons.

209

## World II

World II planning is going to require the orchestration of the same five elements and the use of the five disciplines of Viral Change™. I will not repeat what I have already said in previous chapters, but will focus instead on some rules for each of the five elements.

### Behaviours

**(1) Think of this as 'behavioural warfare'.**
Either (a) you need new behaviours to promote; (b) you need to counteract existing behaviours or (c) both. But behaviours compete for airtime. So the best way to tackle a behavioural epidemic of A is to orchestrate a counter-epidemic of B, with B being the diametrically opposed or incompatible behaviour. Orchestrate an epidemic of kindness as a counter-epidemic to widespread, rough interpersonal relationships. Don't waste your time trying to convince the rough to be less rough. Orchestrate an epidemic of collaboration as a counter-epidemic to widespread individualistic and self-centred behaviour. Do not waste your time trying to teach people how to be less self-centred and more sensitive to others. Orchestrate an epidemic of the use of public transport as a counter-epidemic to one of massive presence of passenger cars on the roads. Do not waste your time waiting for the drivers to 'change their attitude' and figure out how their carbon emissions are causing more harm than good.

These are just examples of counter-epidemics. The principles apply to AIDS, community cohesiveness, indoctrination of bellicose fundamentalism and even absenteeism[3].

---

[3] There may be cases where the direct breaking of the chain of events of a behavioural epidemic is urgent and vital, to the point that a counter-epidemic may need to be 'postponed'. My favourite example is street violence to which I have dedicated a bit more space later on in this chapter.

(2) **Promote the positive (be clear on 'what'), never give airtime to the negative.**

You might not be surprised to hear this, but it is important that you don't find yourself promoting X whilst actually trying to avoid it. I must stress the issue of not highlighting the negative, whether openly or inadvertently. Make sure that your overall plans do not contain the 'don't do that' messages of chapter 3 or that you don't give airtime to the problem you are trying to tackle. Translation: do not glorify desperate suicide bombers or handsome gang members.

(3) **If you can, find as much 'scalable simplicity' as possible.**

'Simple behaviours' that can be easily understood and followed are the best. My best example of this simplicity is the 'pay it forward' concept. You receive a blessing and instead of repaying your giver, you 'pay it forward' by helping out a third person, who will then do the same, always paying it forward[4]. The instructions are clear, the philosophy simple and the effects multiplied exponentially. Instead of 'a blessing/good deed' as currency, you could craft your social change with any other idea instead.

The concept, which has its own 'movement' and 'international day', has an intrinsic social-entrepreneurial power since it seeks to multiply goodness by twisting the social principle of 'reciprocity' and making it forward instead of backwards[5].

The Viral Change™ version of 'pay it forward' entails paying it (you can define the 'it') forward not to one person, but to 3 or

---

[4] See the Wikipedia entry for 'pay it forward' for an historical explanation of the concept which can be traced back to the Greeks.

[5] TSIBA (http://www.tsiba.org.za) is a business school for young people in South Africa entirely run on scholarships adhering to the 'pay it forward' principles. Focused on entrepreneurship and leadership, students will pay (their scholarship) forward by helping other people with specific projects.

5 in your immediate network with each of them repeating the same, reaching exponential growth, not a Chinese-whispers type of chain.

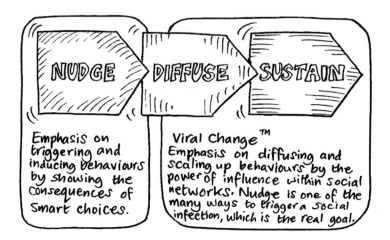

**Scalable influence**

**(1) Nudge if you wish, but plan for the day after.**
Nudge theory[6] has become very popular, amongst other things because of the interest created amongst politicians and policy makers. It shows the advantages of facilitating certain behaviours or, as the authors would put it, of making people make better decisions. The British Government has created a 'Nudge Unit' at 10 Downing Street, the Prime Minister's office, with the hope that it will shape policy on social issues around his project called 'The Big Society'. The roots of nudge are in behavioural economics. Nudge techniques of influence are very valuable. Wearing your social change hat, you need to ensure that you bank on nudge or any other triggering of behaviours to create lasting change. But the comments I made at the beginning of chapter 4.2

---

[6] Thaler, R. H., C.R. Sunstein. 2009. *Nudge: Improving decisions about health, wealth and happiness.* UK: Penguin.

about 'The Fun Theory' apply here. In many cases, where nudge ends, Viral Change™ takes over. Think of what will happen (extension of the infection, behavioural reinforcement, etc.) the day after the nudge, as the nudge in itself is not enough. The weakness of a nudge-only approach is that it puts little emphasis on 'how' the social network will (or won't) support the spread of behaviours. Instead, it puts excessive emphasis (and hope) on the triggering of the behaviours and the immediate advantages of people choosing B instead of A. The immediate logic of 'a better choice' does not guarantee that it will be spreadable, scalable and sustainable.

(2) **Target hubs and bridges, not the population at large.**
Forget the entire population (area, region, social group, society...). Target the highly connected and highly influential nodes/people: the hubs, the super hubs and the ones who are bridges between networks or clusters. Understand where 'the distribution centres' are. If we are talking about positive social epidemics, you need those hubs to be very active for obvious reasons. If we are talking about counter-epidemics, you may need to find a way to isolate them (if you can)[7].

(3) **Activism: Youth to youth, grannies to grannies.**
Again and again think activism, not advocacy. And the best activists are the ones in your peer group. Social infection in youth populations? Find young people. Social infection for grannies? Find grannies. Don't send granny role models to the youth problem or young people to role model for grannies. Think 'people like them'. If Jesus Christ chose fishermen

---

[7] It sounds logical, but in the case of sexually transmitted diseases, targeting the promiscuous members of society in a 'safe-sex' campaign has better chances of success than targeting the population at large. [See: Liljeros, et al. 2001. The web of human sexual contacts. *Nature.* 411 (907-908)]. Similarly, in outbreaks of swine flu, for example, once a case has been detected in a school, it would make a lot of sense to close the school for a few days to avoid a 'hub effect'.

instead of PhDs in Theology, you can find 'normal people' other people can relate to. That usually excludes celebrities who should be sent to world I to raise some money so that 'the revolution' can happen in world II.

Think also immediate networks: friends and friends of friends. Tip: the number of Facebook friends is not the issue. We are talking about real people, friends with whom you interact and who can become activists like you (or your 'patient zero'). Facebook friendship is a conceptual entity in its own right which contains loads of what I would call digital voyeurism. Facebook passivity is greater than 'activism'. Don't bank on the number of 'friends' in a 'Facebook movement' to start a revolution, as people would actually need to do something and not just click the 'Like' button[8]. Remember, it's important not to misunderstand activism. (See previous comments on page 149.)

> Think 'people like them'. If Jesus Christ chose fishermen instead of PhDs in Theology, you can find 'normal people' other people can relate to.

## Informal social networks

**(1) Know your networks.**
Remember the mountains on fire analogy? You have to know your mountains, understand them. Understand the network structure of the targeted social change, its 'rules' and 'spontaneous changes', if any. You will need to know where to perhaps isolate (if you can) or where to start the fire. Don't be superficial about understanding the social network structures, but also don't be obsessed with having extraordinary scientific understanding either. Think mountains and a box of (behavioural) matches.

---

[8] As previously quoted, Malcolm Gladwell put it elegantly in 'Small change: why the revolution will not be tweeted'. *The New Yorker*. October 2010

**(2) Start where there's a better chance now.**

Don't start out with the most difficult side of the network with the most difficult people in the most difficult circumstances. Think probability of success. Both in the 'micro' and 'macro' arenas. Do not wait until you have dotted all your i's and crossed all your t's. In the organizational arena, you are ready once you have a sponsor and other stakeholders are not going to be a barrier. Note: I didn't say all the stakeholders will be in love with you and you will have formal blessing from the Board of Directors, because that's not realistic. Start the fires wherever there is a mountain, a mountain owner and a box of matches.

**(3) Disrupt/wake up silent majorities.**

Silent majorities are responsible for wars and genocides. They need to be disrupted, confronted. Whether there is a 'micro' or a 'macro' silent majority, make challenging, intervening and confronting part of your behavioural currency. A silent majority covering a negative spark of a social change or an epidemic, acts in fact as an infected network that would facilitate the spread of that negative angle.

> Silent majorities are responsible for wars and genocides. They need to be disrupted and confronted. Make challenging, intervening and confronting part of your behavioural currency.

You have a silent majority in an organization when many people are de facto allowing unethical practices or simply turning a blind eye. Or when nobody says anything when people go around saying that Health and Safety is a waste of time, or that safety is only a priority on paper. Be silent yourself at your own risk. You have a silent majority in society when nobody says anything when well-known groups or minorities promote violence. The most dangerous members

215

of that silent majority are the ones who say that 'everybody is entitled to their own opinions'. Like Hitler, I suppose.

## Stories

**(1) Use stories as your WMD.**
Stories are your best Weapons of Mass Diffusion. They have the power to accelerate change, to create identities, to boost self-belief. Invest in uncovering, understanding, analyzing and broadcasting stories of success. Within the organization, re-invent the internal communications section to focus on stories. Outside the firm, imagine the stories you want to hear or capture as a way to double-check (with yourself as a social infector) what your real goals are.

**(2) Stories create cultures, not the other way around.**
Shape the new norms (cultures) by shaping the narrative[9]. This may seem obvious, but the quality and content of the stories coming from the progressive social infection not only

---

[9] As the book is going to print, Egypt is erupting and the 24/7 stream of news leaves you with no doubt about what is going on. People have been cautious this time in attributing the street rallies to the power of Twitter. Fast Company magazine ran an article entitled *Did Twitter, Facebook, and YouTube send people out into the streets? Of course not. Did they speed up the process of protest? Absolutely.* It is spot on. The greatest shaping effect of Twitter et al. was not in the incitement to protest, but in the controlling of the narrative. Whilst it may have been beneficial to government to demonstrate that chaos had taken over life to provide a good reason to 'put an end to it', social media created a quick 'counter-epidemic' by spreading the word that arranged neighbourhood watch groups were taking care of looters. A blogger, being interviewed by CNN, pleaded to the media to avoid the language of chaos and anarchy. As a result CNN changed the headlines from 'Chaos in Egypt' to 'Uprising in Egypt'. These are wonderful—if heroic and painful—examples of world I and world II going hand in hand. It is also a potentially macro-social Viral Change™ in action. We have the demonstration and protest behaviours spread almost 'orphan model'-style. Imitation and social copying spread fast and new critical masses are created. The vast and visible social network of real people is the protagonist. The streets are full of people-like-me. If there is true leadership of the uprising it is certainly backstage. Accelerating a narrative of uprising and liberation has been an intuitive and high level priority as a counter-epidemic to the official narrative. Regardless of how this ends, you can recognize most of the principles that I have tried to discuss in this book.

reinforce the changes and accelerate a new narrative (as discussed before), but also create the new norms and the new culture. As you are aware, I say that 'behaviours create culture, not the other way around'. I say here that stories create culture as well, not the other way around. So be careful which stories you put forward.

(3) **Use stories to explain bridges with world I.**
Be obsessive about establishing the bridge with world I in an orchestrated manner. Crossing the border between the two worlds requires a passport, only given to 'behaviours' (articulated in world I, living in world II) and stories (created in world II, broadcasted in world I).

**Leadership**

(1) **Authority campaigners: not a good idea.**
Actually, it may even backfire. Even when brought in with the best of intentions, a heavy presence of individuals, groups or institutions that hold hierarchical or policy authority inevitably triggers a command-and-control effect which may be counterproductive. The issue is not to make authority invisible and certainly not to expect an unreasonable abdication, but to critically measure the impact that it may have in a social change intervention when compared to alternative sources of leadership. Civil society expects the police to police, the politicians to legislate and the religious leaders to provide a moral compass for their congregations, but when it comes to social infections these leaders need to take a greater backstage leadership role in favour of stronger mechanisms of social influence (see previous comments on activism.) Here, backstage does not mean inactivity, it means staging from the back.

(2) **Celebrities bring money, others change the world.**
Also pay attention to how much the social infection plan relies on the visibility and push of celebrities, because it may

217

backfire. Some of the queens and kings of pop may have great intentions, but their often unsolicited interventions may backfire and cause your infection to collapse. Or, in the best case, there would be no visible change in the social intervention or 'cause' after the peak of excitement caused by the celebrity involvement. People would argue that the visibility and awareness that celebrities may bring is good enough as a solid value, but don't be blind to the potential liabilities. Don't mistake fundraising for social activism.

**(3) The activists are the leaders.**
The real (distributed) leadership power lies in the community(ies) of activists, very often doing invisible peer-to-peer work and not making the front pages. Focus most of your energy as a social infector on supporting and facilitating the work of activists without hijacking their voluntarism or over-formalizing their work. The engine of change is in the peer-to-peer networks, not in the designer rooms of policy, NGO HQs or the boardrooms. As I have repeated several times, this is not about 'letting them loose', but about facilitating, shaping and enabling the informal network activity in whatever form appropriate to the social infection. Activists may need some guidelines and tools, and perhaps some new skills, but you need to provide all this without making them 'professional champions'.

## Some maps

Let's take a look at two very high level maps of social infection plans to illustrate the parallel tracks of worlds I and II. Both are caricatures by design. They do not intend to be comprehensive and will look simplistic to expert eyes. That's because they are. But this kind of thinking is my recommended starting point when planning a social infection, whether on the 'macro' or the 'micro' level.

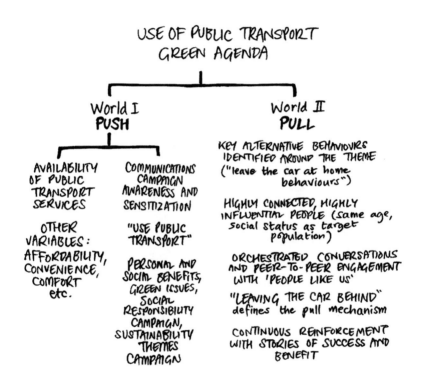

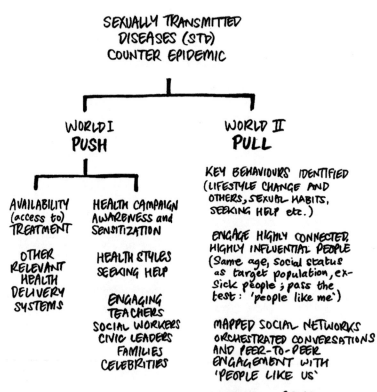

SEXUALLY TRANSMITTED
DISEASES (STD)
COUNTER EPIDEMIC

WORLD I
**PUSH**

WORLD II
**PULL**

AVAILABILITY
(access to)
TREATMENT

HEALTH CAMPAIGN
AWARENESS and
SENSITIZATION

OTHER
RELEVANT
HEALTH
DELIVERY
SYSTEMS

HEALTH STYLES
SEEKING HELP

ENGAGING
TEACHERS
SOCIAL WORKERS
CIVIC LEADERS
FAMILIES
CELEBRITIES

KEY BEHAVIOURS IDENTIFIED
(LIFESTYLE CHANGE AND
OTHERS, SEXUAL HABITS,
SEEKING HELP etc.)

ENGAGE HIGHLY CONNECTED,
HIGHLY INFLUENTIAL PEOPLE
(Same age, social status
as target population, ex-
sick people ; pass the
test : 'people like me')

MAPPED SOCIAL NETWORKS
ORCHESTRATED CONVERSATIONS
AND PEER-TO-PEER
ENGAGEMENT WITH
'PEOPLE LIKE US'

CONTINUOUS REINFORCEMENT
WITH SUCCESS STORIES

## A great example

The following table describes how an 'epidemic of violence in the streets', a common and often chronic phenomenon in some Western cities, can be tackled by applying Viral Change™ principles. One column describes the facts and the next column compares them with Viral Change™ as applied within the organization. I have stressed the latter on purpose to reinforce once more the fact that Homo Imitans lives both in the 'macro' and 'micro' worlds. The street violence example is largely taken from the very successful 'Ceasefire project' based in Chicago[10], but any errors will be mine, including the slight modifications to make it more generic.

|  | 'Violence in the streets' as an endemic problem | Viral Change™ in organizations |
|---|---|---|
| Theoretical base | Epidemiology. Infections. | The five disciplines infections. Network theory and maths, epidemiology, behavioural and social sciences. New change management. |
| One-liner | 'Violence is a contagious behaviour, a social infection' | 'Organizational change as an internal epidemic; only behavioural change is real change' |

---

[10] See Chicago Cease Fire project (http://www.ceasefirechicago.org/). The extraordinary good work done by this project is worth following up by anybody interested in social infections and counter-epidemics, whether the focus is violence or not.

221

|  | 'Violence in the streets' as an endemic problem | Viral Change™ in organizations |
| --- | --- | --- |
| Model | Key influencing individuals within the social group have the power to create high social impact. Community mobilization plays in the background (reinforces), but is not sufficient to stop the violence in itself. | A small set of behaviours, spread by a small number of highly connected and influential people, creates behavioural tipping points of 'new ways of doing' equivalent to sustainable cultural change. It is fast and more efficient. |
| Old model that doesn't work well | Exclusive massive public campaigns appealing to rationality ('Violence is bad, stop it') with focus on awareness and communication versus real time behavioural intervention. | 'Big problems need big change, big initiatives', cascaded down the organization via massive communication programmes trying to reach all and naively expecting behavioural change as a by-product. |
| Model of influence | Community influencer ('one of us') is more effective than authority role models. Law can be enforced by agencies, but behaviours bypass/avoid law enforcement. Law enforcement has a very limited role as behavioural change agency when compared with peer-to-peer intervention. | Peer-to-peer is key. Hierarchical authority works on reward/punishment, but studies consistently show the highest levels of interpersonal trust in the 'one of us' model. Hierarchical authority is far from negligible, but it is not the most efficient source of behavioural modification. |

| | 'Violence in the streets' as an endemic problem | Viral Change™ in organizations |
|---|---|---|
| Their goal | Stop the behavioural circle. 'Stop the shooting' (vs. appeal to rationality to stop violence). Stop retaliation. Real time interruption of the vicious circle. | Spread the new behaviours needed for the organizational change by personal endorsement, personal behavioural modelling and reinforcement of behaviours in others. Joint commitments with peers to be active. |
| Key players | 'Interrupters' and 'Outreach workers' | 'Change champions' |
| How they do it | Break the chain of events and stop the escalation in situ, one-to-one or one-to-group/group-to-group. Avoid tipping points of violence. | Create a chain of events. Informal, often invisible, otherwise well-planned peer-to-peer conversations leading to peers changing behaviours, leading to creating new critical mass. |
| Their profile | Tough, 'being there', often 'on the other side', projecting authority (but not hierarchical) and respect, able to confront. | 'Being there', well-connected and highly influential (not hierarchical). People will listen to; able to confront. Often ex-sceptical and unconventional. |
| Other roles | Community and Faith leaders. They support, articulate, endorse and are visible, but 'work is being done by interrupters'. | Managers and leaders. They support champions and facilitate their activities, but real time social change is being done through the champions and their social networks. |

| | 'Violence in the streets' as an endemic problem | Viral Change™ in organizations |
|---|---|---|
| Additional mechanisms of action | Community mobilization campaigns (including street demonstrations), political and religious public endorsement. These are supporting mechanisms to the person-to-person/group work of the interrupters and outreach workers. Awareness needs to continue, but does not have the power to stop the violence in itself. | 'Big Splash' top-down communication and awareness campaigns (for change), use of corporate Web 2.0/social media. 'Big Splash', world I mechanism does not have the power to create sustainable behavioural change, which only occurs via reinforcement of desirable behaviours, in Viral Change™ called 'non-negotiable behaviours'. |

## Golden rule

If there is one simple overriding golden rule for the Viral Change™ orchestration of social contagion, this is the one: think push and pull all the time. For any planned push (the first thing that will come to your mind), ask yourself where the pull will be. If you find yourself hesitating, I hope you'll feel uncomfortable enough to think twice before spending that massive communication budget or executing that colossal training-all-people plan.

Don't be naive and think that the pull will come from your hierarchical structures, your managerial layers or the formal societal leaders. Whatever they may think, they are seen and felt as 'pushers'. They do have a role, but the amount of power they have in creating culture is debatable.

Leadership 21st century-style contains a high degree of brokerage, up-front invisibility and strong 24/7 support for people who generate trust and followers. Many hierarchical figures can do that and this is to be welcomed. But it is not a universal fact and you can't count on it to scale up.

As stated ad nauseam, cultures are not created by training, although training is the first thing that comes to the managers' mind when confronted with culture-shaping. A culture of training in safety is not the same as a culture of safety[11]. A culture of training in customer-centrism is not the same as a customer-centric culture. A culture of health awareness campaigns is not the same as a culture of health. I am not saying both things are mutually exclusive. I am merely advising you not to be fooled by the automatic assumption that they are the same or the naive hope that they will be if you just keep trying.

> Think push and pull all the time. For any planned push, ask yourself where the pull will be before spending that massive communication budget.

When everybody has been trained in how to greet customers, when everybody has a 'Regulations of Health and Safety' card in their pocket, when your wallpaper has been covered by 'motivational posters' (probably with a lot of 'don't do that' stuff), when all the managers have been injected with 'workshopsterone', when all the PowerPoints have been distributed and presented to staff, when the nomadic leadership team has finished all the road shows, when all the TV ads on safe driving have been paid for, when all the 'debates with leaders' have taken place, when all the celebrities have returned to their respective safe havens, when all the speeches have been delivered and when the noise of the information and awareness bombardment has been transformed into the silence of exhaustion and expectation...you may find yourself asking, "So *where is the revolution?*"

---

[11] And the solution to the recent BP fiasco is not more training!

225

If that's the case, you may have forgotten about the pull. Cultures are created by behaviours (not information), people with real influence on others (not necessarily hierarchical leaders), social copying (not rational indoctrination), social networks (not artificial structures) and stories (not 'Don't-do-that rules').

However, if by doing all or some of the above push you see success of some sort, my sincere congratulations. Seriously, I mean it! But just picture this. For every 'push' dollar you spend, you could have saved 50 cents by using the 'pull' and you would still be a hundred times better off. Just imagine how extraordinarily more successful you would have been if every little piece of 'push' effort had been multiplied by a factor of one hundred through the real power of the (pull) behaviour. Not to mention how much money you would have saved! The gentle 24/7 reminder to your brain of the keyword 'contagion' marks the difference. If you think and act like a broadcaster, you'll just get your messages out there. But if you think and act like an infector, you'll get your epidemic. It is as different as night and day.

# 7

# Viral Change™ cannot fail (it can also fail)

From time to time, my team, my business partners and I get the following question: does Viral Change™ really work? It may surprise you that I still get surprised by that question. After all, it's a good question particularly from people who are genuinely interested in creating true change (and who want to hire us as consultants).

I have wondered a lot about the 'why' of my surprise, far more than about the why of the question. I think I have found an answer. It has to do with the 3 models of change described in chapter 5: 'destination', 'journey' and 'way of life'. In the listener's mind (the interested person, the questioner, the

**227**

potential client), I am presenting, introducing, writing about or putting forward a methodology. And this is a very good question for methodologies: does it work? In my mind, deep in me, in some remote belief system that does not get properly articulated, I see Viral Change™ as a praxis, a way of life, a concept in action in organizations and society, a state of mobilization of influence, a 24/7 culture shaping, an orchestration of goodness, a being and doing, yin and yang all in one. My mind is mostly in the model 3 'way of life' mode, but my mouth is articulating a model 1 'destination'.

> *Viral Change™ can't be compared with the installation of new software or the traditional mechanistic models of 'change management'.*

The question if Viral Change™ works is a good destination question. In other words, is this Viral Change™ a good way to get to B? It is, however, a bad 'way of life' question, because we can make life work or not, it's pretty much up to us (plus the Ortegian circumstance, of course). So when people ask me 'does Viral Change™ work?' it sounds to me like 'does parenthood work?' or 'does marriage work?' Well, the choice is yours. It is logical that people ask 'is it going to work?' I could tell them, *"It depends, we can make it work or we could choose to screw up and fail miserably. We have a choice."* Which is not an elegant answer and in fact, it's very evasive and may even upset the listener!

My engagement with my corporate clients is for the purpose of shaping an entire culture, creating innovation, embedding a value system, enhancing the effectiveness of the organization, etc. And for those purposes, Viral Change™ is the way to achieve the outcomes fast, cost effectively and sustainable.

But it would also be dishonest of me to give a compliant answer straight away ('Yes, of course it works!') without at least

228

attempting to point out that, 'as a method', Viral Change™ can't be compared with the installation of new software or the traditional mechanistic models of 'change management'. Yes, Viral Change™ has a logic, a process and a way of doing which can be replicated which qualifies it as a method. I suppose parenthood also has a logic (or more than one), a process (or several) and ways of doing (lots), but I haven't heard of parenthood as a method to develop kids from diapers to parties. Parenthood is perhaps one of the most beautiful states of man, but it can also go horribly wrong. Mix up the wrong decisions, wrong circumstances, wrong health, wrong ethics and wrong environment and you could easily see the reason why people should not have children.

We can orchestrate Viral Change™ with components shared in this book or we can choose badly articulated behaviours (or no behaviours at all), the wrong champions, over-formalize the process (lots of formal meetings of so-called champions) or just simply have a bit of everything, close our eyes and pray.

The logic of Viral Change™ cannot fail, because it has to do with real people engaging with other real people doing something tangible and reproducing it again. Use the wrong people and the logic remains, but with bad consequences. So, yes, Viral Change™ cannot fail...but it can also fail.

## So what about Viral Change™ as a method?

Ok, this is when we are talking about bringing context to it (which is pretty much all the time): the why, what, where, when, who and how. In method mode, the logic of the things that need to be done to go from A to B is translated into a map, like the one explained in chapter 5.

As a method, the first thing to say is that it creates behavioural change fast. It is typical to see new behaviours being embedded within six to eight months of the champions' community being active.

## Cross-collaboration in a non-collaborative environment

In the case of a medium-sized pharmaceutical company, Viral Change™ was the way to create cross-collaboration between otherwise rather independent sales forces. Collaboration was badly needed due to a restructuring of the business which entailed a massive sharing of customer information which until that point resided in individual pockets of knowledge.

> ● ● ●
> **By month four of the champions' activity as a community most of the collaborative behaviours were visible, not just as a pure observation, but measurable via a simple behavioural survey.**
> ● ● ●

But cross-collaboration was certainly not in the DNA of the organization— largely a sales and marketing apparatus —which had grown via a rather individualistic ethos. To 'solve' the problem, management had invested quite a lot in a Customer Relationship Management (CRM) software system which (surprise, surprise!) was completely underused.

Collaborative behaviours, with heavy emphasis on information and insight sharing, started to appear relatively soon after a small group of champions started a well-crafted peer-to-peer programme. By month eight of the programme (month four of the champions' activity as a community), most of the collaborative behaviours were visible, not just as a pure observation, but measurable via a simple behavioural survey. The percentages revealed an approximate 80% improvement of pre-defined parameters. By the end of year one, the usage of the CRM system had achieved

230

a proud 70%, which is well above the rates seen in many CRM 'implementations'.

### Re-drafting the rules of the game in decision making

In another Viral Change™ programme in an organization of 2,000 people, the change focus was defined around concepts like 'agility' and 'nimbleness'. These were the company's translations in behavioural terms of the opposite they had as 'a description of the problem', a rather common pathology in many organizations: over-inclusiveness (too many people involved in everything) and a very slow and frustrating decision-making process.

The desired behaviours took off in visible ways at around month six and nine. The earliest 'new ways' and 'new cultures' revolved around the number of people involved in decision making. This is how the internal project team summarized the status at the end of year one: "*Monthly meetings reduced from 1 day to ½ day agenda (agreed list of topics/decisions that do not come to the monthly meeting; decisions made elsewhere, 'in between' meetings). Smaller review meetings of X, from 10 to 4 people on average. Process Y (a financial and compliance approval process) reduced from 3 weeks to 5 days.*" In addition, they 'discovered' and brought to the table a 'barrier of the month'. Every time, they would address it and propose a solution (and implement it when possible).

> The behaviours defined took off in visible ways at around month six and nine. The earliest 'new ways' and 'new cultures' revolved around the number of people involved in decision making.

**Broad spectrum cultural change**

Finally, as a third example, in a more complex case of broad cultural change, Viral Change™ was put in place with focus on six behaviours, each of them dealing with a particular identified area of improvement.

The graph below describes the progression of the behaviours over a 12-month period as measured by surveys within the champions' population and others. The title of the behaviours has been slightly modified here for identification issues but the meaning behind them has been respected, so are the scores.

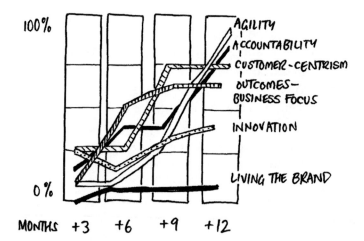

Agility was sub-defined with a series of 'pointers' of what that meant in behavioural terms. As in the previous example, the emphasis was on decision making and over-processing. Note that the behaviour did pretty well very soon. It didn't take much to 'convince' people that fewer of them were needed for particular decisions. As a matter of fact, many people felt relieved!

Note that we are not talking about a dictation from management but 'self-regulation' triggered by the champions' peer-to-peer engagement. And later on, it turned out that management never meant to involve so many people; they just wanted to ensure quality.

Customer-centrism was defined in a very narrow and precise way, distinguishing both customer-facing and HQ/non-customer-facing people. The real breakthrough ('threshold change') took place between months 6 and 9.

> *Customer-centrism was defined in a very narrow and precise way, distinguishing both customer-facing and HQ/non-customer-facing people. The real breakthrough ('threshold change') took place between months 6 and 9.*

Accountability was also expressed in several ways with emphasis on finding out 'who needs to know what'. It started very low and ended quite high, with a threshold change after month 9.

Outcomes and business focus was a behaviour (in several 'scenarios') aimed at trying to change the default position of 'managing by numbers' to managing by 'what it meant for the business'. One of the simple behaviours was the discipline of asking 'why are we doing this?' as a way to check if it was in sync with the business, adding value or just unnecessary 'busyness'.

Many initiatives were stopped as a result of this behaviour being lived by champions and their peers. As a behaviour, it followed a typical adoption curve ending above '50% of the people'.

Innovation was defined not as a typical process of idea generation and qualification, but as a small set of sub-behaviours, one of them as simple as another verbal discipline:

233

ask the question 'can it be done better, faster, cheaper?' In my opinion, the gains of this behaviour were a bit more modest, because people were confused about a parallel initiative on innovation that another part of the company had started, using very traditional methods of 'suggesting ideas' and these being assessed by a Committee. (Somebody needs to tell people that this default position in the understanding of 'innovation' doesn't work!)

The last behaviour, which I have re-named 'living the brand' was about employee identification with the values of the company and a commitment to portraying these values in the external world. Despite being thought of by many as a non-starter, for many reasons it became part of the set of six. As you can see, compared with the significant success of most of the other five behaviours, this one hardly moved over time. In some ways it was good that this happened, because it provided a natural comparison.

Measuring the progression of the behaviours is not the only possible way to track progress of Viral Change™ (stories are another part of the possible scorecard), but it certainly is a key tool.

### Does Viral Change™ work?

- As a method, yes, if the principles are applied correctly. And then it works pretty well.

- As a journey, it is up to you how much you want to discover, challenge and open your eyes and windows to a new reality. Not interested? Viral Change™ doesn't work as a journey. Very interested? Viral Change™ rediscovers and redefines employee engagement, informal connectivity, natural influence, leadership, storytelling and a few other things...

234

- As a way of life? Viral Change™ will be a good life or a bad life depending on you. It doesn't depend on behavioural sciences, network theory, social sciences, storytelling and leadership studies. Or even on us as consultants!

Let me end as I subtitled my previous book. Viral Change™ is the alternative to slow, painful and unsuccessful management of change in organizations...and in society.

# Annex

# The human condition: a guide for the perplexed

# 1. 'Sync' effects

**1.0 Contagious yawning and laughing**

It is a well-known phenomenon that seeing, hearing, reading or thinking about yawning triggers the beginning of a yawn. The same goes for laughing. This contagiousness is backed by neural, behavioural and social sciences. The explanation offered is that the contagion is a response to *stimulus feature detectors* generated particularly by (visual) yawns and (auditory) laughs. It is maintained that yawns and laughs are innate behaviours (i.e. produced by *innate releasing mechanisms*). Mimicking someone who is yawning or laughing does not demand any conscious effort and hence the response of our 'mirror neuron' system activates automatically.

Provine, R. 1996. Contagious yawning and laughter: Significance for sensory feature detection, motor pattern generation, imitation, and the evolution of social behaviour. In Heyes, C.M., Bennett, G. Galef, eds. *Social Learning in Animals: The roots of culture.* San Diego: Academic Press.

**1.1 'La Ola' ('the wave')**

'The wave' was noticed for the first time in 1986 during the World Cup Soccer in Mexico. During this phenomenon, groups of spectators leap up and raise their arms in sequence, then drop back to their seats. It is an exquisite example of a complicated shared behaviour that unfolds without awareness and with no central orchestration in place. To interpret and quantify this collective human behaviour, researchers have applied a model that was originally used to describe excitable media such as cardiac tissue or forests. Prof. Dirk Helbing and his team in Zurich have succeeded in producing a credible mathematical description and impressive simulation of 'La Ola'. Depending on the density and proximity of neighbours and direction of influence (wave coming from the left or right), each person is sitting, but excitable. This phenomenon might be useful to understand the workings of other crowd behaviours like riots, mass demonstrations, collective panic or mourning, etc. It also serves to find ways on how to control groups of excited people in general.

Farkas, I., D. Helbing, T. Vicsek. 2002. Social Behaviour: Mexican waves in an excitable medium. *Nature* 419 : 131-32

See an example of 'La Ola':
http://www.youtube.com/watch?v=FpXlQwBA5Kw
[Accessed May 2010] or a visual simulation: http://angel.elte.hu/wave [Accessed July 2010].

# 2. Panic, collective fear and health scares

**2.0  Copycat poisonings**

In October 1982, when seven people died after taking Tylenol headache capsules laced with cyanide, the tragedy was widely publicized by the national news media. Reports of other 'poisonings' ensued. Elliot Aronson, one of the greatest social psychologists of the 20th century, claims that the media coverage encouraged other people to report similar cases. The reports involved eye drops, nasal sprays, mouthwash, soda pop and even hot-dogs. In turn, these 'copycat poisonings' received equally widespread media attention and hence, the contagion stretched across the nation. In a general state of agitation or panic, people demanded medical help for burns and poisonings, while all they suffered from were ordinary sore throats or stomach-aches. False alarms were seven times as frequent as the actual cases of product tampering. It is claimed that the initial Tylenol incident was almost certainly done by one person only. Subsequent events, however, clearly resulted from the media hype around the Chicago poisonings.

Aronson, E. 1992. *The Social Animal.* New York: WH Freeman Company.

**2.1  Nut allergies in the US**

The buzz around nut allergies in the US displays some characteristics of Mass Psychogenic Illness (MPI). The number of 'nut-free' schools is rising dramatically. Peanut butter and any (homemade) goods without clear labels are prohibited from campus. Measures taken to protect students from 'contamination' are often strict and intense. However, statistically, serious allergic reactions to foods instigate just 2,000 out of 30 million hospitalizations a year and comparatively few deaths (150 a year). These numbers cover all food allergies, not only nuts. This shows that the extremity of reaction to nut allergies in the US is not proportional to the actual danger they pose.

BBC editorial. 2008. Warning of nut allergy 'hysteria' (http://news.bbc.co.uk/1/hi/health/7773210.stm)

| 2.2 | **Collective suicide, Jonestown** | In 1977, Reverend Jim Jones, founder of the Peoples Temple, was facing charges of tax evasion (amongst other things). As a result, he decided to move his followers from San Francisco to a village in Guyana, which he then called Jonestown. In 1978, when faced with a federal investigation for reported acts of child abuse and torture, he talked the whole congregation of followers into poisoning their children and then themselves, claiming this was the only response to the approaching end of the world. Collective fear was at the core. Those who dared to protest were silenced immediately. The next morning, more than 900 bodies were found lying together arm in arm. |

The explanation of this behaviour lies in methods of exerting social and personal influence and conformity. That includes psycho-social theories around personal endorsement, prestige or obedience to authority, direct persuasion, social imitation and social proof. It is suggested that an extreme form of the social conformity phenomenon may well explain many politico-economical events, e.g. Nazism or Communism.

Layton, D. 1999. *Seductive poison: A Jonestown survivor's story of life and death in the Peoples Temple.* New York: Anchor.

Also see a 45min reportage including the recording by Jim Jones himself: http://video.google.com/videoplay?docid=-9111740369454241202# [Accessed May 2010]

# 3. Fads, fashions and consumer behaviours

3.0

Fads and fashions are a novel, homogenous and often non-utilitarian collective behaviour that is spread by imitation or the instigation of latent tendencies in people. Literature gives accounts of mathematical models depicting the social organization of fads and fashions through contagion, convergence behaviour or innovation diffusion. The most important features of these phenomena are homogeneity (fads are consistent in different places and time), as well as their suddenness, rapid spread, quick acceptance and short life span. Fads are short-lived, while fashions tend to stay for a longer and identifiable period. Here is a selection of examples drawn from various domains of social life, prevalent in the last four decades:

**1970s:**
*Fashion:* decade began with the hippie-look continued from 60s: bell-bottoms, wide-legged flare jeans, platform shoes, Saturday-Night fever/Travolta look. The rise of punk with Vivienne Westwood (in response to tough economic situation).
*Society/politics:* Major focus on social activism, breakthroughs in nuclear family vision, sexual revolution, decline of colonial imperialism through new trends in globalization, second wave feminism.
*TV in UK:* peak of *Dr. Who* sci-fi series, *Porridge* (realism in police dramas), *Softly, Softly.*
*TV in US:* social consciousness programming such as *All in the Family, Charlie's Angels, All my Children.* TV shows like *The Sonny and Cher Comedy Hour.*
*Toys:* G.I Joe re-launched as a new, non-military version

**1980s:**
*Society:* neo-conservatism, first panic associated with AIDS.
*Fashion:* 'Miami Vice' look, Madonna's influence,

dancewear (legwarmers), soap opera *Dynasty* with its influence in western fashion, Michael Jackson's 'Thriller' look (red/black leather, glasses, etc), Dr. Martens shoes, post-punk gothic style and designer shoelaces.

**Technology:** Macintosh introduced in 1984, Nintendo's first rise, Super Mario Brothers, Mike Tyson's Punch-Out, Pac-Man obsession.

**Toys:** Cabbage Patch dolls, Koosh balls, Care Bears, Lolo balls.

**Music:** *'Walk-like-an-Egyptian'* craze, *'Lambada'* dance (through to 90s).

**TV:** Smurfs, Garfield, MTV becoming popular, the *'I'll be back'* phenomenon (phrase associated with Arnold Schwarzenegger), *Full House* TV series and the Olsen twins, big come back of *Star Trek*, *Where's the beef?* (from the Wendy's commercial)

**1990s:**

**Fashion:** Wonderbra, Thermochromic dress (changing colours when worn), baseball caps, army/camouflage clothes, bandanas, torn jeans, FUBU clothing.

**Culture:** 'Got Milk?' advertising campaign (increased milk sale by 90%), *'Karaoke* ('Empty Orchestra' in Japanese), Christo's umbrellas phenomenon, best-selling author Kitty Kelley. **Technology:** Windows '95, EBay.

**TV:** *Star Wars* Saga, afterlife films (e.g. *Ghost*), *Family Guy* cartoon.

**Health:** coloured braces, cosmetic surgery for men, mind machines.

**Business:** outdoor training and leadership programmes.

**Food:** ostrich or 'garden' burgers.

**Intellectual debates:** hemp debate, *Who killed JFK?* (the Oliver Stone film made many people believe that Oswald was not alone), SimEarth – The Living Planet (computer programme allowing you to play God according to the Gaia hypothesis).

**Music:** Spanish *Macarena* by Los del Rio, rise of dance music. **Toys:** Tickle-Me-Elmo, Furby, Pokémon and related merchandise.

243

**2000s (the noughties):**
*Reality TV:* Big Brother, Survivor, dating shows, etc.
*Internet*: Twitter, Facebook, MySpace, Foursquare, Chatroulette, Google Earth.
*Technology*: Microsoft's Xbox and Apple's iPod, iPad, Bluetooth earpieces, Crazy Frog ringtones, RAZR cellphones.
*Music*: Ska, ethnic/ world music, rise of reggaeton in Latin America, Hannah Montana phenomenon.
*Culture*: Sudoku, *Numa Numa*-themed videos and dance based on the song *Dragostea din tei* by O-Zone, *JibJab* political cartoons during and after the 2004 elections, LOLcats.
*Fashion*: ironing hair, bob-cuts popularized by Victoria Beckham, beehive (Amy Winehouse), emergence of subcultures such as Emo, Chav, Urban fashion, Lolita in Japan. Ugg boots, pink clothes for men and *Tough Guys Wear Pink* t-shirt, ponchos, low-rise jeans, oversized sunglasses for girls. Livestrong and charity wristbands.

Bikhchandani, S., D. Hirshleifer, I. Welch. 1992. A theory of fads, fashion, custom, and cultural change as informational cascades. *The Journal of Political Economy*. 100(5): 992-1026.

Meyersohn, R., E. Katz. 1957. Notes on a natural history of fads. *The American Journal of Sociology*. 62(6): 594-601.

Hoffmann, F.W., W.G. Bailey. 1994. *Fashion & merchandizing fads*. New York: The Haworth Press Inc.

Aguirre, B.E., E.L. Quarantelli, J.L. Mendoza. 1988. The collective behaviour of fads: The characteristics, effects, and career of streaking. *American Sociological Review*. 53(4): 569-584.

See Fadwiki for list organized by origin and decade (http://fads.wikia.com/wiki/Main_Page) or StateMaster Encyclopedia [Both accessed May 2010]. (http://www.statemaster.com/encyclopedia/2000s)

| 3.1 | 'Monkey see, monkey do' in consumer behaviour | It is said that many consumer demands arise not from their innate needs, but from an ensemble of social pressures. Galbraith, a Canadian-American economist, claimed that the demands ('*wants*' as he calls them) are a result of social aspiration, fashion or simple imitation. He states: "*What others do or have, one should do or have.*" Another example from US fashion trends: the sudden rise in popularity in 1994-95 of Hush Puppies, the classic American suede-shoes. Fads and trends interpreted through microeconomics and/or behaviourism are understood through herd instincts or the bandwagon effect (aka 'cromo effect'). This means that the probability of people adopting a given behaviour increases proportionally to the number of people who have already done so. |

Galbraith, J.K. 1958.*The Affluent Society*. Boston, MA: Houghton Mifflin.

| 3.2 | Imitation in broadcasting | The imitative trends in broadcasting create TV programming fads that could not be explained otherwise. For instance, the wide variety of reality TV shows, *American Idol* and its worldwide counterparts, game shows that appear quickly and disappear even quicker, or the everlasting parabolic tendency of genres such as Sci-Fi. |

| 3.3 | Diffusion of innovations | A sociologist, Everett Rogers, claims that technological advancements diffuse slowly into society at first, then accelerate and then slow down again until they reach the whole society. However, recent research shows that informational flow depends mainly on social network structure. For example, despite the development support to build new latrines in the high Andean community of Tigua, Ecuador, the new utilities were often neglected and the novel technology never gained sufficient popularity. One unusual validating factor was noted: the particular nature of connections between people in Tigua Loma. They did not speak with each other. It is believed that word-of-mouth (WoM) referral behaviour is displayed differently |

according to the strength of a social tie. WoM has an important bridging function and can travel within the broader social system, from one distinct subgroup to another, even if the social ties are weak at the person-to-person level.

Rogers, E.M. 2003. *Diffusion of innovations*, 5th ed. New York: Free Press.

Johnson Brown, J., P.H. Reingen. 1987. Social ties and word-of-mouth referral behaviour. *Journal of Consumer Research.* 14(3): 350-362.

| 3.4 | **Word-of-mouth (including digital one)** | As mentioned before, some of the consumerism-driven manifestations of social epidemics are fads and fashions related to certain products that capture the attention of the general public, but only for a short period of time. Behavioural sciences agree unanimously: without sufficient visibility, no practice or technology can circulate in society. Also, it is false to believe that it is independent thinking that shapes us as a species. Our nature stems from mimicking each other's behaviours and the way we choose to communicate this. Word-of-mouth (WoM) is the key principle (as well as an excellent indication of general business performance) in peer-to-peer or consumer-to-consumer influence. It is also widely used as a tool in online marketing strategies, which led to the rise of viral marketing in recent years. A good example is Windows Live Hotmail, known as Hotmail. This free web-based email service grew to 12 million accounts in its first year and had more than 270 million users all over the world in 2008. The principle is simple: every message contains a Hotmail advertisement. At present, PepsiCo, Tupperware Corporation, Microsoft, etc. have chosen viral marketing as their main marketing mode. This type of marketing uses the strength of already established social networks, sometimes very large and random, which allows for a wide spread of information, quickly, efficiently and at low cost. |

Yang, J., et al. 2010. A study of the spreading scheme for viral marketing based on a complex network model. *Physica A.* 389 (4): 859–870.

Stephen, A.T., J. Berger. Unpublished paper. Creating contagious: How social networks and item characteristics combine to drive persistent social epidemics. http://marketing.wharton.upenn.edu/documents/research/Creating%20Contagious.pdf [Accessed May 2010]

# 4. Political and civic activism

**4.0**  **Contagious voting**

There is a well-documented body of evidence that shows that a single decision to vote might increase the probability of others voting. One decision to vote can trigger dozens of others in a 'turnout cascade' if, firstly, there is a small probability that voters imitate the behaviour of one of their acquaintances, and secondly, if individuals are closely interwoven in social ties within the population. Some studies confirm that media does not touch and influence masses directly when it comes to political campaigning. Instead, those who are the most central to the social network (i.e. 'opinion leaders') filter and interpret the information in order to present it back to the rest. Historically, interconnection in social networks was one of the most important determining factors in the spread of political behaviour. As for voter turnout, it has been proven that when there is a correlation between two people who are socially linked (which also implies they are like-minded) that they imitate each other. One voter copies behaviour of other voters, but at the same time they copy his. On average, one 'independent' decision to vote prompts three others. However, it has also been said that a simple direct request has a strong motivating effect on people. That, however, is subject to passing that request along to the social network.

http://www.pewinternet.org/Reports/2008/The-Internet-and-the-2008-Election.aspx [Accessed May 2010]

Blais, A., R. Young. 1999. Why do people vote? An experiment in Rationality. *Public Choice* 99(1-2): 39-55.

Fowler, J.H. 2005. Turnout in a small world. *Social Logic of Politics*. Philadelphia: Temple University Press, 269-287.

Nelson, P. 2007. Voting and imitative behaviour. Economic Inquiry. 32(1): 92-101.

Beck, P.A. et al. 2002. The social calculus of voting: Interpersonal, media and organizational influences on presidential choices. *American Political Science Review*. 96(1): 57-73.

Huckfeldt, R.R., J. Sprague. 1995. *Citizens, politics and social communication*. New York: Cambridge University Press.

| 4.1 | **'The Kerry cascade'** | Duncan Watts explains John Kerry's 2004 campaign through a classic experiment conducted by Solomon Asch. In a rather humorous way, he says: *"When everyone is looking to someone else for an opinion — trying, for example, to pick the Democratic candidate they think everyone else will pick — it's possible that whatever information other people might have gets lost, and instead we get a cascade of imitation that, like a stampeding herd, can start for no apparent reason and subsequently go in any direction with equal likelihood (…) We think of ourselves as autonomous individuals, each driven by own internal abilities and desires and therefore solely responsible for our own behaviour, particularly when it comes to voting. No voter ever admits — even to herself — that she chose Kerry because he won New Hampshire."* |

Watts, Duncan. "The Kerry cascade: How a '50s psychology experiment can explain the Democratic primaries", *Slate*, February 24, 2004.
http://www.slate.com/id/2095993 [Accessed May 2010]

| 4.2 | **Political activism: 'join the crowd'** | During the time of vigorous protest against the Iraq war in 2004-05, Heaney and Rojas collected information from political activists during selected major protests. Among the events selected were a 500,000-person protest outside the Republican National convention in NY, a protest at G. W. Bush's |

second inauguration in Washington, D.C. and several antiwar rallies. The results yielded notable discrepancies in activists and their objectives. In general, they wanted to achieve their goals either by joining one of the major political parties or by working independently. The choice they made had an impact on how social movements and political parties interacted. Firstly, interconnections between the activists would be defined by partisan attitudes. Unsurprisingly, they would recruit those activists with whom they were ideologically compatible. Secondly, their attitudes would influence others in the way they participated. Finally, decisions to join were driven by the practicalities of activism movement, i.e. an affiliation with a specific group would grant access to government institutions such as Congress.

Heaney, Michael T., F. Rojas. 2007. Partisans, non-partisans, and the antiwar movement in the United States. *American Politics Research.* 35(4): 431-464.

| 4.3 | The 'epidemic' of Methodism | During the 1780s, the Methodist movement became vastly popularized in North America and England, increasing from 20,000 to around 90,000 followers in the US alone. However, the great success of this epidemiological diffusion was not due to the founder of the church, John Wesley. It was George Whitfield, an orator of great power and charisma, who travelled and delivered open-air homilies to thousands of people. In every town, he would stay long enough to organize his converts into religious networks and communities, which in turn, formed smaller subgroups naturally. Social organization of these networks and the strengthening of ties within communities through common practices and beliefs enabled Whitfield to acquire the critical mass and spread the contagion. |

Mathews, Donald G. 1969. The second great awakening as an organizing process, 1780-1830: An hypothesis. *American Quarterly.* 21(1): 23-43

# 5. Collective hysteria

**5.0  Epidemic hysteria in Malaysian schools**

Between 1962 and 1971, twenty-nine rural Malaysian schools and hotels had an outbreak of epidemic hysteria, with a significant rise in 1971 (seventeen schools involved). One particular incident involved 50 schoolgirls suddenly becoming depressed following a series of unfortunate events connected to a flood affecting the school. One girl hyperventilated into a state of titanic spasm. Others followed, displaying seizure-like symptoms (or, as it was believed, a state of spirit possession). When the team from the Ministry of Education met in the school to investigate the outbreak, they were also overcome by a trans-like hysteria. The native interpretation of this collective contagion focused on contamination of the spirit world and the spirits' subsequent offence. That might explain why all hysteria outbreaks stopped after a 'purifying ritual' was performed. It is suggested that the prevalence of outbreaks in Malaysian schools was related to a variety of socio-economical, religious and cultural factors, as well as to the interaction of these factors with the mental balance of girls and other members of the community.

Teoh, J.I., S. Soewondo, M. Sidharta. 1975. "Epidemic hysteria in Malaysian schools: An illustrative episode. *Psychiatry: Journal for the Study of Interpersonal Processes.* 38(3): 258-268.

**5.1  Epidemic of laughter in Tanzania**

This is undoubtedly one of the most noteworthy incidents of MPI. The epidemic of laughing and crying struck villages west of Lake Victoria in 1962. It began at a mission school when 95 out of 159 girls gave way to the same overwhelming compulsion to laugh and sob. When the authorities sent the children back to their villages, the psychic contagion quickly spread to the adult population. Victims laughed for about a week on average. Hundreds of people were affected before the epidemic receded the following year.

Rankin, A.M., P.J. Phillip. 1963. An epidemic of laughing in the Bukoba district of Tanganyika. *Central African Journal of Medicine*. 9: 167-70.

http://www.youtube.com/watch?v=ms7MpUNvAK0

Ebrahim, G.J. 1968. Mass hysteria in schoolchildren: Notes on three outbreaks in East Africa. *Clinical Pediatrics*. 7: 437-438.

| 5.2 | **An outbreak of abdominal pain, UK** | Reported by Newcastle University Hospital, In 1972, at a children's gala, 130 visitors (mainly girls from juvenile jazz bands) developed a sudden illness with common symptoms being stomach cramps and pains. The hysteria did not spread to the local community. Additionally, symptoms did not linger and were not acute. The final investigation found no evidence of a clinical or anatomical cause for the symptoms and the overall case was hailed inconclusive. |

Smith, H.C.T., E.J. Eastham. 1973. Outbreak of abdominal pain. *The Lancet*. 302 (7835): 956-958.

| 5.3 | **Back pain in Germany** | This was a natural experiment provided by the reunification of Germany. Before the Berlin Wall fell, East Germany had much lower rates of back pain than West Germany. But within 10 years of unification, East Germany started copying West Germany's higher rates. It is believed that new available media played a significant role in exacerbating the effect, as well as that the effect might have been culture-related. |

Raspe, H., A. Hueppe, H. Neuhauser, H. 2008. Back pain, a communicable disease? *International Journal of Epidemiology*. 37(1): 69-74.

| 5.4 | **Spasm, fainting hysteria; Blackburn** | In 1965, during a morning assembly, several girls fainted. Teachers, concerned that they might hurt themselves, asked them to lie down on the floor. This only exacerbated the situation and caused an avalanche of panic in other kids. By midday, 141 pupils were experiencing dizziness, nausea, spasms and shortness of breath. 85 of them were hospitalized. A formal week-long investigation |

established that there was no underlying physical cause. A possible explanation evolved around an aggravating effect of authorities on spreading the contagious psychogenic symptoms.

Waller, J. 2008. Falling Down. *The Guardian*. September 18, 2008. [Accessed May 2010]
http://www.guardian.co.uk/science/2008/sep/18/psychology

| 5.5 | **The dancing mania. Mainland Europe** | *"And those who were seen dancing were thought to be insane by those who could not hear the music."* Friedrich Nietzsche |

First major outbreak of the dancing mania was noted in Aachen, Germany on June 24, 1374. People joined hands to form circles and danced for hours in wild delirium until they fell to the ground in exhaustion. Investigators observed that people expressed a range of negative emotions after the incident. They pointed toward an extreme feeling of being oppressed and cried out as if tortured or in anguish.

Hecker, J.F.C., B.G. Babington, trans. 1844. *The Epidemics of Middle Ages*. London: The Sydenham Society.

| 5.6 | **Collective hysteria attributed to toxic exposure. Warren High School, McMinnville, Tennessee, US** | In 1998, a teacher in Tennessee noticed a gasoline-like smell in her classroom. Soon after, she began experiencing a headache, nausea, shortness of breath and dizziness. In a panic, the school was quickly evacuated. 80 students and 19 staff members went to the emergency room at the local hospital. Nearly forty people were kept at the hospital overnight. Government agencies and other appropriate bodies performed an in-depth investigation, but as soon as the school reopened, another 71 persons went to the ER. It was found that the symptoms were reported mainly by females and that they were triggered by mere observation of other people being ill. No medical or environmental causes were found. |

Jones, T.F. et al. 2000. Mass psychogenic illness attributed to toxic exposure at a high school. *The New England Journal of Medicine.* 342(2):96-100.

| 5.7 | 'Phantom anesthetist of Mattoon', Illinois | In her meta-analytic review of epidemic hysteria, Boss states that the majority of the outbreaks that took place between 1973 and 1993 took place in schools, with the rest taking place in small towns and other settings. In 1944, a particular outbreak took place in Mattoon, a village in Illinois. It started with one woman's hysterical report of being gassed and paralyzed at night by an 'evil genius'. The local belief was that the phantom would open the window at night and spray people with a sweet-smelling anaesthetic. That would leave the victim temporarily paralysed. After some scientific reckoning, Johnson concluded that women of slightly lower social status were among the most frequent victims of the 'evil genius' and that their affect led to heightened suggestibility in others. After the attacks were proclaimed to be imaginary, calls to police reporting stalkers and gassers dropped drastically. |
|---|---|---|

Johnson, D. M. 1945. The 'phantom anesthetist' of Mattoon: a field study of mass hysteria. *The Journal of Abnormal and Social Psychology.* 40(2): 175-186

Boss, L.P. 1997. Epidemic hysteria: A review of the published literature. *Epidemiologic Reviews.* 19(2): 233-243.

| 5.8 | Triborough Bridge toll workers | In February 1990, toll workers on the Triborough Bridge began to complain of headaches, abdominal discomfort, dizziness, sore throats and chest pain. Symptoms were spreading, accompanied with a reported sensation of 'sweetness in the air'. 34 workers were taken to hospital. Literature confirms that smells (imagined or not) are frequent triggers of collective hysteria. |
|---|---|---|

Wesseley, S. 2000. Responding to Mass Psychogenic Illness. *The New England Journal of Medicine.* 342: 129-130.

Golden, T., "Bridge illness: anxiety is now the suspect", *The New York Times,* March 12, 1990.

http://www.nytimes.com/1990/03/12/nyregion/bridge-illness-anxiety-is-now-the-suspect.html?pagewanted=1 [Accessed May 2010].

**5.9**    **Koro syndrome**

In a classic example of a culture-bound syndrome, Koro is a condition seen in certain Asian countries. In a state of psychogenic disorder, men collectively experience an intense anxiety that their penises are receding into their bodies and that they may even disappear. Clinical explanation provides some insights into a unique case of depersonalization syndrome. The forms, specificities, occurrence and distribution of this syndrome are moulded by a combination of social and cultural factors.

Yap, P.M. 1965. Koro - A culture-bound depersonalization syndrome. *The British Journal of Psychiatry.* 111: 43-50.

**5.10**    **Fainting outbreak in a school in Tanzania**

In September 2008, about 20 schoolgirls began to faint in a classroom, collapsing to the floor and losing consciousness. After witnessing this, others acted hysterically, screamed and ran amok. A local education officer was quoted in the news stating calmly that such events were very common here. According to some qualitative reports, many Central African schoolchildren are often exposed to emotionally straining situations (cultural, economic or other) which may result in chronic stress. In a state of emotional vulnerability, mass psychogenic illness (or a collective anxiety attack) is more likely to occur and collective behaviour can involve an unusual somatic response.

Bartholomew, R.E., Victor, J.S. 2004. A social-psychological theory of collective anxiety attacks: The 'mad gasser' re-examined. *The Sociological Quarterly.* 45 (2): 229-248.

# 6. Suicide

**6.0** **Suicide cluster in a small Manitoba community**

Between 3<sup>rd</sup> February and 5<sup>th</sup> May 1995, an isolated northern Manitoba First Nations community had 6 suicides in a population of less than 1500. As there are numerous reports of suicides occurring in groups/clusters, it is now believed that *cluster suicide* is a serious psychiatric and public health issue that adds a social angle to an issue that was otherwise perceived as an individualistic matter.

Wilkie, C., S. Macdonald, K. Hildahl. 1998. Community case study: Suicide cluster in a small Manitoba community. *Canadian Journal of psychiatry.* 43: 823-828.

**6.1** **Suicides in Micronesia and Samoa.**

An extraordinary increase in youth suicide rates was noted in several Pacific countries with Micronesia having the highest rates in the world. The general suicide rate for Truk is 40 per 100,000. The rate for Trukese males between 15 and 25 is 250 per 100,000 (which constitutes twenty times the youth rate in the US). Besides an epidemiological explanation, a social change factor is considered, or more specifically, the impact of these changes on cultural development and mental health.

http://www.nytimes.com/1983/03/06/us/micronesia-s-male-suicide-rate-defies-solution.html [Accessed May 2010]

Rubinstein, D.H. 1992. Suicide in Micronesia and Samoa: A critique of explanations. *Pacific Studies.* 15(1): 51-75.

**6.2** **Copycat teenage suicides, NY**

The number of cases increased significantly within four weeks after an article about a suicide was published on the front page of the New York Times. Clusters shared certain characteristics and they all occurred in small towns infecting school networks and teenagers. There is a strong conviction that the way suicides are depicted in the press plays an important role in promoting the spread of suicides contagion. It has been proved that certain media highlights may generate copycat effects. That is most visibly evinced in the suicides rates, which polarize geographically – numbers increase especially in areas where the story was printed and popularized.

Phillips, D.P. 1974. The influence of suggestion on suicide: Substantive and theoretical implications of the Werther effect. *American Sociological Review*. 39(3): 340-354.

**6.3    Suicidal outbreak in high school, Pennsylvania**

In a high school of 1,496 students, two students committed suicide within four days. During the following eighteen days, seven more students attempted suicide and an additional twenty-three displayed suicidal intent. These totals were significantly higher than the expected rates. Moreover, 75% of these people had at least one major psychiatric disorder prior to the exposure. 110 high-risk students underwent a psychopathological screening. It was found that students who became suicidal after exposure were more likely than their non-suicidal counterparts to be presently depressed or to have had manifested depression or suicidality in the past. Friendship was another factor that was said to heighten the chances of suicidal behaviour. The closer a friend was to the victims, the lower the threshold would be for manifesting suicidal intents.

Brent, D.A., et al. 1989. An outbreak of suicide and suicidal behaviour in a high school. *Journal of the American Academy of Child and Adolescent Psychiatry*. 28(6): 918-924.

**6.4    Suicides vs. friendship, US**

The research conducted by Bearman and Moody analyzed data from 13,465 adolescents from the National Longitudinal Survey of Adolescent Health. They looked into a threefold relationship between friendship, suicidal ideation and the actual attempts. Not surprisingly, having had a friend who committed suicide significantly increased the chances of suicidal intent and endeavours. This was true for both sexes. Social isolation (individual's position in the social network) was among the most prevalent triggers of suicidal thought. The research demonstrated that, in general terms, suicide attempts appear not to be determined by any statistical regularities.

Bearman, P.S., J. Moody. 2004. Suicide and friendships among American adolescents. *American Journal of Public Health*. 9(1): 89-95.

**6.5 Suicide epidemic in US**

This 1997 report is a first report from the National Longitudinal Study on Adolescent Health (Add Health study). It gave a valuable overview of facts and figures related to the health status of adolescents, their social context and any risk behaviours associated with that social context. In relation to the suicide epidemic, it provided proof that 13% of American adolescents were seriously considering suicide in 1997 and that 4% of them went through with it. Additionally, it was found that the context of family and school had a significant impact on managing the balance between health and risk behaviours in adolescents.

Resnick, M., et. al. 1997. Protecting adolescents from harm. Findings from the National Longitudinal Study on Adolescent Health. *The Journal of the American Medical Association*. 278: 823-32.

**6.6 France Télécom suicide wave**

During 2008 and 2009, 25 employees of France Télécom, a European telecommunications giant, committed suicide. General consensus amongst trade unions was that the main cause could be attributed to emotional strain, stressful working conditions and, resulting from that, deteriorated mental health of employees. However, since 2009 the issue was looked at on a more general level and attracted the attention of occupational psychiatrists. It was concluded that these occurrences could be interpreted as 'suicide clusters' that did not stem from individual mental ills in the group, but from a broader context of organizational culture where suicide became contagious. On an organizational level, prevention that focuses on the mental well-being of employees is generally seen as a more realistic strategy for changing the image and other aspects of the whole corporate culture. The French press also stated that the suicide numbers within France Télécom made statistical sense. The annual total of 10,423 suicides in France equates to 16 for every 100,000 inhabitants. Therefore, 25 suicides in 2 years for 102,254 employees in France Télécom equates to 11.7 for every 100,000 employees annually.

Kivimäki, M., M. Hotopf, M. Henderson. 2010. Do stressful working conditions cause psychiatric disorders? *Occupational Medicine.* 60(2): 86-87.

Bonde, J.P. 2008. Psychosocial factors at work and risk of depression: a systematic review of the epidemiological evidence. *Occupational and Environmental Medicine.* 65(7):438–445.

Krug, F. Est-ce qu'on se suicide plus à France Télécom qu'ailleurs? *Eco89*, 17 September, 2009, 11H56. http://eco.rue89.com/2009/09/17/est-ce-quon-se-suicide-plus-a-france-telecom-quailleurs [Accessed May 2010]

# 7. Health and well-being habits

| 7.0 | **Sexual behaviour in adolescents, US** | These two papers report on studies based on the National Longitudinal Study of Adolescent Health (Add Health) which was conducted in 1994 with 90,118 students. The papers examine: |

1) the influence of friends' religiosity on the probability of the first sexual encounter.
2) the impact of the friendship network's characteristics and pubertal timing on girls' sexual debut.

Overall results share a common ground for the view that group influence on a girl increases in strength in proportion to her level of embeddedness within her social networks. Also, it is claimed that habits in sexual behaviour can spread from one person to another or can even be imitated. Here again, the embeddedness and interconnections within the social networks determine the routes for influence and the degree of social mimicry.

Adamczyk, A. 2006. Friends' religiosity and first sex. *Social Science Research.* 35 (4): 924-47.

Cavanagh, S.E. 2004. The sexual debut of girls in early adolescence: The intersection of race, pubertal timing, and friendship group characteristics. *Journal of research on adolescence.* 14(3): 285-312.

**7.1**   **'Chicago Sex Survey' (The National Health and Social Life Survey)**

The National Health and Social Life Survey was conducted in 1992, interviewing 3,432 adults aged 18 to 59. The survey is a very precise and inclusive description of romantic and sexual behaviours in the US, including how people met and who they were drawn to. Initial findings yielded that 68% met after being introduced by someone they knew. For short-term sexual encounters 53% were introduced by a third party. Speculations evolved around the link between the ways people meet versus how quickly they have sex. Data reveals the tendency in people to utilize their connections and networks accordingly to the type of relationship they pursue. It was shown that, typically, family tend to instigate long-term, as opposed to short-term, relationships. Regardless of the network, the study shows that people search for homogamy in their relationships. Individuals want to spend time with someone they resemble, with whom they share qualities, traits, beliefs, characteristics (even physique) and so on. As proof of that, 72% of marriages follow these rules of homophily, compared to only 53-60% for other types of sexual relationship.

Laumann, E.O., et al. 1994. *The social organization of sexuality: Sexual practices in the United States.* Chicago: University of Chicago Press.

**7.2**   **The Framingham Study: Overview**

The Framingham Study was initiated in 1948 to investigate an epidemic of coronary disease in the USA. The researchers used a forthcoming epidemiological approach. Main research results provided a variety of insights into the occurrence, the full clinical range, as well as predisposing factors. It also provided a deeper understanding of the biggest 'risk factors' (a term coined by the Framingham Study) for diseases such as stroke, coronary disease, peripheral artery disease and heart failure. .

Kannel, W.B. 2000. The Framingham Study: ITS 50-year legacy and future promise. *Journal of atherosclerosis and thrombosis.* 6(2): 60-6.

**7.3**    **The Framingham Heart Study: obesity epidemic**

This study by Fowler and Christakis confirmed that the nature of social ties plays an important role in shaping the person-to-person spread of obesity in social networks. Drawing on available body-mass index details, the researchers used a longitudinal statistical model to examine whether weight gain in one person was associated with weight gain in other people in their network (such as friends, brothers and sisters, colleagues or neighbours). Results illustrated vividly that clusters of obese individuals were noticeable and present in social networks. This, the researchers concluded, meant that the network phenomenon, both biological and behavioural, appeared to be significant to the trait of obesity. An obese person was more likely to have obese friends and this tendency typically extended to three degrees of separation. The epidemic can also be triggered by an event in an individual's life. Divorce, distress, stopping smoking, exercising less, losing a loved one may also contribute to the concentric spread of the epidemic.

Another implication to consider is the spread of eating disorders, specifically anorexia and bulimia. Female binge-eaters are socially perceived to be more popular and move to the centre of network naturally. In turn, that results in encouraging imitative behaviour and copycat effects.

The most striking finding from The Framingham Heart Study still remains that obesity displays epidemic-like characteristics, which allows it to travel across close social networks. Having an obese friend increases our chances of gaining weight.

Fowler, J.H., N.A. Christakis. 2007. The spread of obesity in a large social network over 32 years. *The New England Journal of Medicine.* 357 (4): 370-79.

Fowler, J.H., N.A. Christakis. 2008. Estimating peer effects on health in social networks: A response to Cohen-Cole and Fletcher; and Trogdon, Nonnemaker, and Pais. *Journal of Health Economics*. 27 (5): 1400–1405.

| 7.4 | **The Framingham Heart Study: happiness spread** | This fascinating study on happiness confirms: |
|---|---|---|

- that people's happiness depends on the happiness of others with whom they are connected.
- that 'islands' of happy people can form within social networks.

Regularity of social interactions can be benchmarked by geographical distance. Distance is therefore crucial in influencing speed and effectiveness of the spread of emotional contagion. What Christakis and Fowler found, was that people's happiness extends up to three degrees of separation in networks. Those positioned centrally in the network and encircled by many happy people are more likely to be happy in the future. The important conclusion from this study is that the human tendency to homophily is not the only explanation behind forming clusters of happiness. Longitudinal statistical models confirm that the 'happy niches' are a result of the spread of happiness through the network. For instance, someone who becomes happy and lives within a mile of his friends increases the probability of his friends being happy by 4 times. The effects perish with time and with geographical separation.

Happiness, like obesity, is a collective phenomenon. If people are connected with each other via social networks, their happiness depends on the happiness of others in their networks.

Fowler, J.H., N.A. Christakis. 2008. Dynamic spread of happiness in a large social network: Longitudinal analysis over 20 years in the Framingham Heart Study. *British Medical Journal*. 337: a2338.

| 7.5 | **The Framingham Heart Study: smoking** | Despite the substantial decrease in smoking in the population in the last 30 years, the size of clusters of smokers has not changed. Looking at this phenomenon more closely, Fowler and Christakis hypothesized that individuals are not acting in isolation when it comes to quitting. They have proven that whole groups of people are acting together, following the choices made by groups of individuals who are, more or less directly, connected to each other. The results confirmed that smoking behaviour spreads through close, as well as distant, social ties and that this fact is well-reflected when groups of interconnected people copy each others' non-smoking behaviour roughly at the same time. |

Once more, the social network and interconnectedness of people seem to be relevant for smoking cessation.

Fowler, J.H., N.A. Christakis. 2008. The collective dynamic of smoking in a large social network. *The New England Journal of Medicine.* 358 (21): 2249-2258.

| 7.6 | **The Framingham Heart Study: drinking in adolescents** | As with smoking and obesity, the Framingham population revealed that drinking behaviour similarly extends to three degrees of separation. Interestingly enough, it was noticed that drinking behaviour was greatly influenced by women. In another study, it was found that binge drinking in the UK spreads on an interpersonal basis and is transmitted within the peer group (although the type of relationship matters a lot). In other words, assuming that adolescents have random contacts with each other each year, alcohol use prevalence fits closely to a logistic curve used to model an epidemic progression. |

Careful analysis of drinking patterns reveals that there is an interpersonal aspect in transmission of drinking behaviour. This, however, is biased by gender, education and type of relationship.

Rowe, D.C., J. L. Rodgers. 1991. Adolescent smoking and

drinking: Are they epidemics? *Journal of Studies on Alcohol.* 55(2): 110-117.

Rosenquist, J.N., et al. 2010. The spread of alcohol consumption behaviour in a large social network. *Annals of Internal Medicine.* 152 (7): 426-433.

Animation of dynamic changes in the Framingham social network over the time of the study: http://www.annals.org/content/suppl/2010/04/07/152.7.426.D C3/fhssn_drink_v1.mov [Accessed June 2010]

Ormerod, P., G. Wiltshire. 2009. 'Binge' drinking in the UK: A social network phenomenon. *Mind and Society.* 8(2):135-152.

| | | |
|---|---|---|
| 7.7 | **The Framingham Heart Study: loneliness** | The more connections people have, the less lonely they feel. However, little is known about how the loneliness spreads and how it is positioned within social networks. This study demonstrates that loneliness, like health behaviours or happiness, occurs in groups and extends to 3 degrees of separation. Due to the fact that it happens through emotional and cognitive contagion processes, it is excessively represented at the periphery of social networks. This effect was found to be stronger for friends than for family, and stronger for women than for men. One of the possible implications authors suggest, is that by knowing the broad social forces that drive loneliness, we can decrease loneliness phenomena in our society. We could start by repairing social ties of the people who remain on the periphery of the network and the positive avalanche should ensue. Therefore, loneliness, even though it appears to be quintessentially a personal experience, is a result of groups of people. |

Cacioppo, J.T., J.H. Fowler, N.A. Christakis. 2009. Alone in the crowd: The structure and spread of loneliness in a large social network. *Journal of Personality and Social Psychology.* 97(6): 977–991.

| 7.8 | **Happiness survey in rural China** | By means of a survey administered in rural China, this paper attempts to answer the question whether happiness depends on the happiness of a reference group. The evidence is consistent with the hypothesis that happiness is infectious. Furthermore, it was found that happiness is not a mere reflection of someone else's state. There is a clear methodologically indentified fundamental explanation for this interdependence. Although it is not clear what exactly causes the happiness to spread, it is suggested that it may involve increased socio-economic conditions, positive biological effects or an enhanced sense of fellowship within the groups of individuals. |
|---|---|---|

Knight, J., R. Gunatilaka. 2009. Is happiness infectious? Unpublished paper.

| 7.9 | **Money vs. happiness** | In this paper, it is shown that an increase in income, and thus in the goods one owns, does not bring a lasting increase in happiness. Having happy friends and family is a far better predictor of being happy than earning more money. Social and evolutionary psychologists claim that it is on account of the negative effect it holds on hedonic adaptation and social comparison. |
|---|---|---|

Easterlin, R.A. Explaining Happiness. 2003. *Proceedings of the Natural Academy of Sciences of the United States.* 100(19): 11,176-11,183.

| 7.10 | **Farr's study on marriage vs. longevity and health** | William Farr, a British epidemiologist, was the first one to analyse the data of 25 million French to ascertain what the effects of conjugality are on the life expectancy of the larger population. His conclusions encompassed the fact that marriage extends life and improves health. This was a turning point in the forthcoming research on how a dyad of connections can affect health and on how health status in marriage can constitute a network marker for the spread of contagions. |
|---|---|---|

Farr, W. 1858. The influence of marriage on the mortality of the French people. In Hastings, G.W., ed. 1862. *Transactions of the National Association for the Promotion of social science.* London: John W. Parker and son. pp: 504-13.

**7.11**    **Syphilis epidemic, Rockdale County**

For public health officials and most inhabitants of Atlanta, it was a surprise to see a sudden outbreak of syphilis among middle-class teenagers in 1996. The outbreak received great media attention and left many parents and citizens bewildered about how little they knew about the sexual and social behaviour of their children. A formal investigation reconstructed the network of people connected to one another sexually. A group of white girls under 16 appeared to be at the core of this network, linking different clusters of boys by participating in group sex. The epidemic stopped when the network structure changed.

Aral, S.K., Berman, S.M., Aral, S.O. 2002. Anticipating outbreaks: A prevention role for integrated information systems. *Sexually Transmitted Diseases.* 29(1): 6-12.

**7.12**    **Mindless eating**

Other people have a significant impact on our eating behaviour. Not only do we imitate people sitting next to us, but also those who are much farther away. It is claimed that people are generally unaware of the influence that 'hidden persuaders' in our environment have on our behaviour or the role of these persuaders on 'mindless eating'. The concept of self-control also makes a reference to neuro-economics where people choose mindlessly when they act on 'auto pilot' (under the Automatic System, as opposed to the Reflective one). A famous example of this is where people ate 34% more stale popcorn, just because the bucket they received was bigger.

Wansink, B., Ferko-Adams, D. 2008. Mindless eating: Why we eat more than we think. *Vegetarian Nutrition Update.* XVI (III): 1-2.

Wansink, B. 2007. *Mindless eating: Why we eat more than we think.* New York: Bantam Dell.

**7.13**  **Weight-loss with friends**  There is a lot of evidence that smoking- or alcohol-cessation programmes are much more successful when provided with group support and not aimed at isolated individuals. In this study of 166 participants, researchers wanted to see what the benefits were of social support for weight loss and maintenance. At the end of the 4-month treatment, the overall outcome was that 95% of participants that were recruited together with 3 friends or family members, lost more weight. Additionally, this exceptional result was maintained even after 6 months. On the other hand, only 76% of lone recruiters completed treatment and only one fourth of them sustained their weight loss. Other studies have also confirmed the power of the interpersonal aspect in maintaining a healthy state. For example: 357 randomly assigned people lost weight, which was, unexpectedly, followed by their 357 untreated spouses! Here, a broader range of explanatory mechanisms is probable, but the primary one is simply copying the eating behaviour of the treated spouse.

Wing, R.R., R.W. Jeffery.1999. Benefits of recruiting participants with friends and increasing social support for weight loss and maintenance. *Journal of consulting and clinical psychology.* 67(1): 132-138

**7.14**  **Group support in AA**  When treating alcoholism, social contact is crucial. This starts during the first treatment and continues through to the post-treatment follow-ups. Undeniably, one of the strongest predictors of relapse is the number of heavy drinkers in a recovering alcoholic's network. Their presence is especially influential within the first year after treatment. Conversely, having a social network that supports non-drinking behaviour leads to very favourable outcomes. This was made clear in this study: outcomes were particularly favourable when the source of support came from AA (Alcoholics Anonymous) or friends (as compared with non-AA or family support). Interestingly, it is said that this kind of alcohol-specific support appears to be more important for maintaining abstinence than any other, more general social support (like emotional or financial support).

Bond, J., L.A. Kaskutas, C. Weisner 2003. The persistent influence of social networks and Alcoholics Anonymous on abstinence. *Journal of studies on alcohol*. 64(4): 579-88.

| | | |
|---|---|---|
| 7.15 | **Socializing non-drinking** | A survey by the Harvard School of Public Health revealed that about 44% of college students engaged in binge drinking two weeks or less before the survey was taken. However, if the error of availability heuristics is taken under consideration, these perceptions can seem exaggerated. Beliefs of how much others drink may be false. In this case, if the students misperceive how much others drink, alcohol abuse will inevitably increase given that their actions will follow their beliefs. Knowing this, Montana adopted a major educational health campaign that hailed 81% of citizens in Montana alcohol-free. It also claimed that most college students consume no more than 4 alcoholic drinks per week. It also published advertisements suggesting that 70% of teens do not smoke. These strategies have considerably lowered the numbers of smokers and also ameliorated the level of correctness in social perception. |

Perkins, H.W. 2002. Social norms and the prevention of alcohol misuse in collegiate contexts. *Journal of Studies on Alcohol. Supplement*. 14: 164-172.

| | | |
|---|---|---|
| 7.16 | **Contagious pregnancy in teenagers** | Alarming trends have emerged in US (and other western countries) over the past 30 years. Even though contraception became accessible to the general public in the 70s, single motherhood and the feminization of poverty began to grow. As a result, United States poverty rates have been steadily rising for the last quarter century. Quantitative work by economists and sociologists suggests that the volume of these changes is too vast and complex to be explained solely on the basis of the increase in welfare and social benefits. This paper discusses where the changes in sexual and marital practice occurred. One of the |

explanations given is that teenage girls imitate other teenagers' sexual behaviour. Therefore, they are more at risk of having children themselves when they observe their pregnant peers.

Akerlof, G.A., J.L. Yellen, M.L. Katz. 1996. An analysis of out-of-wedlock childbearing in the United States. *The Quarterly Journal of Economics.* 111(2): 277-317.

| | | |
|---|---|---|
| **7.17** | **Self-injury in teenagers vs. online community 'support'** | Self-injurious behaviour like 'cutting' has increased drastically in recent years and is now observed in 4% of teenagers. Social contagion is proposed as a viable explanation for this because many behaviours of this type tend to follow an epidemic-like pattern. In a study of online community message boards, researchers investigated how adolescents enquire about and share information related to self-injurious behaviour. More than 400 self-injury message boards were identified. Findings summarize that online social networks provide new ways for influence and social contagion to spread as they give an illusion of support and sense of affiliation to otherwise isolated individuals. On the other hand, these boards can constitute a normalizing and encouraging factor for those in search of self-identity or some 'reputable' options for self-injurious behaviour. |

Whitlock, J.L., J.L. Powers, J. Eckenrode. 2006. The virtual cutting edge: The internet and adolescent self-injury. *Developmental Psychology.* 42(3): 407-417.

# 8. Violence/aggressive behaviour

| | | |
|---|---|---|
| **8.0** | **Mob violence, Sydney** | To illustrate the transmission perspective in herd behaviour (see item 9.5 in this Annex), researchers evoked mass behaviour: riots, demonstrations and mob rule. An example of this is what happened in December 2005. Approx. 5,000 people gathered at Cronulla beach (Sydney, Australia) after receiving an SMS asking them to assemble there to reclaim the beach from non-locals. Earlier that day, aggressive behaviour from some Middle Eastern |

individuals had been reported. The initially festive atmosphere turned bad when a 'non-local' was chased into a hotel, surrounded and then attacked. Soon after, a full riot broke out: 25 people were injured and 12 arrested. But it didn't stop there. Later that evening, cars and windows were smashed, property damaged and a gang of 10 men of Middle Eastern appearance stabbed an Australian man. Violence conquered the periphery of Sydney. After another wave of SMS messages calling for retaliation, 1,000 gathered outside a mosque to protect it. But when nothing happened, they diverted to southern suburbs vandalizing property on the way. Most locals barricaded themselves at home, but those who found themselves in the way of the enraged mob were attacked with iron bars, baseball bats, Molotov cocktails, etc. The violence continued sporadically for a week, but after that, the attacks vanished as quickly as they appeared.

Goggin, G. 2006. SMS riot: Transmitting race on a Sydney beach, December 2005. *M/C, A Journal of media and Culture.* 9(1).

**8.1 Epidemic of violence, Chicago**

Aggregate homicide rates, as well as gang murders and other violent endeavours, are best exposed through an action-reaction response within the network structure. It is indeed through a web of connections that the contagion process begins and this network represents a crucial determinant for the practical and emotional consequences of homicide. This network is further sustained by hostility, dispute and interaction. In the literature is it said that gangs assess and measure the evident proceedings of others and negotiate local dominance through an epidemic-like process.

Papachristos, A.V. 2009. Murder by structure: Dominance relations and the social Structure of gang homicide in Chicago. *American Journal of Sociology.* 115 (1): 74–128.

**8.2 Crime in time and space**

*"Quelquefois aussi le crime prend sa source dans l'esprit d'imitation, que l'homme possède à un haut*

*degré et qu'il manifeste en toutes choses."*
A. Quételet

The most bewildering aspect of crime is not its overall intensity or the interconnections, it is its huge inconsistency across time and space. Throughout history we have observed drastic changes in the rise and fall of crime rates in many corners of the world. For example, in the United States between 1933 and 1961, homicide rates declined by 50%. In Philadelphia, an equally substantial drop was noted during the late nineteenth century. Indisputably, however, certain crimes spread more easily than others. For instance, in Ridgewood Village, New Jersey there are only 0.008 serious crimes per capita, but 0.384 in nearby Atlantic City. Researchers attempt to explain this phenomenon by the fact that when criminal acts are committed in a certain place and time, they increase the probability that others (who are in close proximity) will do the same. They call it informational polarization echoing within social networks. That escalation causes a multiplication of crime incidents and a rise of rates to an extent that would otherwise not be predictable.

Glaeser, E.L., B. Sacerdote, J.A. Scheinkman. 1996. Crime and social interaction. *The Quarterly Journal of Economics.* 111(2): 507-548.

## 9. Financial contagion and behavioural economy

9.0    **'Behaviour' of the price-story-price loop and market making system**    Social influences matter to the economy. Economists claim that there are three kinds of market participants: a (representative) market maker a speculator and irrational feedback traders. The behaviour of feedback traders is determined by price trends: they buy stocks now after observing an earlier price gain. The loop starts here: they buy stock due to the price gain, which in turn inflicts a future price gain. This produces a vicious circle that raises market prices and leads to the creation of a price bubble. Robert Shiller, a Yale economist, claims that the most critical component in understanding the *behaviour* in volatile markets is the social contagion of boom thinking. He claims that this contagion is biased by the popular perception of rapidly rising prices. In the process, public knowledge displays a functional self-imitating tendency. Optimistic views are collectively taken on as accurate just because everyone else seems to accept them. The price-story-price loop repeats continuously, but, as Shiller asserts, it will eventually break down, as popular judgment is unstable and unlikely to be maintained for a long period of time.

Shiller, R.J. 1998. Human behaviour and the efficiency of the financial system. NBER Working Paper No. W6375. Available at SSRN: http://ssrn.com/abstract=226124 [Accessed May 2010]

**9.1 Market contagion**

The 'Efficient Market Hypothesis' (EMH) defines a market in which prices fully reflect the available information, i.e. is 'informationally efficient'. The alternatives to EMH are based on social imitation. Schoenberg and his team concluded that in a financial environment, the imitative behaviour is more likely to be the default response when the target of judgment is subjective. This means that people's decisions are influenced by strategies that seem to be more successful (read: more visible) in a market environment at a given time. The price-value ratio often ends up disproportioned as a result of the market contagion spread.

Schoenberg, E.J. 2007. Beauty is in the eye of the other beholders: Imitation in financial markets. Unpublished paper. Department of Psychology, Columbia University. https://vlab2.gsb.columbia.edu/decisionsciences.columbia.edu/uploads/Beauty%20and%20Beholders%20v5.doc. [Accessed May 2010]

**9.2 Financial crisis 2008**

One of the main principles of behavioural economy, alongside bounded rationality and self-control, is social influence. In finding the origin of the financial crisis in 2008, one can turn to the example of investments in subprime mortgages: loans to people who do not qualify for market interest rates. Situation was as follows: up to 2004, there was a significant increase in house prices and by 2008, many mortgagees were under foreclosure. This caused an interruption in liquidity for many investment and mortgage companies, which in turn triggered a decrease in stock values. From the perspective of behavioural economy it was noted that many people were under the false impression that house prices would always increase. Therefore, their behaviour pursued this belief, creating new ways for the social contagion to act. This false belief produced unrealistic projections with obvious consequences for home purchases and mortgage choices. A survey conducted in 2005 showed that people were expecting the median increase of 9% per year. The optimism was based on the recent increase in prices and positive emotional contagion seen in others as well as the media.

Schiller, R. 2008. *The subprime solution: How today's global financial crisis happened, and what to do about it*. Princeton: Princeton University Press.

| | | |
|---|---|---|
| **9.3** | **Northern Rock 'financial contagion'** | On 12 September 2007, Northern Rock (a UK bank) sought and received a liquidity support facility from the Bank of England. When the bank reopened two days later, long queues formed. People wanted to withdraw their money, scared they would lose their savings. The direct, person-to-person interaction caused other people to join in the frenzy. The anxiety that overwhelmed the crowd was similar in quality to the one in mass psychogenic illness. |

BBC editorial. 2007 Northern Rock panic in papers. http://news.bbc.co.uk/1/hi/uk/6997174.stm [Accessed May 2010]

http://www.reuters.com/news/video?videoId=66505 [Accessed May 2010]

| | | |
|---|---|---|
| **9.4** | **Financial contagion continued** | Researchers investigated the spread of panic among Irish depositors at a New York bank (Emigrant Industrial Savings Bank) during two |

financial panics in the 1850s. As recent immigrants, their social network was heavily determined by their place of origin in Ireland and, subsequently, by where they lived in New York. It was found that the decision of closing an account was influenced more by social networks (local communities, etc.) than by how long the account had been open or by how much money they had in it.

Kelly, M., C. O'Gráda. 2000. Market Contagion: Evidence from the Panics of 1854 and 1857. The *American Economic Review*. 90(5): 1110-1124.

| 9.5 | Herd behaviour: theory and practice |
|---|---|

Herd behaviour (herding) is well-documented and most often used in the economical context of stock market bubbles, financial speculation, consumer preferences and political choice. However, it is suggested that it is a largely interdisciplinary concept that reaches far beyond the economic area. The core mathematical and behavioural principles behind herd behaviour are parallel to the ones in La Ola ('the wave'). Herding is a form of convergent social behaviour that is powered by (spatially restricted) interaction and self-ordinance, but without centralized coordination. Thus, it could be relevant to anything from decision-making processes, to mass hysteria, social influence, collective instinct and mob violence.

Due to the wide range of conceptual backgrounds behind herd mentality, a recent meta-analytic study by Raafat, Chater and Firth summarizes the diverse approaches and proposes a classification based on two standards:
1. the transmission of a particular thought between people (with sub-categories of automatic contagion and rational deliberation)
2. the pattern of these transmissions.

The pattern standard stresses the inert and imitative modes of interaction and structure of the system (real-life examples include analysis of traffic jams and crowds, financial market analysis or the analysis of tracing obesity in social networks). On the contrary, the transmission perspective absorbs mainly the cognitive and affective components of information transfer (i.e. mentalizing, emotional contagion, social contagion, priming, conformity and the like).

The researchers concluded this paper by claiming that to fully comprehend the phenomenon of herd behaviour, a further move from one conceptual framework to another is required.

Raafat, R.M., N. Chater, C. Frith.2009. Herding in humans. *Trends in Cognitive Sciences.* 13(10): 420-428.

# 10. Conformity & contagion experimental phenomena

**10.0**  **Asch conformity paradigm**

The classic Asch experiments published in the 1950s demonstrated the power of conformity in groups for the first time in history. Subjects were placed with a group of confederates who deliberately gave false estimations for measurements of a line. Asch measured whether the subject would modify their interpretation based on the majority opinion. About one third of the responses conformed to the erroneous majority.

To illustrate the strong prevalence of this principle in the present day, researchers carried out a study on tax compliance. A real-world experiment was conducted by officials in Minnesota where 4 groups of tax payers were given different information. Group 1 was told the tax collected was going to be used for a good cause. Group 2 was threatened with punishment for noncompliance. Group 3 was given tips on how to get information or help with filling out their tax forms. Group 4 was told that 90% of Minnesotans had already obeyed. Only one intervention exerted a considerable impact on the tax compliance decision: the last one.

Asch, S. E. 1956. Studies of independence and conformity: I. A minority of one against a unanimous majority. *Psychological Monographs.* 70(9) complete 416.

Coleman, S. Unpublished paper. The Minnesota income tax compliance experiment: State tax results. Minnesota Department of Revenue. http://mpra.ub.uni-muenchen.de/4827/1/MPRA_paper_4827.pdf. [Accessed May 2010]

**10.1 Milgram's sidewalk experiment, NY**

In this study, Stanley Milgram gives an account of the relationship between the size of a stimulus crowd (1 to 15 people standing on a busy city street looking up at a building) and the response of passersby. As the size of the stimulus crowd was increased, a greater proportion of passersby adopted the same behaviour. About 1 in every 25 passersby stopped to look up when 5 volunteers were sky-gazing. A stimulus crowd of 15 people, however, made nearly 1 in every 5 people stop. . Clearly, the decision of passersby to mimic others' behaviour was contingent on the size of the crowd exhibiting the behaviour.

Milgram, S., L. Bickman, L. Berkowitz. 1969. Note on the drawing power of crowds of different size. *Journal of Personality and Social Psychology.* 13(2): 79-82.

**10.2 Zimbardo's Stanford Experiment**

In 1971, Philip Zimbardo decided to investigate a concept similar to Milgram's study on obedience. Zimbardo wanted to investigate how readily people would conform to new roles in a simulation of a prison environment. 24 students were selected to play the roles of either guards or prisoners in a mock prison in the basement of Stanford University. The results shocked everyone: guards started to display abusive and authoritative behaviour, harassing and punishing the prisoners. This led some of the prisoners to rebel, while some became depressed or even quit the experiment. The situation got out of hand quickly, and the experiment was discontinued after only 6 days.

Even though the Stanford prison experiment remains one of the most ethically controversial, similarities are found in real life situations where people conform to social roles they are expected to play (e.g. the military prison torture in Abu Ghraib in March 2004 or the recent French TV game

show experiment administering near lethal electric shocks to contestants).

de Moraes, L. 2010. Reality show contestants willing to kill in French experiment. *The Washington Post.* http://www.washingtonpost.com/wp-dyn/content/article/2010/03/17/AR2010031703594.html [Accessed May 2010]

Zimbardo, P.G. 1973. On the ethics of intervention in human psychological research: With special reference to the Stanford prison experiment. *Cognition.* 2(2): 243-256.

| 10.3 | **Experiment on emotional modelling** |
|---|---|

A meta-analysis of 40 findings from 36 studies has provided unquestionably substantial evidence for the proposition that depressive symptoms and mood are contagious.

In one study, college freshmen were assigned to live with mildly depressed students. Over a period of three months, their levels of depressive mood rose. This state possibly stems from direct day-to-day contact, which incites a modelling process or augments general feelings of dysphoria resulting from an unsatisfactory relationship with the roommate. In another study, a similar pattern was found while exploring the interdependence between academic performance and the dormitory assignments of first-year students.

Howes, M.J., J.E.Hokanson, D.A. Loewenstein. 1985. Induction of depressive affect after prolonged exposure to a mildly depressed individual. *Journal of personality and social psychology.* 49(4): 1110-1113.

Sacerdote, B. 2001. Peer effects with random assignment: Results for Dartmouth roommates. *The Quarterly Journal of Economics.* 116(2): 681-704.

Joiner, T.E., J. Katz. 2006. Contagion of depressive symptoms and mood: Meta-analytic review and explanations from cognitive, behavioural, and interpersonal viewpoints. *Clinical Psychology: Science and Practice.* 6 (2): 149-164.

| 10.4 | Experiment on emotional contagion | A more instinctive and less sophisticated process of emotional contagion is described as an affective afference: a kind of instinctive empathy rooted in facial-feedback theory. It relates to the path of the signals from the muscles to the brain. Practically, it means that a simple facial expression can have an impact on people's mood. This is one of the reasons why telemarketers and cold-calling teams are trained to smile when they talk to customers, even though they don't see each other. |
|---|---|---|

In this experiment, subjects listened to recordings of nonverbal vocal reactions communicating two positive and two negative emotions. MRI scans showed that hearing those cues stimulated parts of the brain that correspond with the same command that is responsible for facial expressions, even though participants were asked not to respond. As with the yawning and laughing principles mentioned earlier, the triggered action is an imitative response of our 'mirror neuron' system.

Warren J.E., et al.2006. 2006. Positive emotions preferentially engage an auditory–motor 'mirror' system. *The Journal of Neuroscience.* 26(50):13067-13075.

| 10.5 | Service with a smile | When waiters smile while dealing with customers, customers tend to report being more satisfied. There is also a better chance that they will leave a bigger tip. Again, a possible neuropsychological explanation is the 'mirror neuron' system. |
|---|---|---|

Pugh, S.D. 2001. Service with a smile: Emotional contagion in the service encounter. *Academy of Management Journal.* 44(5): 1018-1027.

| 10.6 | Social transmission of face preferences | Previous studies found copying patterns in the mating choices of some non-human species. In this study, it was found that when women were looking at other women who were looking at men and smiling (rather than retaining a neutral expression), the women's preferences towards those men would increase significantly. By contrast, the reverse was true for male participants. This latter |
|---|---|---|

finding exposed the rules of within-sex competition. Men develop negative attitudes towards other men who receive more of women's positive affirmation.

Jones, B.C., et al. 2007. Social transmission of face preferences among humans. *Proceedings of the Royal Society. Biological Sciences.* 274 (1611):899-903.

**10.7 Emotional contagion vs. product attitude**

In this experiment, proof was found for emotional contagion, i.e. positive emotion coming from 'senders' was caught by 'receivers'. The fact that these 'receivers' were mimicking smiling and developed positive emotions towards the 'senders', resulted in the same positive bias towards a product. The researchers in this study confirmed also that the mere observation of facial expression was a sufficient condition for emotional contagion to take place.

Howard, D.J., C. Gengler. 2001. Emotional contagion effects on product attitudes. *Journal of consumer research.* 28(2): 189-201.

**10.8 Social contagion of memory**

This is a study on how people influence each other's memories and how this memory contagion is implanted by social influence. In the same way that an individual conforms to the majority in error, one individual's memory may be contaminated by another person's misperceptions.

Roediger, H.L. III, M.L. Meade, E.T. Bergman. 2001. Social contagion of memory. *Psychonomic Bulletin & Review.* 8(2): 365-371.

**10.9 Cheating contagion experiment**

At Carnegie Mellon University, a group of students were asked to take a difficult math test. To explore the contagion behaviour in this situation, researchers placed a confederate in the middle of the room and asked him to openly and visibly cheat on the test. Seeing that, others began to cheat too. However, this behaviour increased only when the cheater was someone to whom others felt connected.

When the cheater, for example, wore a T-shirt with a rival university logo, the unethical copying decreased.

Gino, F., S. Ayal, D. Ariely. 2009. Contagion and differentiation in unethical behaviour. The effect of one bad apple on the barrel. *Psychological Science*. 20(3): 393-398.

| 10.10 | **Minority power effect** | A small group of influential, credible people can consistently influence decision processes and behaviour of the majority. The speed with which the consensus is reached depends on the network structure and, as in other studies on minority influence, on consistency of behavioural style (such as 'stubbornness'), presence of 'extremist' individuals and the awareness of opposing incentives. This phenomenon is evident, for example, in voting behaviour or certain religious gatherings. |

Kearns, M., et. al. 2009. Behavioural experiments on biased voting in networks. *Proceeding of the National Academy of Sciences of the USA*. 106(5):1347-52.

| 10.11 | **Informational cascade** | This research suggests an alternative explanation to social influence, 'geographic' conformity or short-lived booms, fads or fashions (such as religious movements, riots, reformations and the forming of social attitudes towards cigarettes, smoking, drugs, junk food and many more). Researchers claim that an individual, having observed the actions of those who went before him, is likely to ignore his own informational input and follow the behaviour of others, causing the social equilibrium to shift (sometimes radically). The researchers concluded that this is one of the reasons why mass behaviour is so vulnerable in the sense that minor impacts can cause considerable changes. The informational cascade assumes that the rationality of other agents is a sufficient reason to conform. Today, economists and behavioural scientists apply the informational cascade in exploring herd behaviour. |

Bikhchandani, S., D. Hirshleifer, I. Welch. 1992. A theory of fads, fashion, custom, and cultural change as informational cascades. *The Journal of Political Economy.* 100(5): 992-1026.

**10.12 Tracking the spread of emotions experiment**

In this study, the method of experience-sampling was used to determine whether adolescents' emotions were in fact interrelated with the immediate emotions of their parents. Emotional states were recorded when participants were beeped. Various associations in emotional influence were indeed observed. These associations also showed a bias by gender and age.

Larson, R.W., M.H. Richards. 1994. Family emotions: Do young adolescents and their parents experience the same states? *Journal of Research on Adolescence.* 4(4): 567-583.

# Bibliography

Adams, Tyrone, and Stephen A. Smith. *Electronic tribes: the virtual worlds of geeks, gamers, shamans, and scammers.* Austin: University of Texas Press, 2008.

Ackerman Anderson, Linda, and Dean Anderson. *The Change Leader's Roadmap.* San Francisco: Pfeiffer, 2001.

———. *Beyond Change Management.* San Francisco: Pfeiffer, 2001.

Anderson, Dean, and Linda S. Anderson. *Beyond change management: advanced strategies for today's transformational leaders.* San Francisco: Jossey-Bass/Pfeiffer, 2001.

Ariely, Dan. *Predictably irrational: the hidden forces that shape our decisions.* New York, NY: Harper, 2008.

———. *The upside of irrationality: the unexpected benefits of defying logic at work and at home.* New York, NY: Harper, 2010.

Astuti, Rita, Jonathan P. Parry, and Charles Stafford. *Questions of anthropology.* Oxford, UK: Berg, 2007.

Autissier, David, and Jean-Michel Moutot. *Pratique de la conduite du Changement.* Paris, France: Dunod, 2003.

Bakker, Hans, Martijn Babeliowsky, and Frank Stevenaar. *The Next Leap: Achieving Growth Through Global Networks, Partnerships and Co-operation.* London, UK: Cyan Communications, 2005.

Bandura, Albert. *Social learning theory.* Englewood Cliffs, N.J.: Prentice Hall, 1977.

Barabási, Albert-László. *Linked: The New Science of Networks.* Cambridge, MA: Perseus Books Group, 2002.

Bartlett, Christopher A., and Sumantra Ghoshal. *Managing Across Borders: The Transnational Solution.* New York, NY: Random House Business Books, 1989.

Beer, Michael, and Nitin Nohria. *Breaking the Code of Change.* Boston, MA: Harvard Business School Press, 2000.

Bell, Catherine M. *Ritual theory, ritual practice.* New York, NY: Oxford University Press, 1992.

Benedict Bunker, Barbara, and Billie T. Alban. *Large Group Interventions: Engaging the Whole System for Rapid Change.* San Fransisco: Jossey-Bass, Inc., 1996.

Binney, George, and Colin Williams. *Leaning into the Future: Changing the Way People Change Organisations.* Boston, MA: Nicholas Brealey Publishing, 1997.

Boéri, Daniel, and Stéphane Bernard. *Organisation & changement.* Paris, France: Maxima, 1998.

Bon, Michel for Harvard Business Review. *Le Changement*. Paris, France: Editions d'organisation, 2000.

Bonner, William, and Lila Rajiva. *Mobs, messiahs, and markets surviving the public spectacle in finance and politics*. Hoboken, N.J.: John Wiley & Sons, 2007.

Booker, Christopher. *The seven basic plots: why we tell stories*. London: Continuum, 2004.

Boyd, Robert, and Peter J. Richerson. *The origin and evolution of cultures*. Oxford: Oxford University Press, 2005.

Bridges, William. *Managing Transitions: Making the Most of Change*. New York, NY: Da Capo Press, 1991.

Brogan, Chris, and Julien Smith. *Trust agents: using the web to build influence, improve reputation, and earn trust*. Hoboken, N.J.: John Wiley & Sons, 2009.

Brown, Tim. *Change by design: how design thinking transforms organizations and inspires innovation*. New York, NY: Harper Business, 2009.

Bruggeman, Jeroen. *Social networks: an introduction*. London: Routledge, 2008.

Buchanan, Mark. *Nexus: Small Worlds and the Groundbreaking Science of Networks*. New York, NY: W. W. Norton & Company, 2002.

Burnes, Bernard. *Managing Change*. Upper Saddle River, NJ: Prentice Hall, 2004.

Cameron, Esther, and Mike Green. *Making sense of change management: a complete guide to the models, tools & techniques of organizational change*. London, UK: Kogan Page, 2009.

Capra, Fritjof. *The Web of Life: A New Synthesis of Mind and Matter*. New York, NY: HarperCollins, 1996.

Carnall, Colin, and C.A. Carnall. Managing Change in Organizations. Upper Saddle River, NJ: Prentice Hall, 1990.

Carter, Louis, et al. *Best Practices in Organization Development and Change Handbook: Culture, Leadership, Retention, Performance, Consulting*. San Francisco: Jossey-Bass/Pfeiffer, 2001.

Casey, Conerly, and Robert B. Edgerton. *A companion to psychological anthropology: modernity and psychocultural change*. Malden, MA: Blackwell Pub., 2005.

Castells, Manuel. *The Information Age: Economy, Society and Culture: Volumes I,II & III*. Oxford, UK: Blackwell Publishers, 1999.

Christakis, Nicholas A., and James H. Fowler. *Connected: the surprising power of our social networks and how they shape our lives*. New York, NY: Little, Brown and Co., 2009.

Christensen, Clayton M., and Michael E. Raynor. *The innovator's solution: creating and sustaining successful growth*. Boston, MA: Harvard Business School Press, 2003.

———, Michael B. Horn, and Curtis W. Johnson. *Disrupting class: how disruptive innovation will change the way the world learns*. New York, NY: McGraw-Hill, 2008.

Cialdini, Robert B. *Influence: the psychology of persuasion*. New York, NY: Collins, 2007.

Coleman, Loren. *The copycat effect: how the media and popular culture trigger the mayhem in tomorrow's headlines*. New York, NY: Paraview Pocket Books, 2004.

Collins, Randall. *The Sociology of Philosophies: A Global Theory of Intellectual Change*. Cambridge, MA: Belknap Press, 2000.

Cross, Rob, and Andrew Parker. *The Hidden Power of Social Networks: Understanding How Work Really Gets Done in Organizations*. Boston, MA: Harvard Business School Press, 2004.

Csermely, Peter. *Weak Links*. New York, NY: Springer-Verlag, 2006.

Dannemiller Tyson Associates. *Whole-Scale Change Toolkit*. San Francisco: Berrett-Koehler Publishers, 2000.

Davidson, Jeff. *The Complete Idiot's Guide to Change Management*. Indianapolis, IN: Alpha Books, 2002.

Dawson, Ross. *Living Networks: Leading Your Company, Customers, and Partners in the Hyper-Connected Economy*. Upper Saddle River, NJ: Financial Times Prentice Hall, 2002.

Earls, Mark. *Herd: how to change mass behaviour by harnessing our true nature*. Chichester, England: John Wiley & Sons, 2007.

Ebers, Mark. *The Formation of Inter-Organizational Networks*. New York, NY: Oxford University Press, 1999.

Ehin, Charles. *Hidden Assets: Harnessing the Power of Informal Networks*. New York, NY: Springer, 2005.

Elster, Jon. *Explaining social behaviour: more nuts and bolts for the social sciences*. New York, NY: Cambridge University Press, 2007.

Farmer, Neil. *The invisible organization: how informal networks can lead organizational change*. Farnham, UK: Gower, 2008.

Ferrazzi, Keith, and Tahl Raz. *Never Eat Alone: And Other Secrets to Success, One Relationship at a Time*. New York, NY: Crown Business, 2005.

Fisher, Len. *Rock, paper, scissors: game theory in everyday life*. New York, NY: Basic Books, 2008.

Fisher, Len. *The perfect swarm: the science of complexity in everyday life*. New York, NY: Basic Books, 2009.

Gellner, David N., and Eric Hirsch. *Inside organizations: anthropologists at work*. Oxford: Berg, 2001.

Giovagnoli, Melissam, and Jocelyn Carter-Miller. *Networlding: Building Relationships and Opportunities for Success*. San Francisco: Jossey-Bass/Pfeiffer, 2000.

Hagel, John, John Seely Brown, and Lang Davison. *The power of pull: how small moves, smartly made, can set big things in motion*. New York, NY: Basic Books, 2010.

Harrigan, Kathryn Rudie. *Strategic Flexibility: A Management Guide for Changing Times*. Lexington, MA: DC Heath & Company, 1985.

Haskins, Gay, and Allan Mitchell. *Making and Managing change and Innovation*. London, UK: The Economist Intelligence Unit, 1989.

Hazy, James K., Jeffrey Goldstein, and Benyamin B. Lichtenstein. *Complex systems leadership theory: new perspectives from complexity science on social and organizational effectiveness*. Mansfield, MA: ISCE Pub., 2007.

Heath, Chip, and Dan Heath. *Switch: how to change things when change is hard*. New York, NY: Broadway Books, 2010.

Heller, R. *Gérer le changement*. Paris, France: Mango Pratique, 1999.

Herrero, Leandro. *The Leader With Seven Faces*. Beaconsfield, UK: meetingminds, 2006.

——— *Viral Change™: The Alternative to Slow, Painful and Unsuccessful Management of Change in Organisations* . 2nd ed. Beaconsfield, UK: meetingminds, 2008.

——— *Disruptive ideas - 10+10+10=1000: The maths of viral change that transform organisations*. Beaconsfield, UK: meetingminds, 2008.

——— *New Leaders Wanted - Now Hiring! 12 kinds of People You Must Find, Seduce, Hire and Create a Job for*. Beaconsfield, UK: meetingminds, 2007

Hofstede, Geert H. *Culture's consequences: comparing values, behaviors, institutions, and organizations across nations*. 2nd ed. Thousand Oaks, Calif.: Sage Publications, 2001.

———, and Michael Minkov. *Cultures and organizations: software of the mind: intercultural cooperation and its importance for survival*. New York, NY: McGraw-Hill, 2010.

Howe, Jeff. *Crowdsourcing: why the power of the crowd is driving the future of business*. New York, NY: Crown Business, 2008.

Jacobs, Robert W. *Real-Time Strategic Change*. San Francisco: Berrett-Koehler Publishers, 1997.

James, Wendy. *The ceremonial animal: a new portrait of anthropology*. Oxford: Oxford University Press, 2003.

Jarillo, J. Carlos. *Strategic Networks*. Oxford, UK: Butterworth-Heinemann, 1995.

Jarrett, Michael. *Changeability: why some companies are ready for change - and others aren't*. Harlow, England: Financial Times/Prentice Hall, 2009.

Joerges, Barbara. *Narrating the organization: dramas of institutional identity*. Chicago: University Of Chicago Press, 1997.

Kanter, Rosabeth Moss. *The Change Masters: Corporate Entrepreneurs at Work*. New York, NY: Taylor & Francis Books Ltd, 1985.

———— *When Giants Learn to Dance: Managing the Challenges of Strategy, Management and Careers in the 1990's*. New York, NY: Simon & Schuster, 1989.

————, Barry A. Stein and Todd D. Jick. *The Challenge of Organizational Change: How People Experience It and Manage It*. New York, NY: The Free Press, 1992.

Katzenbach, Jon R., and Zia Khan. *Leading outside the lines: how to mobilize the (in)formal organization, energize your team, and get better results*. San Francisco: Jossey-Bass, 2010.

Keidel, Robert W. *Corporate players: designs for working and winning together*. New York: Wiley, 1988.

Kelly, Kevin. *New Rules for the New Economy: 10 Radical Strategies for a Connected World*. New York, NY: Viking Books, 1998.

Kilduff, Martin, and Wenpin Tsai. *Social Networks and Organizations*. London, UK: SAGE Publications, 2003.

Koch, Richard, and Greg Lockwood. *Superconnect: harnessing the power of networks and the strength of weak links*. New York, NY: W.W. Norton & Co., 2010.

Kotter, John P. *Leading Change*. Boston, MA: Harvard Business School Press, 1996.

Kramer, Jitske. *Managing cultural dynamics*. Utrecht: HumanDimensions Publications, 2009.

Larking, T.J., and Sandar Larkin. *Communicating Change: Winning Employee Support for New Business Goals*. New York, NY: McGraw-Hill, 1994.

Linkage Inc. *The Courage to change*. Ponte Vedra Beach, FL: Work Systems Ass. Inc., 1996.

Levine, Robert. *The power of persuasion: how we're bought and sold*. Hoboken, N.J.: John Wiley & Sons, 2003.

Low, Setha M., and Denise Lawrence-Zunigais. *The anthropology of space and place: locating culture*. Malden, MA: Blackwell Publishing, 2003.

Lunn, Pete. *Basic instincts: human nature and the new economics*. London: Marshall Cavendish, 2008.

Manns, Mary Lynn, and Linda Rising. Fearless Change: Patterns for Introducing New Ideas. Indianapolis, IN: Addison-Wesley Professional, 2004.

Morozov, Evgeny. *The net delusion: the dark side of internet freedom.* New York, NY: Public Affairs, 2011.

Neuhauser, Peg. *Tribal warfare in organizations.* Cambridge, Mass.: Ballinger Pub. Co., 1988.

Newman, Mark, Albert-László Barabási, and Duncan J. Watts. *The Structure and Dynamics of Networks: Princeton Studies in Complexity.* Princeton, NJ: Princeton University Press, 2006.

Olson, Edwin E., and Glenda H. Eoyang. *Facilitating Organization Change: Lessons from Complexity Science.* San Francisco: Jossey-Bass/Pfeiffer, 2001.

O'Toole, James. *Leading Change.* New York, NY: Ballantine Books, 1996.

Pfeffer, Jeffrey. *Power: why some people have it--and others don't.* New York, NY: Harperbusiness, 2010.

Porta, Donatella, and Mario Diani. *Social movements: an introduction.* Malden, MA: Blackwell, 2006.

Price Waterhouse Change Integration Team. *Better Change: Best Practices for Transforming Your Organization.* New York, NY: McGraw-Hill Trade, 1994.

Pritchett, Price. *The Employee Handbook of New Work Habits for a Radically Changing World: 13 Ground Rules for Job Success in the Information Age.* Plano, TX: Pritchett & Hull Associates, Inc., 1996.

Rodgers, Chris. *Informal coalitions: mastering the hidden dynamics of organizational change.* Basingstoke [England: Palgrave Macmillan, 2007.

Schelling, Thomas C. *Micromotives and macrobehavior.* New York, NY: Norton, 1978.

Scott, John P. *Social Network Analysis: A Handbook.* London, UK: SAGE Publications, 2001.

Shirky, Clay. *Here comes everybody the power of organisation without organizations.* London: Allen Lane, 2008.

Snow, David A., Sarah Anne Soule, and Hanspeter Kriesi. *The Blackwell companion to social movements.* Malden, MA: Blackwell Pub., 2004.

Sproull, Lee, and Sara Kiesler. *Connections: New Ways of Working in the Networked Organization.* Cambridge, MA: The MIT Press, 1992.

Sutherland, Stuart. *Irrationality.* London: Pinter & Martin, 2007.

Thaler, Richard H., and Cass R. Sunstein. *Nudge: improving decisions about health, wealth, and happiness.* New Haven: Yale University Press, 2008.

Thomas, Martin, and David Brain. *Crowd surfing: surviving and thriving in the age of consumer empowerment.* London: A & C Black, 2008.

Tidd, Joseph, J. R. Bessant, and Keith Pavitt. *Managing innovation: integrating technological, market and organizational change.* Chichester, UK: John Wiley, 2001.

Watters, Ethan. *Urban tribes: are friends the new family?* London: Bloomsbury, 2004.

Watts, Duncan J. *Six Degrees: The Science of a Connected Age.* New York, NY: W. W. Norton & Company, 2004.

———— *Small Worlds: The Dynamics of Networks Between Order and Randomness* (Princeton Studies in Complexity). Princeton, NJ: Princeton University Press, 1999.

Weiss, Joseph W. *The Management of Change: Administrative Logistics and* Actions. Santa Barbara, CA: Praeger Publishers, 1986.

Zentall, Thomas R., and Bennett G. Galef. *Social learning: psychological and biological perspectives.* Hillsdale, N.J.: Lawrence Erlbaum Associates, 1988.

# I acknowledge...

As a practitioner, I am indebted to my clients, business partners and our growing network of Associated Practices across the world (UK, Italy, Belgium, Holland, Germany, Sweden, South Africa, Canada and Brazil) for the continuous learning.

Claus Maron and Søren Jakobsen, senior partners in our Viral Change™ company, supported my continuous crafting of ideas and the articulation in this book of the work we do for clients. From their base in Denmark they work with me in our global consulting practice, assisted by Thomas Prehn. Caroline Tierney and Ian Garrard are always ready to support my frequent need for a reality check in multiple areas of my two business practices, The Chalfont Project Ltd and Viral Change LLP (UK). Allison Spargo, business and client relationship lead, put gentle, but efficient pressure on me and kept everything else on track while I was writing. Anna Torun did a great job as my research assistant. David Lewis created great cartoons, not only for the book, but for many presentations. Many thanks to all.

The colleagues in our network of practitioners enriched everything by their interaction with us. We share a rich and challenging journey. I am grateful for this to David Trickey, Ariane Vanderlinden, Thierry Bouckaert, Carl Buyck, Jitske Kramer, Jan and Mike Emerton, Silse Martell, Mari Lategan, Nolan Beudeker, Anne Stenbom, Tony Bradley, Sue Tupling, Maureen Rabotin, Richard Morrice, Colin Nelson, Drissia Schroeder-Hohenwarth, Stefan Meister, Jayne Royden, David Hart, Carol Sharpe and many others.

Sharon Warre-Dymond at Pfizer and Davide Scotti at Saipem were generous in allowing the reproduction of some materials used in Viral Change™ programmes in their organizations.

Clients and ex-clients are a source of inspiration. I am grateful for their trust. During the last year some interactions in particular have shaped the direction of *Homo Imitans*, sometimes without specifically talking about the book! I am privileged to interact with high calibre business leaders such as Pierre Morgon (Sanofi Pasteur),  Philip Watts (Pfizer), Louise Makin (BTG plc), Stephen Connock, Dean Finch and David Duke (National Express), Davide Scotti, Darren Matkin, Andrea Forzan and Sabatino de Sanctis (Saipem), Steve Gates (The Gap Partnership),  Geoff Carss (element8),  Frank Dybdal Lilleøre (Danske Bank), Lars Thomander (Abbott Sweden), Euclides Coimbra (Kaizen Institute), Karen Brown (HSBC), Jose Maria Martinez (Asisa), Joost Knoll (Hertel), Joyce Geir, Chuck Chada and Mark Stewart (Xerox), Klaas Schuring, (Suzlon), Frank Coenen (Tessenderlo) and many others, including people in their own teams.

Finally, I am particularly grateful to my many keepers. To my children for keeping me young. To my wife for keeping up with me. To my clients for keeping me. To my corporate ex-employers for not keeping me. To my business partners for keeping me excited. To my colleagues in the business for keeping me on track. To my readers and audiences for keeping me productive. To my dearest friends, the monks of the Benedictine abbey of Pluscarden in Scotland, for keeping me sane.

Leandro Herrero
Pluscarden Abbey, November 2010

## About the author

**Leandro Herrero** practiced as a psychiatrist for more than fifteen years before taking up senior leadership positions in several top league global companies, both in Europe and the US. He is co-founder and CEO of The Chalfont Project Ltd, an international consulting firm of organizational architects, and managing partner of Viral Change LLP, part of the Global Viral Change Network.

Taking advantage of his behavioural sciences background—coupled with his hands-on business experience—he works with organizations of many kinds on structural and behavioural change, leadership and human collaboration.

His books include *The Leader with Seven Faces, Viral Change™, New Leaders Wanted: Now Hiring!, Disruptive Ideas* and *Homo Imitans.* He is currently working on a new book, *The beta organization.*

Other than his medical and psychiatry qualifications he holds an MBA and he is Fellow of the Chartered Management Institute and the Institute of Directors in the UK

He lives in England with his family and can be contacted via www.thechalfontproject.com

# Company Information

**The Chalfont Project Ltd**

The Chalfont Project is a UK-based international consultancy with leading expertise in organizational architecture. Founded in 2000 by Leandro Herrero and Caroline Tierney, the company specializes in organizational strategy and implementation, particularly in the areas of collective leadership, organizational effectiveness and innovation, behavioural branding (organizations) and human collaboration. Its client base is broad and global, and the company's strong foundations are based on behavioural and social sciences applied to the challenges of the modern organization (public or private, small or large). Due to the success and growth of programmes in behavioural change management applied to the organization and the increasing global presence of Viral Change™, the Chalfont Project Ltd spun off this area of consulting services and created Viral Change LLP.

**Viral Change companies**

Viral Change LLP (UK) is a spinoff from The Chalfont Project Ltd, with exclusive focus on the creation of large-scale change. This is done following the Viral Change™ methodology, the principles of which define a particular understanding of the modern organization in which change is a status, a way of life and in which the readiness to change and constantly reinvent itself is a key core competence.

The company is part of a large Global Viral Change Network composed of both Viral Change companies and a network of accredited practices and practitioners. The companies within the network provide professional consulting services, both strategic and implementation, in a diverse spectrum of organizational challenges, from large-scale cultural change and broad organizational transformation, to specific focus in areas such as innovation, effectiveness, employee engagement or behavioural change in health and safety.

**Resources and contacts**

www.thechalfontproject.com
www.viralchange.com
www.viralchange.net
www.leandroherrero.com
www.homoimitans.com

# Index

**Viral Change™:**
**The alternative to slow, painful and unsuccessful management of change in organizations**
By Leandro Herrero

Many 'Change Management' initiatives end in fiasco, because they only focus on processes and systems. But there is no change, unless the change is behavioural.

*Viral Change*™ is THE manager's handbook on how to create sustainable and long-lasting change in organizations.

The author says: *"If change is needed, the traditional 'change management models' may not be the most effective vehicle. Most of those change management systems fail because they do not deliver behavioural change in the individuals. Viral Change*™ *is different... and it works!"*

You can listen to the author talk about *Viral Change*™ at **www.meetingminds.com**, where you can also read excerpts, reviews and much more.

*Viral Change*™ is available from Amazon, Barnes and Noble, Blackwell, WH Smith, Borders, Books Etc. and many other (online) bookshops, as well as from www.meetingminds.com.

**Disruptive Ideas**
**10+10+10=1000: the maths of Viral Change that transform organizations**
By Leandro Herrero

In a time when organizations simultaneously run multiple corporate initiatives and large change programmes, *Disruptive Ideas* tells us that—contrary to the collective mindset that says that big problems need big solutions—all you need is a small set of powerful rules to create big impact.

In his previous book, *Viral Change*™, Leandro Herrero described how a small set of behaviours, spread by a small number of people could create sustainable change. In this follow-up book, the author suggests a menu of 10 'structures', 10 'processes' and 10 'behaviours' that have the power to transform an organization.

These 30 'ideas' can be implemented at any time and at almost no cost; and what's more...you don't even need them all. But their compound effect will be more powerful than vast corporate programmes with dozens of objectives and efficiency targets...

You can read excerpts, reviews and much more information about the book at **www.meetingminds.com**.

*Disruptive Ideas* is available from Amazon, Barnes and Noble, Blackwell, WH Smith, Borders, Books Etc. and many other (online) bookshops, as well as from www.meetingminds.com.

**The Leader with Seven Faces:**
**Finding your own ways of practicing leadership in today's**
**organization**
By Leandro Herrero

After all the books written about leadership, you'd think we
know a thing or two about leadership. However, nothing seems
to be further from the truth.

*The Leader with Seven Faces* provides a
novel approach to leadership where the
questions to ask (about what leaders say,
where they go, what they build, care about,
do, how they do it and 'what' they are) take
priority over producing 'universal answers'.

For anybody interested in leadership of
organizations... and in seeing things
through a new pair of glasses.

You can read excerpts, reviews and much more information
about the book at **www.meetingminds.com**.

*The Leader with Seven Faces* is available from Amazon, Barnes
and Noble, Blackwell, WH Smith, Borders, Books Etc. and many
other (online) bookshops, as well as from
www.meetingminds.com.

**New Leaders Wanted: Now Hiring!**
**12 kinds of people you must find, seduce, hire and create a job for**
By Leandro Herrero

A small percentage of the workforce has the key to success. A selected group of managers make all the difference. But what are the skills these people have that enable them to create business success?

The job advertising pages don't often describe those new skills. There is a tendency to play safe and look for people with a conventional set of skills and a proven track record. However, to get spectacular success, you need an 'internal engine' of people who think and behave differently. Who are these people? Where could they be? Do I have them already or do I need to find them? You cannot ignore these questions and your number one priority should be to find these people.

*New Leaders Wanted* explores those new skills and new approaches to reality and will guide you in your search to find those people.

You can read excerpts, reviews and much more information about the book at **www.meetingminds.com**.

*New Leaders Wanted: Now Hiring!* is available from Amazon, Barnes and Noble, Blackwell, WH Smith, Borders, Books Etc. and many other (online) bookshops, as well as from www.meetingminds.com.

# meetingminds
## ideas worth printing

**To order extra copies of** *Homo Imitans* or any of our other books, contact us at sales@meetingminds.com. The books are also available from Amazon, Barnes and Noble, Blackwell, WH Smith, Borders, Books Etc. and many other (online) bookshops. For bulk orders, please contact us directly for more information on discounts and shipping costs.

**Customized editions:** These are special editions created for a particular audience such as a specific company or organization. The core materials of the book are maintained, but relevant company-specific resources, such as in-house case studies or tool-kits, are added. A special foreword or tailored introduction, written either by the author or by your company's leadership, may be added as well. The book cover could also be adapted. Using modern printing technology, we can supply virtually any number of copies, from small runs to bulk production. If you are interested, please contact us.

**Continue the conversation:** There are many ways you can engage the author, from speaking opportunities to consulting services facilitating a change process and/or enabling your internal resources to drive change and leadership. Details can be obtained via the author's consulting website: **www.thechalfontproject.com**, through which you can also contact the author.

PO Box 1192, HP9 1YQ, United Kingdom
Tel. +44 (0)208 123 8910 - **www.meetingminds.com**
**info@meetingminds.com**